The Autism-Friendly Cookbook

of related interest

The Young Autistic Adult's Independence Handbook
Haley Moss
ISBN 978 1 78775 757 8
eISBN 978 1 78775 758 5

Shake It Up!
How to be Young, Autistic, and Make an Impact
Quincy Hansen.
ISBN 978 1 78775 979 4
eISBN 978 1 78775 980 0

The Autism and Neurodiversity Self Advocacy Handbook
Developing the Skills to Determine Your Own Future
Barb Cook and Yenn Purkis
ISBN 978 1 78775 575 8
eISBN 978 1 78775 576 5

The Autism-Friendly Cookbook

LYDIA WILKINS

Illustrated by Emily of @21andsensory

Jessica Kingsley Publishers
London and Philadelphia

First published in Great Britain in 2023 by Jessica Kingsley Publishers
An imprint of Hodder & Stoughton Ltd
An Hachette Company

1

A CIP catalogue record for this title is available from
the British Library and the Library of Congress

ISBN 978 1 83997 082 5
eISBN 978 1 83997 083 2

Printed and bound in Great Britain by TJ Books Limited

Jessica Kingsley Publishers' policy is to use papers that are natural,
renewable and recyclable products and made from wood grown in
sustainable forests. The logging and manufacturing processes are expected
to conform to the environmental regulations of the country of origin.

Jessica Kingsley Publishers
Carmelite House
50 Victoria Embankment
London EC4Y 0DZ

www.jkp.com

In memory of Sir Harold 'Harry' Matthew Evans (1928–2020), an individual who never stopped trying to shine a little light. Without him, this book would have never happened. Wherever you are, Harry, I hope 'upstairs' is all you wanted it to be, with the 'lost journalists' you spent your life speaking up for. May the Thalidomiders' quest for justice, led by Mikey Argy, Guy Tweedy and Nick Dobrik, be one day prosperous. It is still not too late to do the morally right thing, for those remaining of the worldwide thalidomide survivors, even though we are now but six decades on.

And last of all to Pete Taylor. For the first time in my life I had been fully understood and actually embraced for what others had called and still call 'my weirdness'. He saw me as a journalist first when others saw and still only see 'the label'. If there is something you can do for anyone, acceptance – even in a classroom setting – is a wonderful thing to do. The power of a simple gesture like that should never be underestimated.

Contents

Acknowledgements

In the days after Harold Evans died, I received reciprocal messages from all around the world. I am indebted in particular to Dr Martin Johnson, who kindly emailed me to say keep writing, because 'that would be your tribute'. It is his wisdom and patience that I am grateful for after all this time, even if I have – and still do – put that to the test.

Cindy Quillinan also deserves my thanks for her legendary patience, too; it is my wish that we may one day cross paths again. Izzy Evans also belongs here, for being so kind on reading an initial draft, as well as director Jacqui Morris, one of my 'partners in crime', who acts as the guiding 'voice of reason'. Jacqui's guidance has been invaluable since the day we met. Her documentary, *Attacking the Devil: Harold Evans and the Last Nazi War Crime*, is a testament to what the power of words and good honest reporting can achieve. It should be watched by everyone, everywhere.

William 'Bill' Kuhn and Violet Fenn helped in the assisting of getting 'the show on the road', such as when it came to advice about contracts, how to not worry about word counts, and just how to keep going when slogging it out. It was an unexpected kindness; I hope to pay that back in due course, too.

Lalaine Jones is my oldest friend, someone to rely on for laughter, as well as enforcing perspective keeping, often through sarcastic nicknames such as 'Madam De Journalism' or 'Mrs Jesus' (that's a long story). Humiliating DWP (Department for Work and Pensions) assessments were made better with jokes like 'the patch', a response to the idiocy of an assessor asking if I take pills for 'my condition'. Yep. Sometimes you just have to laugh or you will cry. As well as this, the wonderful women who made up my NCTJ class somewhat shocked me when writing this as they asked to read the draft, expressing how excited they were – to the point of asking a lot of questions about it. They are the people that make me want to be better and braver; I cherish them. The same goes for Eloise Barry, a brilliant journalist who would read through drafts – sending back copious notes – while swapping WhatsApp voice notes with me about our various stories into the early hours while I worked.

Pete Taylor taught me media law, as well as adding in an occasional (read: unorthodox) grounding in ethics. It was one of the only times an educator 'got it'. He never asked me about being autistic, much to his credit – only balking at the occasional (madcap) challenge. Ann Bannister, a teacher I hadn't seen for over a decade, also found me while writing this. She's the teacher that taught me to love language and history. We need more teachers like this, across the board.

Salena Godden is a poet and the author of *Mrs Death Misses Death*, a wonderful celebration of life. That book had a huge influence on me; a conversation with her while writing this significantly changed my outlook and my world view. There is a power in optimism, in looking for those tiny glimmers of hope. The same goes for Deeivya and Chameli Meir, two very talented individuals who took me under their wing around the same time. I am grateful to them all.

Julia and Alex at Assert also deserve their place here. For the first time in my life, I was given some of the support I needed. Likewise, every autistic person who came forward to offer their recipes, insights and wishes for accessible requirements ought to have a place here. I thought I was the 'only one' who struggled with cooking; I hope this book begins to bridge the gap of such common experiences. You can find all of their names at the back of this book.

To the DWP, for giving me the idea for this book in the first place, after their humiliating 'assessments' forced me to go to a tribunal. I am not 'sick' because of my disability. No pills are available to 'cure' autism; that is just downright offensive. Knowing or having an autistic relative gives you no right to determine what I may or may not be capable of, either, because we are not all the same. Autism is not a mental illness, nor is it a form of suffering you can just penalize just 'because'. The blocks placed as hurdles by society, enabled by organizations such as yours, are discriminatory, unethical and an injustice to us all. The act of ignorance is not an excuse to be callous or cruel.

And last of all, to my family. Words can never truly express how thankful I am, not ever, not really. Very simply, thank you.

Disclaimer

This book is written by a journalist, who is also on the autistic spectrum and has written about and researched the autistic spectrum previously. All efforts have been made to make this book as accessible as possible; read-throughs of the recipes have also been offered to all the contributors to this book. The author and all those associated with the production of this book bear no responsibility for any decisions made as a result of reading it. Similarly, one autistic person does not speak for everyone. While language of a collective nature has been used, this is to retain continuity; the premise of this book is to avoid gatekeeping of resources, therefore allowing anyone who reads this to pick the parts most relevant to them.

In order to be as inclusive as possible, individuals have been left to choose how they describe themselves. Asperger's syndrome is not an official diagnosis in some places now, but people diagnosed before it was written out of the diagnostic criteria are still autistic but may prefer to use this term. Other countries still use Asperger's syndrome as a diagnosis. Others may prefer identity-first language, while others may prefer person-first language. This is not intended to cause offence; it was put in place to be as inclusive as possible to people from all over the globe who have contributed to this book.

The Equality Act (2010) is a piece of legislation in the UK that gives autism the legal status of a disability. To retain continuity throughout, this is the definition we have used, with emphasis on the social model of disability.

Preface

At the age of almost 90, Sir Harold 'Harry' Evans had the quality of a child captivated by a story – the stage where you begin to see the characters dancing through the air in front of you, constructed from fragments, words. A master of holding an audience in the palm of his hands, it was surreal that such an individual had agreed to speak openly for an interview. His hands would clap together while he rocked back in his chair, his blue eyes laughing, suddenly twisting forward to listen intently, ready to pepper the unsuspecting with so many questions. A former editor responsible for *The Sunday Times* newspaper scoring scoops such as uncovering the activities of Kim Philby and exposing the enormity of the thalidomide catastrophe, he was unlike anything you could have ever imagined. Insisting I call him Harry, he gestured at me: 'Go on, shoot.'

There is a paradox here – to be autistic, I mean – in conducting such an interview. It isn't what you may regard as being 'obvious'. My ability to manage relatively 'complex' things, such as arranging and conducting interviews, creating features for national newspapers or setting up a website, may not necessarily be indicators of my support needs. Up until that day I had felt like a failure – for not being enough or being too much, not understanding the coded language and customs people speak in called 'normal'. Societally, we tend not to like difference, and we have created many synonyms for it, suggesting a lack of comfort. Speak on the phone? Hours of preparation are behind that, with more for recovery time due to exhaustion. Cook a meal? Don't make me laugh. How about a 'spiky profile' – being good at just one particular thing – instead, with limited social skills and strange so-called 'obsessions'?

That shame – of being told I could never be a journalist for the crime of 'difference', that I apparently suffer from a terrible illness or ailment that is out of my control – was taken away in mere minutes after this meeting, which overran by almost an hour. Diversity is crucial in this industry, Harry explained, and there is no shame in the 'asset' of being 'obsessive', either. That is actually very useful, he said.

Every person with a disability is capable of having a degree of independence within their own needs and abilities – or should at least be given the chance, such as if they need support to enable this. Support needs should not have to be justified constantly. For example, I cannot 'just learn' how to do something. An 'attainment gap' between me and other people my age will always exist when it comes to skills, and while it's the nature of the beast, it is frustrating not to feel a part of things often as a result. Support is a necessity, a basic right, as are the very basics of food education.

By 2020, the more I looked into it, the more my experience seemed almost universal: not knowing how to cook or bake, accessibility not a great prospect, instructions being inaccessible, information having to be researched tirelessly – like what specific adaptations are available. 'Special diets' were what I found when looking for an accessible cookbook, alongside horrific content around the 'curing'/prevention of autism. Other neurodiverse conditions were apparently curable by eating specific foods, while others ostensibly act as 'poisons' to our brains, a sign of junk science being accepted as standard. It's time that this horrible myth is no longer accepted, for us to actually celebrate our differences, the one common denominator that makes us all human. We are better in Technicolor, not the grey of conformity. Disabled individuals are also more likely to experience food poverty, yet taking away funding equates to taking away access. If we start having a conversation to make the right information available, our support needs can also start to be addressed, such as when it comes to education or medical care. But I digress.

In the years after I graduated, Harry and I worked together; I later went on to cover other disability issues for *The Metro* and Refinery29. The UK Thalidomiders by then had also taught me a lot. Snobbery — being looked down upon for disability, class or any 'other' characteristic — is not for you to worry about, because it is incumbent on the snob to worry about themselves. (That insecurity is not to be internalized.) You are here to do a job, in a higher position in a grand scheme of things. Hold your head high, and don't you dare look back. Self-deprecation is not worth it. Try, try and try again — because if it is the right thing to do, you hold the moral high ground. Assert your needs if needed. You have every right to ask questions, and to demand accountability when needed.

When I asked how he would like to be remembered, Harry immediately told me off while laughing at my impertinence, reprimanding me because the question sounded as if he had passed on. He then answered seriously, a thoughtful look on his face while speaking directly into the recording device: 'As Harry.' As a father, a husband, a brother, a grandfather, he said. Not the editor, not the journalist, not the book editor. He did not belong to the journalists in the end; he was so very human.

The last phone call came in around November 2019 — midnight UK time — from the back of transport returning to Manhattan. Another book I was potentially going to write at the time came up in conversation, and the response was almost immediate, the excitement almost palpable. The instructions were quick, direct, precise — to the point of instructing how to draw out the shy subject, someone we both knew — and if a contract to write the book was ever going to be signed, 'send it to me', he said. Knowing that someone, somewhere has faith is powerful — and you wouldn't be reading this book if that conversation had not happened. This is the man that I knew, someone who bridged two very different worlds, who loved his craft, who turned up and never stopped showing up. He was my friend, my mentor and also an editor; I'd like to think that, wherever he is, Harry would be proud of this book. 'Upstairs' — his word, not mine — is lucky to have him — along with the 'lost generation' of journalists he spent a lifetime speaking up for. This is my 'salute' to him, for having taught me so much. I miss him, still. More than I can ever truly express.

Rewriting the rule book

How to Use This Book

As a standard practice, accessibility should be at the core of everything and anything, and to make this book as accessible as possible, a few things need to be kept in mind when reading.

First of all, this is a book for autistic individuals first and foremost, but there is information to help other people, too. Some autistic individuals need help with support workers, for example, and may need guidance with this book or an element of supervision while preparing or working with food. As a journalist who covers disability and 'social justice' issues, I have often written about – and criticized – how we cover the topic of disability. The publishing world has only just started to publish the voices of autistic individuals, yet there is still a heavy emphasis on memoirs by parents or carers. Well-meaning individuals may even think that asking a parent or carer about how to be more accessible is appropriate – when it very often is not. The 'gap' in between the two demographics is slowly beginning to be bridged; strides have been made within recent years, such as with the landmark memoir *Odd Girl Out* by Laura James, the work of Siena Castellon and illustrator Megan Rhiannon, as well as countless other autistic creative types. There is a long way to go, but we are eventually getting there. That autistic individuals are doing it for themselves is absolutely marvellous, yet this diagnosis has often been co-opted. This is why everyone involved with this book is autistic or at least has some appropriate experience. Those who have made this book happen – who are not on the autistic spectrum — are fully 'on board' with neurodiversity as a core value as a default position.

In order to best serve autistic individuals, this book has also been written with others in mind as well, such as if extra support has to be provided in the kitchen, as I have just explained. There is information for parents – perhaps if they have a teenager with sensory sensitivities – as well as teachers, in order to aid food education in the classroom. Those I have interviewed for the 'research' side of this book work in some capacity with autistic adults, including one individual who has personally supported me rather extensively.

❋ ❋ ❋

'Self-awareness' – knowledge about ourselves, such as under-standing our strengths and weaknesses – can have a hugely pos-itive impact. Knowledge is typically described as something that makes us powerful; this needs to become standard practice when it comes to the topic of disability, in order to aid accessibility in the long run. We need to not be shy around using terms such as autism, or even when just describing issues we experience. Being equipped with the appropriate vocabulary is a 'must'.

To illustrate further, I would like to share a little bit about my own diagnosis. The process of getting the diagnosis was very abrupt, with one meeting to talk through my diagnostic assess-ment – every facet of what makes me 'me' was dissected, labelled, documented, much to my humiliation. This was the 'what' part of 'what makes Lydia autistic', but missing from this is the 'how we can help her'. There were some basic recommendations to help me through my GCSE exams, and a lot of that was not put into practice, and not much else about life after leaving school at 16. However, autism is a lifelong condition, one outlasting exams and the awkward stage of 'growing up'. The only advice that was really given was to watch *The Big Bang Theory*, as Sheldon Cooper apparently shows autism well, held up as an example of great representation. (I disagree hugely about such a narcissistic character.)

Nothing much else happened after that – a few measures, but not much. The tangible 'getting of' the label was hugely anticli-mactic; I was still autistic – just without strategies or adaptations in place, without a lot of much-needed support.

Assert, the charity that supported me socially and in terms of skills development, is somewhat different and unconventional in its approach; every autistic client whom they help – me included – should be able to develop some self-awareness, and therefore some knowledge about themselves, to enable a positive impact.

Julia Martinez is the leader of the life skills courses run by Assert, which supports autistic adults in Brighton and surrounding areas. The charity has neurodiversity as one of its core values, with the philosophy that everyone should have some self-aware-ness in order to be able to learn skills that are healthy, to cope a bit better. She said:

> I understand self-awareness as being able to *identify* our own feel-ings, and to *understand* the way our feelings affect our actions, as well as being able to identify our own strengths. It also helps us to *regulate* our feelings and actions in different situations. Self-discovery (working on understanding all of the above) directly affects our self-esteem and helps us feel more connected to our-selves and others. I believe self-development and self-actualization – working on becoming the best version of ourselves – is key to leading a happier life and supporting others in achieving this too.

To me, it was something of a revelation. I was no longer resentful or frustrated at myself, and what makes me 'me' was not some-thing I perceived to be detrimental, in need of covering up, to be hidden away. Contrary to how I'd been made to feel by other organizations, I was not a 'charitable case' who had been asked to 'come and make a special friend' at a gathering or event. (Yes, really – this is a true story. The words 'safeguarding risk' clearly had never been flagged when designing such a poster, as that phrase has other insidious meanings.) I was not going to have someone 'grow alongside me' when they should have been assist-ing me; emotional labour – to be expected to educate everyone about everything to do with autism – is an unfair expectation, but is often the default when individuals generally have not met a walking, talking female. (Also another true anecdote that was deemed 'appropriate'.)

Taking this into account, I have compiled as much information as possible all in one place, to try to create a reference point for anything to do with cooking, baking and food preparation; to be aware of challenges we may experience while cooking and why is important. If we have this knowledge, we can work to adapt and learn how to manage our support needs.

❇ ❇ ❇

Being accessible often means rewriting the 'rule book' – which means that the recipes you find here are not written in a conventional format. They are instead designed to aid autistic individuals, just like those interviewed for this book who spoke candidly about their experiences of struggling.

There are many things that can throw up a roadblock while trying to cook. Anecdotally, I know many autistic people who have several common experiences such as struggling to 'time sequence' a meal so everything is cooked at the same time, ensuring everything is cooked properly or 'decoding' the language a recipe is written in. The language we use in cookbooks can be difficult to interpret, and some things may not always be explicit, so you have to guess what the 'obvious' is. Language is strange because it is fluid and open to interpretation. Why would heat have a weight, for example? One interviewee described her frustration at the language of recipes and questioned what a 'light heat' was. While the English language has sometimes adapted with strange idioms – such as 'it's raining cats and dogs' – this can be unhelpful to someone who may be literal, who may be left having to learn (and memorize) the meanings of such phrases. Some non-autistic early readers described their own frustration with this exact same context, too. Accessibility is not just 'preferential treatment' – quote marks intended – because it positively impacts everyone. To be accommodating is to level up, to enable everyone to do the same job to the best of their ability, regardless.

Everyone has a level of energy that is available in only limited supply, but this is also likely to be even more limited for autistic individuals. We are having to cope with a world that is not built for us, and therefore our energy is in shorter supply. How can you decide what to cook and when to cook when your energy may already be far too depleted from having to mask, cope with being social, as well as dealing with feeling 'overwhelmed'? Unless you have made a recipe a hundred times before, you may not realize that your energy is running low, or that the recipe may 'cost' you far more, and then even more energy has been lost. Having a degree of self-awareness would mean knowing how much energy you have and learning how to manage to prepare food in line with your needs, which is a continual process.

Methods have been adopted by autistic individuals to express how our energy levels may be significantly lower as more is spent on 'coping' – masking in various situations, dealing with over-load, trying to manually decode the nuances of social codes and language. Each recipe in this book has information about the amount of energy it will cost. Working with food takes a lot of energy – which we may not always have. Constructing a complex meal may not be possible after a meltdown. More information – along with an energy scale and what this entails – is available at the beginning of all the recipes.

Along with this – taking into account the use of energy – each recipe is also given a skill level. The more energy you have, the more feasible it is to construct a more complex meal. Cooking is an imprecise science, said one interviewee, and therefore these descriptors are guidelines, designed to accommodate as many individuals as possible.

EASY   MEDIUM   COMPLEX

Easy

- Minimal use of physical skills (e.g. cutting/chopping and stirring) is required.
- One or two adaptations in the kitchen will be needed.

- Only one component of the recipe will be cooking or baking to complete the meal.

Medium

- Moderate use of physical skills (e.g. cutting/chopping and stirring) is required.
- Three or four adaptations in the kitchen might be needed.
- Between two and four components of the recipe will be cooking or baking at one time to complete the meal.

Complex

- Maximum use of physical skills (e.g. cutting/chopping and stirring) is required.
- Five or six adaptations in the kitchen might be needed.
- Five or more components of the recipe will be cooking or baking at one time to complete the meal.

To assist further, notes are included where you need to plan ahead of time when creating a recipe. For example, ice cream will not just automatically freeze; it takes eight hours to become ice cream. If you fancy it right in the moment, this will be fairly useless! This will also help with executive functioning challenges; unless told explicitly, some autistic individuals may not necessarily know how to sequence a recipe if this is not clear.

Feedback has been taken on board to make the book as inclusive and as accessible as possible.

When I was able to finally announce on Twitter that I was writing this book, the response was overwhelming. It was incredible to see the number of people who said that this book was something they needed — and that they would be putting it on their Christmas wish list for whenever it would arrive! My inbox was filled with people wanting to read the book before I'd even written it or who wanted to be interviewed to contribute a recipe. As a result, feedback from every possible source has been taken into account – from taking note of Twitter users and private Facebook groups, to asking those who were interviewed for this book about their challenges and experiences. A book is poorer without interviews, as there's a wealth of experience you could miss; this was something I had practised a lot as a journalist anyway. But there needs to be a caveat to this.

In taking in feedback as I was writing, I have tried to be as inclusive of everyone – but there may be some gaps. I cannot claim to speak for every autistic person. Autism is a spectrum, and every autistic person is an individual – in the same way that every human being is different from every other person. I do not know every autistic person just because I am on the spectrum, and by proxy, I cannot speak for everyone. This applies to every characteristic of those who are classed as being marginalized or tick the box that says 'other'; human beings speak not for a collective, only themselves, when it comes to such a topic, unless specifically designated to do so – for example, if they sit on a council of some kind or are giving evidence to a House of Commons Select Committee.

All efforts have been made to be as inclusive and as accessible as possible while writing this book. Those who contributed recipes were also given the chance to read through their recipe, in order to ensure it stayed true to how they described it. Changes were also made – for example, if the interviewee was non-verbal, or if a conversational structure was needed – to allow for 'scripting'. We are all works in progress, and this may not be a book for everyone, for this reason. However, it would also be inappropriate for me to write about other conditions – I am only autistic and yet I was often criticized for not writing 'The Neurodiverse Cookbook'. It would be inappropriate for me to write such a book when I only have the one diagnosed condition – and it would have gone on forever!

Five Golden Rules to Remember

These five rules should make up the 'common ground' of what any autistic individual needs to remember while using this book and cooking, baking or working with food.

1. Knowing how to help yourself can be helpful

From the point of diagnosis, there seems to be this odd idea about how to deal with acknowledging that someone is on the autistic spectrum. I know of parents who have hidden their child's diagnosis, only for the child to later find out as an adult, having spent years wondering why they were different, unable to articulate or understand why. This seems to so often be dismissed as 'typical teenage angst' – whatever that means – when there is an actual underlying reason. Anecdotally, there are stories where the child – now a 'grown-up' – would later argue that difficulties they struggled with in the present went back to having spent so much time struggling, having lived under a cloud of 'not knowing' and feeling out of place. The justification that often came up? 'I don't want my child to experience stigma.' But that is allowing a struggle to go on and is arguably worse than a stigma that is in need of challenging in the first place.

Knowing yourself, your strengths and challenges you face has a huge range of benefits. 'Stigma' is more of a 'what if' concept – 'what if I experience this?' – a hypothetical scenario. While I understand why some may suggest they want to shield others from stigma, you cannot live life in a perpetual state of 'what if'. You will never know what will happen; you may even later wonder,

'What could have been if...?' It also suggests that stigma is the responsibility of the autistic individual.

Understanding yourself – what you find difficult or easy, your preferred textures, your sensory profile, possible triggers for distress – can have a hugely positive impact, as we can start to help ourselves when it comes to adapting the kitchen and making food accessible. We will be delving more into this in the next chapter, by way of 'lifting the lid' on all things sensory. It can be difficult, and there is never just a stage of 'I have learned everything'. We are all works in progress, after all.

2. There is no shame in the 'not knowing' of something

My job relies on asking questions, which is not just in the context of an interview. Information is what empowers all of us and is what we all effectively run on; we give and receive information on a day-by-day basis. We tweet it, blog it, Facebook it, WhatsApp it, exchange it in conversation; it is the very basis of what constitutes a society of people. It is the very fabric that binds us all together as a species.

There is a huge gap in 'food education' when it comes to autistic individuals, but research has yet to quantify this. At the time of writing, there is no data to officially provide context, but it is blindingly obvious from anecdotes, interviews or just friendly conversations with autistic people. Many autistic people spoke or wrote to me about how they did not learn how to cook or prepare food because lessons were not accessible – or that they had not learned because they were perceived as not needing to know how to prepare food, on the basis of their condition. Another common theme was bullying and discrimination, very often connected to the state of 'not knowing'. Some also had another condition that meant an extra layer of support was needed, which can happen when someone is on the autistic spectrum, but with infantilization added to the mix. All played a part in making the kitchen a place where many were extremely uncomfortable and/or anxious/apprehensive at times. There is no shame in the 'not knowing' – we are all entitled, by the basic right of being a human being, to information. Information empowers us, and it is how we learn.

Inaccessibility, discrimination and bullying have no place in the twenty-first century.

3. Cook for yourself – and not for the approval of anyone else

We are all familiar with those moments where something is just bound to go wrong, when we end up asking, 'Why me?' I have had many of those while baking and cooking, preparing the most basic of meals. For example, during one of the Covid 19 lockdowns, virtually everyone in the UK tried baking banana bread. Mine leaked out of the improvised cake tin, as the bottom was not screwed properly into place. Not bad for a first attempt, perhaps, but it did go badly wrong and was a lot smaller than it should have been and more shrivelled as a result.

At the suggestion of a lecturer, I baked a weekly cake for a particular class while attending college. It was a way to make friends, apparently – my social skills are not the best, after all – but I would argue people just talked to me because of the prospect of free cake. I was baking every week for approval, which became something quite stressful. (I also remained relatively lonely, more likely to turn to books as a result.) Each and every single cake would have a satirical, tongue-in-cheek theme. It was the year Donald Trump was elected, and some of us felt really sad – we got through it on the basis of buns. Cake can do a lot for misery, sometimes. Just something to bear in mind.

The more I cooked or baked for approval, the more I found that something was liable to go wrong. This is just one example of *that* manifesting itself. Or, failing that, I could always see the faults and the flaws of what I had (imperfectly) produced. My nature can be a little too perfectionist, thanks to often trying to compensate for my executive functioning challenges. So, learn from my mistake: cook for yourself, and only yourself. The moment I did this, my self-confidence began to improve massively. And if someone criticizes that delicious, chocolate sponge cake you tried to create, because you turned it into something that looked a little like a monster to cover up some very noticeable flaws, they can always go without a slice.

4. To be accessible, we are going to have to let go of the neurotypical standards most kitchens go by

It is something that should not have to be said, let alone written in a book. We should not have to wear lanyards just to ensure basic standards, or even phone ahead to get access to venues. We should not have to lobby constantly for a basic 'levelling up' of standards we are eligible for, just to reach the same standards set for a very niche demographic society holds up as 'normal'. We should not have to prove that we are autistic enough when applying for Personal Independence Payment, a specific benefit in the UK, to try to avoid a tribunal yet still be set up to fail.

Can I let you into a secret? Come closer...closer. *Whispers* Accessibility matters – and to make the kitchen accessible, we are going to have to rewrite neurotypical standards of what it means to be accessible. It also will have a positive impact for everyone, and is not just 'preferential treatment', a phrase that seems to crop up in justifications to not provide basic accessible arrangements, when legally they should already be in place.

It took me so many years to realize that I judged myself too harshly by marking myself against neurotypical standards, such as when it came to productivity, fitness or any other ability. The feeling of 'I am not good enough but what is it that is wrong with me?' was – and still is – immense at times. The same can be said for my 'hit and miss' style of working – well, trying to work – in the kitchen. This is a story that I see so very often when it comes to other autistic folk, too. The frustration was almost palpable; it was the taste of metal in your mouth, the feel of a balled-up fist just before a meltdown, the lack of follow-through.

We will keep rules that define things such as safety, as well as keeping standards of food care in place, too. But we will not keep the standard of 'everything having to be perfect' – from the presentation of a recipe to the food combinations. Mistakes happen. And people sometimes have tastes that may seem outlandish to some of us – such as peanut butter on sliced apple. (That's my sibling who likes that. Now, *that* is something we will never see eye to eye on. Yuck.) Cook for yourself and try to learn to let go of impossible standards. You will feel so much better for it, trust me.

5. We are but a tapestry in progress

The world would be a very boring place if we were all the same, with no difference, no creativity, no originality. It is the in-between where what makes us human begins and ends. We all have our faults and flaws, our better sides and more positive days. It may be frustrating at times to acquire new skills over time, but there is something beautiful in that. Be kind to yourself.

Five Ground Rules for Parents/Guardians/ Carers, Teachers, Support Staff and Others

I am aware that there will be other people who will also read this book, including parents, teachers and support workers. I also wanted to provide five ground rules for this particular demographic, too.

1. Failure is not a bad thing: If you are in a supervisory role, you need to let us fail in order to improve

Take a leaf out of the book of Elizabeth Day, a journalist and podcast host who is perhaps best known for her books including *How to Fail* and *Failosophy*. Failure is not a bad thing and is something that we all have to cope with while we live on this small but utterly wonderful planet. But there is something I need to emphasize, too: we all are in need of being allowed to fail, which is a slightly different concept. Karl Knights, an autistic writer who also has attention deficit hyperactivity disorder (ADHD) and cerebral palsy, agreed. When asked what he struggles with most when working with food, he said:

> I think for me it's almost a psychological thing, it's almost like the thing that I struggle with the most is just feeling comfortable, at home in a kitchen. And for me at least — I know this will be true of a lot of autistic people — where the kitchen will sort of

historically, in childhood, in adolescence or whenever, have been a kind of battleground really, would have been a battlefield that you would have had to navigate.

He further suggested that this has a further negative impact of being in the kitchen and having to deal with inaccessibility, as well as food in general, such as having to battle with issues over and over when little accessibility is put in place.

Asking Karl what he'd say to someone in a supervisory role retrospectively, he replied, 'We'll get there eventually' – adding that time needed to be created to allow for mistakes. He further said, 'I think the key thing really is to create an environment where failure or what we might call failure is just a natural part of the process', citing environments where 'failure' is just an 'end point', where it is a part of the process to learn. 'Mistakes are just part of the process,' he said.

Growing up, the dots had not been joined together. I knew I was 'different' from a young age, yet I lacked the emotional sophistication and language to articulate this. Being diagnosed was somewhat the same, and the process took years. I knew I was autistic – which is the 'how' – but the 'why' as to cooking and the associated difficulties had just not clicked for some reason. No one bothers to explain the 'why' – you struggle to work out if you're cold due to poor interoception recognition. A diagnostic report in the UK may not draw the dots to line up, which leaves you to discover your own strengths and weaknesses, what you struggle with and what you need little help with.

It is beyond frustrating for others to take over what you are doing, to be twitching and hovering around while you are trying to complete whatever recipe you want to make. It is also arguably a sign of infantilization, in taking away and undermining that inde-pendence, and therefore preventing further learning. Although supervision is needed at times, we need to be able to learn freely. Very often, I was not allowed to fail, and I can think of multiple occasions when I was prevented from completing various recipes, without an explanation.

Step in when appropriate, if help is urgently needed or if there is a fire hazard. Decide the appropriate level of instruction, too – and you can sometimes do that by talking to us! But failure is not a bad thing, and you need to let us learn from mistakes.

2. Telling us to be careful will probably not make us more careful when we are already trying to be careful

The kitchen was loud, the lights too bright. The oven was hissing, almost like bellows from an old accordion slowly wheezing into life. I was too hot; the early warning signs of overload were starting to show. Too much sensory 'stuff' was having an impact physically, on my speech and gestures. Overwhelmed and frazzled, the impact was beginning to manifest.

'Okay, go slowly,' the voice instructed me. My inner monologue was aware of me being watched, going into hyper-drive. My arms became heavy, topped off with my cumbersome motor skills, in an attempt to make it look as though the stirring was being done neatly. My mouth quirked into a nondescript expression to try to avoid attracting attention. In other words, I was attempting to be careful and putting a lot of work into meeting an invisible standard being placed on me by somebody else.

'Careful, Lydia.' I continued stirring, mouth still in a weird position, arms still heavy. All was going okay, or so it seemed – the contents of the bowl were contained within the bowl, after all. It wasn't as if I had flung ingredients on to the ceiling of the fastidious person supervising. This time, the emphasis in their tone changed.

'Lydia, be careful!' It was more direct, curt. But I was trying my best, to the extent that my head was starting to hurt with too much input. An irritated sigh was directed at me and my apparently lacking skills, and the pot of what was being stirred was physically taken away from me. My cooking activities were curtailed as that individual took over and finished the recipe. I was left feeling annoyed and upset at having been infantilized once again, because of something well outside of my control – and for a non-specific issue (apparently, my 'awkwardness' and 'slowness' were just too much). Karl Knights also identified with this. Describing the kitchen as a contentious space, he said, 'For whatever reason, we might not have that knowledge that's considered basic [in the kitchen] or considered a bedrock.' He gave the example of wishing to fade into the background while being taught how to cook in education, because of the space not being accommodating enough.

Telling us to be careful is counterproductive sometimes. It is probably highly likely that we are already trying to be careful and using a lot of our already reduced energy to meet an impossible standard. Instead, try saying directly what the issue is or be direct with the instruction, rather than leaving us to try to guess what we need to do. We cannot read minds, after all.

3. Mistake in the classroom? Do not draw everyone's attention to it

This does not really need explaining does it? If there is a catastrophe in the classroom, do not draw attention to it – just deal with it calmly and professionally, and deflect attention if needed. In retrospect, I wish this is something I could have told virtually every teacher who was supposed to teach me how to cook and bake.

4. Encourage, encourage, encourage

For a long time, I felt quite ashamed of 'it', the thing that no one talked to me directly about until recently. 'It' was scary, 'it' was trouble, 'it' was apparently a problem to just about everyone. Being a diagnosed autistic female meant having to confront what was framed as a problematic flaw, something that would mark me out as 'other'. 'It' finally had a name, but it did not do a lot for my self-confidence or esteem to begin with. I would be lying to say otherwise. It is indicative of us as a society when this is also a frequently shared experience.

We need to reframe the way we see ourselves, as well as how you – someone not on the autistic spectrum – may see autistic people. Think that they talk about one particular subject a lot, and that they are a 'boffin' or a 'know it all' as a result? That is something that will be very useful one day – whether it is being able to recite the names of all the Doctor Who aliens or passages of Sylvia Plath verbatim. (Go on, ask me. I dare you. It's been years but I can still do it.) It is just how you see 'it' and how you reframe the viewpoint. 'Flaws' make for strengths a lot of the time.

Think about being in the classroom or kitchen. Sometimes 'fine motor skills' can be an issue for us; I know I definitely have this issue. It can make some tasks tricky, such as grating cheese as a topping for a jacket potato. (Might be easy for some, but not for me.) Other things, such as how the environment is, or even just executive functioning, can be challenging on the best of the 'good' days. It may be incredibly frustrating, but it is not something to laugh at, to judge, to make prejudiced comments about or to 'tease' about.

If there are issues like this, it is probably not an isolated issue. It could be used as an opportunity to get classmates to work together, to learn a little bit more than usual. If the language of a recipe is difficult to understand, I would bet that it is not just one person who thinks the same. Some neurotypical people told me while writing this book that they actually found it easier to understand my way of working when language was adapted. Sometimes the characteristics we have are assets – but it may take longer to find out how that will work. Trial and error is the way to go.

5. Talk to us as if we are human beings

Just like the internet meme, let's say it louder for the people at the back: being autistic, having a diagnosis of autism, self-diagnosing, being a 'suspected' autistic or being in the bubble of waiting for a diagnostic assessment does not make you stupid, an idiot or any other horrible stereotype. If I could, emojis would be added to that one sentence, in the shape of hands clapping between words, just to underline and punctuate the point.

It is strange to assume that autism equates to having a 'lack of intelligence' or to confuse it with an unassociated condition. For example, people very often assume I am hard of hearing – and will take to me loudly, in a childish tone, with child-appropriate language to converse with me. (Talking through me to my parent is another 'low'.) Sometimes I have been shouted at, even by professionals, who assume I am *winces* of a 'low-functioning level of autism'. (Ick!) Trust me, I can understand you – and this is never appropriate behaviour. As a general rule, being age-appropriate, regardless of disability, is what you should be doing. Using the term 'disabled' or naming the condition is also probably a good way to go. Ask us how we prefer to describe ourselves.

Autistic individuals may just need help when it comes to communication at times. That is down to their own individual diagnostic profile that describes them as an individual, what their needs are and what they may need support with. But if you teach an autistic person, please just talk to them like a human being. It will make the world of difference to use respectful and age-appropriate language in line with their support needs, and will contribute to a more productive lesson/baking session as well.

A Note on Equity vs Equality

The concept of equality is something that we are all familiar with, and we have probably been parroting the word since we were old enough to speak, think and understand the world around us. I certainly remember being taught what it means when I was little: to be treated as equals, regardless of characteristics that are protected, such as race, religion, class, etc.

Ironically, this has been taken somewhat literally, in that it has come to mean treated exactly the same, regardless of whatever issue there was in the first place. A common photo that circulates online shows a classroom of different individuals – sometimes they are animals given human characteristics. One has broken a leg, one has a cut and one is totally fine. All of them are given a plaster. This illustrates an extreme and literal form of equality in practice, underlining how our interpretations have sometimes come to lose all meaning or reason with time. It may be equal to give everyone a plaster, but it doesn't much help someone with a broken leg.

Everyone in the same classroom may be given the same equipment at the same time in the interests of equality, but that does nothing to solve the issues and challenges autistic people find themselves having to battle and grapple with constantly. (We may need adapted equipment, after all!) That is not equality; instead, it is Inaccessibility with a capital I.

Equity is a different concept that ought to take precedence, so that we can achieve equality. It means that everyone is treated according to their needs, so that everyone reaches the same standard of equality and accessibility. This book is written with this principle in mind.

This should not be confused with the term 'preferential treatment', a phrase that we have seen a lot of in some newspapers and occasionally in policy. I have lost count – much to my disgust as a journalist – of the many newspapers that have used this expression, some with the view that they are somehow being helpful to the world of special educational needs. (Spoiler: It is probably not at all helpful. And it embodies exactly why we need a diverse, representative media. But that's a conversation for another time.)

Accessibility means, within the context of this book, to 'level up' – a phrase deployed here without any intended irony. There is no such thing as 'preferential treatment'; all that means is that there is no barrier to you and your access. To 'level up' in the realm of this book means to give access to everyone, regardless, in line with the needs of the individual. Because that is the true meaning of equality; you cannot have one without the other.

Why Cooking and Baking May Be Difficult for Autistic People

When I applied for Personal Independence Payment, a specific type of disability benefit here in the UK, it was always likely it would result in a tribunal, simply on the grounds of probability. I am used to autism often being regarded as something that can be 'switched off', being told that I could just 'do better' while being 'more communicative', 'making more of an effort'. An assessment came back, reflecting nothing of my distress, and it was beyond inaccurate. One line that stood out was the suggestion that I could 'just learn' to cook – which reflected nothing of my reality or lived experience. If I can 'just learn', then maybe I can just learn to 'be normal' and not be autistic! (Sarcasm intended.) It also suggested I had no issues with communication. Again, that was not a true reflection of the amount of time and energy that I spend trying to communicate on a daily basis.

Having read that ridiculous report, I was looking for confirmation that my experience was real, that there was a universal experience in what I found when it came to cooking. Many others had many of the same challenges I still experience, and those who were able to cook seemed only to have learned as a result of working with food as part of a special interest, to which time was (often extensively) devoted. That is exceptional and cannot be the same for everyone. Autism is a spectrum, after all.

There are three recurring areas that were continually flagged by interviewees for this book and was supported by my research into why autistic people often find working with food to be difficult. These may not be the same for everyone, and this just scratches the surface of an issue, too. Strategies practised by autistic individuals are in the chapter 'Solo Strategies for Cooking: In Their Own Words'.

What is a sensory profile and how does it affect working with food?

Imagine this. You find yourself planted in a region unknown to you previously. The environment is strange; boxy structures are all around you, emitting some kind of odd light. No matter how much you shield yourself, it's so bright that it hurts your eyes. The ground is fuzzy beneath your feet; the texture is unpleasant, and your feet make a noise that grates on your teeth when you walk. Nearby, there is noise playing; someone thinks it's music, but it's modern rap music at an intolerable, disorientating level. To you it sounds just like shouting, an incomprehensible mix of sounds, and the pain it causes lasts for hours afterwards. The bass and the voices become indistinguishable, loud, painful. This is just a little bit of what it is like to be autistic, with ever-present sensory issues. And this was what it was like to be cooking at secondary school. There are strategies to work with this, however, rather than expecting autistic people to 'just cope'. Everyone has eight different senses. There are the five that we all know about – smell, sound, touch, taste and sight. There are three additional senses that need to be taken into consideration, too. They are:

- **Proprioception.** This means how the body senses things such as movement and location. However, it may be impaired in autistic individuals. From my own experience, if there are two tables in front of me, I logically know I need to navigate between them, but I will almost certainly still end up bashing into at least one table.
- **Interoception.** This is the sense of what is going on inside the body. Sensory markers send signals to the brain; they

interpret sensations and sometimes turn this into an emotion or feeling. Stomach rumbling and making gurgly noises? You got it – you must be hungry and ready for it to be lunch time! Yawning all the time and finding it hard to keep your eyes open? You probably need an early night. Autistic individuals may have an impaired interoceptive sense, which can look like not knowing if they are hungry or full up, for example, or not being able to interpret temperature very well.

- **Vestibular.** This refers to balance and movement.

What is important to know and to take into consideration is that we have different sensitivity levels when it comes to each sense. Struggle with a lot of noise in one place? You may be hypersensitive – too much input is overwhelming. That would make you a sensory avoider in this context. However, are you a big fan of spicy food, enough to liberally sprinkle your dinner plate? That is a classic sign of being hyposensitive – looking for extra input. This would make you a sensory seeker. Each individual can have different sensory sensitivity levels for each sense; this is what makes up a sensory profile.

Sensory issues can pose an extra layer of challenges to contend with when it comes to cooking, baking and working with food. Occasionally, there can be hideous smells and textures that assault our senses, sounds that are impossible to deal with, things that taste disgusting. Imagine all the extra input of cooking with your peers – the talking, socializing, cooking sounds, instructions from your teacher, squeaking of tables... It can be a bit much at times, and it may begin to have a more visible impact – for example, problems with focusing, productivity, speaking and more.

When it comes to eating, there is such a stereotype around 'picky eaters'. This is often a lazy catch-all for when an issue has gone unaddressed – tastes and textures that may go against a sensory preference. Sometimes just changing the form of the food served can help – such as blending cooked vegetables into a sauce or serving all of the food elements clearly and separately.

Executive functioning: when the little PA inside our brain decides not to work

Being able to follow a recipe through to the end, to construct a meal from raw ingredients, can be a challenge for most people. However, there is a scientific reason that explains why autistic people may find it significantly harder.

Julia Martinez, leader of the life skills courses run by Assert, a charity that supports autistic adults in Brighton and surrounding areas, was asked to describe executive functioning, and the impact it may have when it's impaired. She said: 'The way I see executive functioning is like a little PA, so a personal assistant in our brain, like an office person, trying to organize, prioritize tasks.' It is the part of the brain that oversees basic task functions, ensuring that things get done, tasks are completed and sequenced correctly, all the while keeping appointments and staying up to date with the day-to-day grind we all have to contend with. Autistic individuals may experience what is called executive dysfunction, thanks to the PA not being quite up to the job. This will have an impact when cooking, baking or even just attempting to work with the most basic of food items. It is not the individual's fault and is often an issue outside their control.

Difficulties with executive functioning could look like: difficulty starting/initiating tasks; being unable to sequence a task (e.g. to make a cup of tea, following through the steps in the right order to arrive at the desired ending of the drink itself); struggling with tasks to maintain basic hygiene practices such as washing, keeping your living space clean or knowing when and how to change your bedding; paying bills on time, and more.

This can create various issues in the kitchen, which are very often not seen, and may not be immediately obvious. If a recipe has instructions that are written in a non-accessible way, sequencing the recipe in order to get to the final dish is likely going to be difficult. It could even be as simple as struggling to time two pots on a stove which are cooking at the exact same time – a common issue expressed by the people interviewed for this book.

Language

Autistic individuals have a bad reputation for being literal. If you think about it, the English language is filled with some pretty strange turns of phrases, images and metaphors, such as 'it's raining cats and dogs'. Rather than talking more loudly or more slowly, which can be infantalizing, the presentation of the information needs to change – such as being more direct, asking either/or type questions.

Julia Martinez had previously been a primary school teacher and was used to working with young children prior to working with autistic adults in the UK. She said, 'I wouldn't necessarily use different language with children than I would when I'm with adults, when I'm talking to adults.' She added that this was a matter of showing respect and kindness, while suggesting that, although well meaning, this can come from conflating autism with a learning disability or difficulty.

Robin Van Creveld is the founder and director of Community Chef, a not-for-profit organization based in Sussex, UK, that has the mission statement of 'good food for all is a fundamental human right'. With over 20 years' experience in the food industry, he also teaches in-person workshops and demonstrations. He said:

> Use the power of asking questions to get people to share who they are, but also to build trust. It's a good way to be a good facilitator. For me a key thing is [to] keep asking questions – be open hearted, be empathic, and ask questions. You learn so much more about people when you ask them something personal than when you ask them something didactic or specific.

He added: 'I think [a] really important way of creating an environment where anyone can learn is by making people feel super comfortable, super safe.' This empowers individuals to ask questions and advocate for themselves if needed. This can be done by asking questions and making written language – for example, in ingredients lists – as clear as possible.

Language that is implied – not explicit – is unlikely to work well. It has always seemed to me that people who are not on the autistic spectrum have an innate skill to just 'get' what is implied – such as when it comes to social codes to make friends. There is so much that is implied in language, but unless an instruction is made abundantly clear, it is very unlikely that an autistic individual will just 'know' it. This is important when it comes to instructions and interpreting recipes that are written down.

Says Martinez: 'It wouldn't be so much changing the tone to speak to someone, but maybe choosing clear words, and being specific about instructions, reducing the information we use to communicate, and using the essential, clear words.'

Instructions need to be kept clear and straight to the point. Keeping expressions simple and cutting out fancy language like silly metaphors will help a lot. Martinez also made the point about allowing time for processing communication: 'The moment you hear the information doesn't necessarily mean you're understanding or making sense of that information. So frequent pauses to allow for individuals with slow processing time to catch up...just allowing for this time, to process language.'

Add in frequent breaks and pace a lesson if you're a teacher; this will enable better communication and information retention. This is beneficial for everyone, not just autistic individuals. Live demonstrations are all very well and good, but instructions also need to be written down.

How You Can Help an Autistic Person When They Are Working with Food

We are all likely to need a little bit of help sometimes – there's no shame in admitting that. In the UK, the Equality Act stipulates that autism is a disability. Some people may not like this – we are all entitled to use our preferred ways of describing ourselves – but it means that in a legal context organizations and institutions are obliged to provide reasonable adjustments. We need to accept that we have extra challenges that we may need help with. Sometimes autistic individuals have additional help such as a carer, guardian or a personal assistant (PA).

There are some basic things that you can do to help an autistic person when cooking, and they are often inexpensive and simple. Adaptations will be covered further on; they can also help out a lot when working in the kitchen, or even just when it comes to consuming food. Keep in mind, autism is a spectrum, so this may not work for everyone. Trial and error can help to map out how to help.

Be aware of sensory profiles
Sometimes there is a cultural expectation of 'not wanting to label' your child, yourself, your relative or your student in terms of an autism diagnosis, to avoid the associated stigma, but this may lead to another kind of stigma. The 'not knowing' leads to other labels such as 'lazy', 'clumsy', 'disorganized' and other negative terms. In knowing and accepting that an individual is on

the autistic spectrum, they can begin to develop self-awareness, advocate for themselves and learn crucial skills that fit within their own access/support needs and abilities.

We have already briefly looked at sensory profiles in the previous chapter – what they are, what they mean and how they can potentially create another layer of challenge in the kitchen. However, being aware of a sensory profile means being aware of potential issues further down the line, which can be worked around while working with food. While writing this book, I undertook a baking course that was run by Robin Van Creveld. I cannot abide the feel of some textures on my hands, particularly when working with dough – especially if it is cold and squishy, with the possibility of being sticky. Robin suggested using a butter knife to stir instead of kneading, which worked well to get around my sensory issue of aversion to the texture. This is just a small example of being aware of a sensory profile, and therefore being aware enough to work around a situation and find an adaptive solution. Being aware of sensory issues and adapting could include small measures such as wearing ear plugs or headphones to guard against certain sounds, using disposable gloves when working with particular types of food such as meat, nose plugs and more.

Instructions

Instructions can pose a problem if there is a lack of adaptation for an autistic person or if they are poorly written. (This happens a lot. And it can be a hindrance to anyone, regardless of where they sit on the spectrum.) Instructions can be communicated by writing down a recipe or verbally – if there is an emergency or if you are part of a class. Instructions can also be delivered in other forms such as a demonstration (when you'll have to replicate later what you were shown) or a cook-along (where everyone does the same action together, right through to the end of a recipe).

The language instructions are written in can sometimes be problematic, and it makes interpreting recipes difficult sometimes. There is a lot of jargon and it is just assumed that everyone knows what it means. Some language also can be a bit tricky to understand, especially if the context is about hypotheticals or it is non-explicit. One of the people interviewed for this book spoke about how they felt frustrated when trying to understand instructions for cooking with a hob. What exactly is a 'light heat', and how can you cook with it? Heat does not have a weight, so what does a 'light heat' mean? If you're presenting a recipe, try to ensure the language of the instructions is simple and straight to the point. This should also be the rule when you are teaching or directing an individual or a class. I have tried to do this to the best of my ability throughout this book.

Allow questions to be asked; if someone does not understand, do not just repeat the same instruction. Repeating will not mean that we suddenly understand what you are trying to tell us! (Personally, this annoys me a lot, especially when people think they are being helpful, but their tone changes to how they would talk to a child. It's inappropriate, shows a lack of respect and is patronizing.) Keep calm, be patient, and if reassurance is needed, give it. And for autistic individuals, there is a list of terminology with definitions at the end of this book.

In a classroom/teaching setting

Classrooms are not known for being accessible environments. Period. A lot has been written about this in recent years, so I'm not going to re-hash the same research/knowledge here. There are other books that are written by experts that would do the topic more justice than I ever could.

To help an autistic individual in these settings, keeping the communication open – especially in terms of instructions – can be very helpful. If you are demonstrating how to make a particular dish, allowing questions to be asked at each stage can be very helpful; explaining more than just the instructions can build up skills and confidence. Robin's teaching method is especially helpful – for example, he explains the basic chemistry of dough. This allows his students to adapt and build on what they are taught. Keep to the schedule/routine and check in on people now and again. Some may be afraid to ask for help.

Solo Strategies for Cooking: In Their Own Words

In the course of writing this book, there were a few universal themes that needed to be addressed. When I began looking for recipes, it was really quite striking how so many individuals experienced the same issues when cooking, baking and working with food. The majority expressed frustration that although they had been willing to learn how to cook, they were often mocked or discriminated against, or those teaching – whether a teacher, parent or carer – had quickly lost patience, assuming that any challenges were 'insolence', rather than a legitimate struggle. Alongside this, there was a lack of knowing how to help themselves among so many participants; other people got in touch over many months to express that they had no idea about strategies or potential adaptations. Others did not have the vocabulary to describe their own experiences – or, if they did, it was not until much later in life that they had been equipped to do that, and they had been left to play 'catch up'.

In the UK, you are more likely to experience food poverty if you have a disability; in terms of the relevant legislation, autism is considered to be a part of this definition, thanks to the Equality Act 2010. For this very reason alone, equipping autistic people with the right skills and knowledge should be hugely important, along with other disabled demographics. It would enable better levels of independence, as well as arguably having a positive knock-on impact in terms of nutritional health, mental health, etc.

This wonderfully unique demographic of individuals is so often spoken over in media terms and the way we talk about autism;

we still spend so much time telling the stories of parents and guardians, for example, when they are not the story of an autistic person. Individuals interviewed for this book were given the chance to speak to their own experience, and it was important that they could do that while not being moderated. A small collection of experiences has been collated here; please note that not all strategies will work for everyone.

Adaptations in the kitchen

There are small adaptive changes that can be made to the kitchen in terms of tools, as well as the surrounding environment; it's a matter of 'trial and error' to work out what works best for you. The next chapter includes a list of potential adaptations for autistic individuals – such as meal separators that can be used when an individual does not like different foods touching each other. There is no shame in using adaptations to prepare or consume food with; they are there to help.

Barb Cook is a developmental educator and the founder of *Spectrum Women Magazine*. She is also the co-author of the book Spectrum *Women*. She expressed her frustration with cooking due to dexterity-related issues: 'If I'm cutting something and holding on to it, I do okay sometimes, but other times I can't hold on to things, so they roll off.' She also finds tasks such as getting something out of a frying pan to be difficult, due to dexterity-related issues.

Visual prompts can aid language interpretation and so much more. Visual prompts mean exactly that – an object to visually prompt you to do something or to help you to understand something better. These constitute a multiplicity of objects. For example, liquid timers can be very useful when cooking; time is visually represented by the dripping of the liquid. Some autistic individuals may also describe this in the sense of time becoming much more of a tangible concept, too.

April Lloyd is a sports producer for Radio Clatterbridge, as well as being a disability fellow for Journo Resources. She is also the co-founder of Empoword Journos. A self-confessed foodie, she said: 'What I suppose I find really difficult is not having a visual for what each step in a recipe needs to look like. Say, for example, if I am making fudge, I need to have a visual to tell me what mixtures look like when they "lose their shine" or have a "play dough texture".' Here, there is no visual prompt to aid April's understanding of what the fudge was supposed to look like while she was making it.

Karl Knights reflected on his own cooking experience: 'If I was cooking, I would often ask, "Okay, why does it do that?"' he said, laughing. 'Or, "Why does this happen?" And I would need to know why. I'd say, "Why does bread rise?"' He professed this was not being awkward but trying to actively understand, visually, what was happening to the food in front of him.

So think of potential challenges you may face and having to deal with multiple parts of a recipe at once. Use a visual aid to help, such as a liquid timer or a written-down recipe. If you're teaching individuals, being specific about changes to look out for – such as changes in the texture of the fudge, the example cited by April Lloyd – can be helpful to autistic individuals.

Think of the environment

Autistic individuals are sensory beings. What that means is that we may have different sensitivities from people who are neuro-typical – those not on the autistic spectrum. We can be hypersensitive – experiencing too much sensory input – which would make us a sensory avoider. We can also be hyposensitive – wishing for more sensory input – which would make us a sensory seeker. This is sense-dependent, in that you could be hypersensitive to noise but be hyposensitive in terms of taste. This presents in a variety of ways that depends on the individual.

Maia Osborne is a laboratory scientist. She said:

> It makes me anxious, uncomfortable and I struggle to concentrate when other people are in the kitchen while I'm trying to cook. I'd be much happier, faster and accurate when cooking if I was left alone in the kitchen for that period of time.

Karl Knights agreed with this. Mentioning cooking classes in secondary school, he reflected: 'People pick up on that, they pick up on any kind of "difference", and they'd sort of persecute that.' He cited backgrounds of bullying and discrimination, both common themes that cropped up while researching this book. Knights also suggested that criticism from parents or guardians can have an additional negative impact, creating an environment of 'not belonging'. He suggested that those in a supervisory role – who have to be comfortable, by nature, when working with food – might not necessarily be able to fathom the experience of those who would not be. He added: 'It would be really useful as well, I think, to put autistic people's experiences into context' in a scenario such as teaching, to empower students more.

There are a host of different sounds in a kitchen; there is also a lot more sensory input that may become very overwhelming – sometimes very quickly. As someone who is hypersensitive to noise, I find working in a crowded space quite difficult; too much noise can have an impact in terms of my ability to carry on, even at a base level of behaviour.

For individuals who are hypersensitive to noise, there are small and discreet earplugs you can purchase; these still allow you to hear if somebody needs to interact with you directly. You can also purchase ear defenders, but these will almost completely block out all sound. Having a quiet space or pacing yourself – for example, cooking in 15-minute intervals – could also potentially be good strategies to follow.

Instructions

Indulge me a metaphor to explain this section a little bit. Sometimes people ask me, 'What is it like to be autistic?' In the context of instructions, this is important to highlight. To be autistic is to fundamentally know that you will likely be misunderstood from the moment you wake up until the moment you go to sleep. You have to attempt to 'translate' social codes, expectations, boundaries that everyone else just seems to innately know, but every mistake may involve some kind of social penalty. Instructions are a little bit like that, especially when it comes to interacting with recipes. Many of the interviewees for this book expressed frustration. A lot of the time, there will be language that would be known to people who regularly cook and bake – 'crimping' or 'sweating the vegetables'. To help with potential challenges around odd baking terms, there is a list at the back of this book; rewriting a recipe can also help.

At other times, the expectation to fit one method of teaching – and therefore follow one mode of instructions – caused significant distress. Maia Osborne commented: 'Particularly for longer recipes, I have to spend time studying them and rewriting them in a way that I understand. Most commonly, I find that in recipes a "single step" actually consists of multiple actions that would be better suited to being split into multiple, shorter (but clearer!) steps.' Maia is not alone in using the strategy of rewriting recipes that aren't clearly understood. She also expressed that this helps her in another way, as cookbooks tend not to stay open, and a laptop or tablet can also go on standby.

Barb Cook had some additional thoughts to add, specifically about 'one size fits all' teaching methods. 'We all learn differently,' she said, noting we all have different ways of completing tasks. She continued:

> If you're causing more distress to the person by changing how they do something, or handle something, or carry something, or flip an egg, then you're not helping that person. You're making that experience more distressing by changing the way they do something that works for them. So you don't want to be doing that.

Having more than one form of instructions can help; some of the contributors to this book expressed how, in a classroom setting, they were expected to replicate a live demonstration after being shown by a teacher, without any instructions to help or to remember multiple steps, ingredients or the amounts/quantities that were needed. Even without being autistic, that would be a complex task.

Chris Bonnello is the award-winning author of the acclaimed *Underdogs* series and is also an international speaker and autistic advocate. He expressed a different challenge that was connected to instructions: in taking things such as quantities that need to be precise, and thus becoming bogged down in tiny details. Bonnello expressed that his way around this potential challenge is 'having the understanding that cooking is an art, it is not a science', adding that 'recipes by and large are a guide, not a rule book'.

When it comes to instructions and interpreting, a general rule of thumb would be to keep to measurements and quantities as much as possible, as this can have an impact – for example, when it comes to making dough (an experiment while writing this book went horribly wrong due to excessive flour). However, it does not matter if you go slightly over or slightly under the required quantity – for example, 5 grams under or over, but no more than this.

Accessibility benefits everyone and is not just special treatment for one particular demographic. Having accessible instructions will benefit everyone, not just autistic individuals. When it comes to interpreting instructions, some individuals may benefit from a polite redirect that is patient in tone.

Adaptations Everyone Should Know About and Use on a Regular Basis

Adaptations are incredibly useful when you experience extra challenges in the kitchen. By adaptations, I mean physical objects, not just simple strategies that can be put in place. These are just a few examples of what you could consider; they all have their own benefits, and some were even suggested by people interviewed for this book.

Food separators

Sometimes sensory avoiders prefer to keep all the different components of their meal separate, so that none of them touch. Sometimes this is because there are too many flavours combining, which can be overwhelming. Food separators can be purchased cheaply from places like Amazon; they keep all the different ingredients of a meal on a plate apart and may help with such an aversion.

Handheld grater

Need to grate cheese or a carrot? A handheld grater – avoiding the need to use a downward motion while another hand anchors the top – can be easier for some individuals to use.

Jar opener

Sensory integration issues may mean that an autistic individual has trouble with tasks such as opening doors, packaging and other things that are seen as 'simple'. I find opening jars difficult, and it takes me longer to do than people who are neurotypical. A jar opener is inexpensive and time-saving. It is one of the most helpful disability-related aids and one of the best Christmas presents I have ever been given.

Liquid timer

Executive functioning issues may mean you have trouble when it comes to sequencing tasks and keeping time. A liquid timer acts as a visual prompt and is also a potential 'stim', too.

Timer

Making time visual in the kitchen can be very helpful to autistic individuals. Having the right timer can be useful – such as on your phone or a loud egg timer. It's worth just checking the sound to avoid potential alarm or sudden movements when they are set off.

Weighted cutlery

Two things kept coming up while researching this book: sensory integration issues that impact motor skills and/ or having a comorbidity that also affects your hands and movement. Weighted cutlery can sometimes be a bit more expensive, but it was a recommended adaptation of a handful of the interviewees for this book.

Weighted cups

These follow the exact same logic as above. If you find moving cutlery or other objects a bit more of a challenge, due to autism or other condition, a weighted cup could be really helpful.

Spoon keyring

Measuring anything will need spoons and these keyrings usually have four or five spoons of different sizes. These also usually have a label of the unit and name on them too; this is both a practical adaptation and a visual prompt. We will be looking at the spoon keyring again in a minute, with some helpful tips everyone needs to know when it comes to volume and mass.

Spring-loaded cookie scoop (or an ice-cream scoop as it's known in the UK)

Miranda Dressler specifically recommended this when submitting her recipe for this book. A spring-loaded cookie scoop – known as an ice-cream scoop in the UK – can be useful to mitigate sensory issues when working with things like cookie dough. You will find out more about that when you read her delicious cookie recipe in the desserts part of this book.

Common Cooking Implements

It's always helpful to know what we are using to cook, especially when it comes to the tools of the trade. Having the right vocabulary has so many advantages, not least being able to ask for something precisely, because this can be useful for asserting our needs. These are some common cooking implements that we should all know about.

Corer
Sometimes cutting up apples and similar fruit can be difficult – this is an example of where I take so much longer than a neurotypical person. A corer is a simple tool that allows you to 'core' out the centre of just about anything – apples, pineapples, etc. It's handheld and will mean this task should take seconds, rather than the minutes stacking up.

Digital scales
If you find measuring ingredients a bit difficult, especially when it comes to accuracy, having a set of digital scales could help to improve measurements. They don't have to be expensive or flashy, and they usually last for years. I know someone who has had a set of digital scales for as long as I have been alive!

Wooden spoons
Helpful for folding (more on that below) ingredients into mixtures you're creating.

Silicone tools

Silicone has similar properties to non-stick coating, in that food doesn't tend to stick to it. If you find cleaning up a bit of a chore, or don't want to waste a lot of mixture – this is a bit of a sensory peeve for me – then having a set of silicone tools in your arsenal is very useful.

Colander

We all need to drain pasta or vegetables at some point; this is easier than draining them over a sink with the saucepan and the saucepan lid.

Mixing bowl

Because we also need to mix something, too. I would suggest having at least two.

Saucepan

Usually for handling boiled water or to heat something up. These are a basic necessity.

Peeler

Using a knife to peel something like a carrot or a potato is, well, fraught with risk; I know that if I did that, I would raise a huge number of concerns. (My fingers would also be promptly shredded.) A peeler is arguably a necessity for when it comes to vegetables like carrots and potatoes.

Whisk

This will make many tasks so much easier! And not just the occasional whisked egg.

Kettle

You don't need a kettle, but if you need to boil water, a kettle will speed up the process. It took me months to actually own one when I started to live independently – and that was only because my mum gave me one so she could have a cup of tea when visiting!

Ladle
For ladling liquid-based food on to a plate or into a bowl.

Palette knife
For scraping or when you need to extract a cake or a banana loaf from its tin. Or for spreading buttercream on a cake.

Set of knives
One knife doesn't fit all tasks, and having the right knife will make some tasks a lot easier. We will be looking at the different kinds of knives and their functions later in the book.

Scraper
Usually a small piece of hard plastic for getting the last remnants out of a bowl, it's useful, cheap, and prevents the need to use metal spoons to scrape out bowls. (The horrible clanging noise! Who wants that?! No one.)

Butter knife
Robin, the Community Chef who has been mentioned previously, taught me the trick of mixing dough with a butter knife if you don't want to touch it! Which is great if you have sensory issues. And it can also be used for buttering bread.

Chopping board
Pretty self-explanatory. You need a board to chop and prepare ingredients on, to protect your kitchen surfaces.

Spoons in a range of sizes
We have already looked at this in the chapter about adaptations autistic individuals may find useful in the kitchen; incorporating them can save time and energy, and make the kitchen just that little bit more bearable. However, some things are not entirely obvious when it comes to the kitchen and cooking – such as how spoons line up perfectly in terms of ratios. Knowing this will be really helpful – to the extent that I'd argue it's crucial to know. More on this below.

Blender

Autistic individuals may find that their energy is a lot more limited compared with people who are not on the spectrum; I know I do, and we will talk about this again later. A blender can help in a range of recipes – smoothies, milkshakes, soups, sauces, even ice cream. This is a really useful piece of kit to have; they also don't have to be that expensive. I think mine was about £45. It's an investment, but really worth it.

Masher

To mash potatoes and similar foods to a fluffy pulp! Spoons and forks are tricky and cumbersome to do this – go for gold and mash away!

There are also some 'extras' which you might not have but it might be worth collecting and acquiring in the future if you wish to expand your skill set or if you wish to learn more.

Pipette

For measuring small amounts of liquid!

Bread tin

Depending on what type of bread you are making, a bread tin is used to make sure that a loaf of bread will be loaf-shaped once baked.

Baking beans

If you need to blind-bake pastry – more on that later – it will shift about in the oven. Ceramic baking beans keep the pastry in place!

Slotted spoon

A slotted spoon is for lifting solid food, such as a bagel, out of liquid.

Cake tin

A cake tin was my first 'adult' purchase with my own money when I began to live independently; a friend of mine was celebrating her birthday, and she is very 'big' on cake. However, if you want to be baking cakes and other treats regularly, this needs to become standard. One will suffice, even if you want a layered cake – just chop in half and add icing in the middle, thus sandwiching the two halves back together.

Meat thermometer

This piece can look vaguely terrifying, but it allows you to measure the internal temperature of cakes, bread and other delicious things, to ensure that they are cooked.

A Note on Knives

In order to learn as well as to articulate and advocate for our access needs, we need the right words and vocabulary. Generally, that will help with staying safe, picking up new skills, working with food – and, in a wider and more general context, improving communication. (Instead of words such as 'thing', being specific – 'I want that pen' – can be more helpful.)

Knives are fundamental to working with food. As a pre-teen, I wish, retrospectively, someone had gone through the purposes of each kind of knife; it would have helped with various issues, especially at the point of interacting with food. While my motor skills leave a lot to be desired, and tasks like cutting bread quickly become difficult and frustrating if, say, I have limited time, it would have been helpful to know what kind of knife to use, rather than being left floundering. (The choruses of 'slow down' at various intervals were well meaning, but it can be frustrating to be reminded.)

People reading this, I imagine, may even have other conditions such as dyspraxia, which add more in terms of challenges. (Statistics suggest this is very likely, due to comorbidities frequently occurring with autism.) They might also need a bit of help. Instead of being shouted at or laughed at for the way I grip things, someone calmly talking through with me what to do would have been great. For that reason, the illustration on the next page was included in this book, to try to address potential issues head on. These are the basic knives that everyone should have and work with, what they are for and why. The best piece of advice I was given was to 'hold the knife like you mean it'. That will make chopping easier; looking at the intensity of your own grip could help. That was the 'jackpot' for me – although I still struggle, it helped a lot.

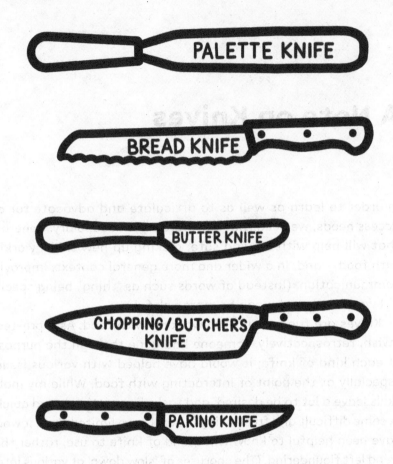

A chopping knife – sometimes referred to as a butcher's knife – is used for sturdier food preparation, such as dicing onions, chopping carrots and the like. The sharper and bigger blade of the knife makes this more attainable.

A bread knife is longer and the blade has a serrated edge; it doesn't quite cut as smoothly as a chopping knife, and it takes more of a carving motion to cut bread. Holding the bread steady with your other hand will be needed.

A small paring knife (usually around 7–9 centimetres long) was recommended by Robin Van Creveld, as this can be useful for general food preparation. Having these in a variety of sizes can also help in terms of navigating food preparation – simply because sometimes different-sized blades are needed, in order to make chopping and cutting a lot easier.

Common Cooking Techniques Everyone Needs to Know

The world of cooking can feel a bit daunting at times; it's almost as if it is assumed that everyone knows all the different names of specific cooking techniques. This was one of the biggest frustrations autistic individuals expressed – the lack of understanding what was being asked of them, especially in terms of cooking techniques! At the end of this book is a list of other terms that might crop up in cooking, but below are some techniques, what they mean and how to go about it, explained in detail.

Bain-marie
Bain-marie involves heating up water to the point of boiling, then using it to melt something, usually chocolate. You need a kettle, a saucepan and a mixing bowl that just rests inside the saucepan, but without touching the bottom of it. Pour the boiling water into the pan; add the bowl into the saucepan, so that they connect. The water should be underneath it; the bowl should not be immersed and floating in the water but balanced on the saucepan. The chocolate in the bowl will slowly begin to melt.

Blind baking
While working with pastry – for example, if you want to make an apple pie – 'blind baking' means to bake the pastry twice, in order to retain the shape. This can also mean that you may be using baking beans.

Broil

Used commonly when working with chicken breasts. Water and a small amount of butter are heated in a large pan (with a lid that goes over the top). Turn the chicken breasts over and cook on a low heat; they should be fully cooked when the water has evaporated. However, do note that this method does not colour the chicken – you can do that using other methods.

Claw hold

The shape of your hand when working with a large chopping knife on items such as an onion and other things like that. The 'claw' of your hand will keep the knife in place to stop it sliding while cutting the onion.

Crimping

The use of a fork to create a 'crimp', often when sealing a filling inside pastry. Think of the edges of a Cornish pasty; this is what you'd be creating.

Dicing

This usually refers to cutting up vegetables – as in 'dice the onion'. It means chopping into slices, then again into tiny, cube-shaped pieces. Using the onion as an example, peel it and chop it in half. Then chop into the onion halfway from the bottom. Then cut from top to bottom to create the tiny cubes.

Folding

Folding is not mixing, and mixing is definitely not folding, and the reason for this is usually connected to flour. Flour has two parts to it – starch and gluten. Too much manipulation, such as from stirring or mixing, will make it tougher and a lot harder to work with. Using your non-stick or wooden spoon, imagine the mixture is like paper. Where the base of the bowl starts to circle round, angle the spoon to create a corner, which will then 'fold' into the middle. (If you're still stuck, look this up on YouTube – describing the technique of folding is quite difficult.)

Incorporate

Folding into the centre or mixing all ingredients in together.

Kneading

Kneading means using your palms of your hands to work with dough. Sprinkle flour over the surface and then put the dough on top. Use your palms to stretch out the dough and then work it back into the same shape; this increases how elastic the dough is. Kneading bread dough, for example, adds air, thus allowing it to ferment and rise a bit better. (If you need a visual of kneading, YouTube it – again, it's difficult to describe on paper without being able to demonstrate it!)

Mixing

This usually means combining two or more ingredients, to create something like a soup, or to add an extra 'something' to rice. This is also mostly with a whisk or a wooden spoon.

Rolling pin roll-up

(**Note:** this is not the official name – no one seems to know what this is actually called!) Putting pastry on top of something, such as an apple pie, can be very difficult. So put a little flour on your rolling pin and wrap the pastry around it, starting from the side furthest away from you. Then reverse this step to drape it over the pie. This technique will prevent the pastry cracking.

Rubbing in

If you want to create something like pastry from scratch, the main ingredients, usually butter and flour, need to be rubbed together – with your thumb and fingers – to create a sand-like consistency. This can also make the dough lighter.

Scoring

Usually connected to bread, this means adding your own personal mark to the dough as a type of 'stamp'. Historically, it was used to distinguish ownership of loaves when people shared ovens.

Cut into the dough slightly, at a depth of 2 centimetres maximum. This adds more of a crust to bread these days.

Stirring

In terms of language, this seems to be used more with 'wet' recipes. For example, when breaking up egg yolks, you stir them with a metal fork or a whisk.

Sweating

This usually refers to vegetables that you are cooking in oil in a frying pan. You are sweating them so steam appears, so that they are eventually cooked. (I like to imagine this as sweat pouring out of the ingredients.)

Conversion Chart

Being autistic means that you may have a comorbid condition – statistically, it is very likely. (Right now I am waiting for a referral for an assessment of dyscalculia, something I have always been told I have but have never been tested for.) For this reason, a conversion chart is included – with some helpful hints along the way, too.

Conversion chart

WET INGREDIENTS

Wet ingredients are those that have a wet texture – such as water, olive oil or sunflower oil, melted butter, milk – and are usually a liquid.

1 centilitre (cl) = 10 millilitres (ml)

1 litre (L) = 1000 millilitres (ml)

DRY INGREDIENTS

Dry ingredients are those that have a dry texture – such as flour (all kinds) and sugar – and are in the form of a solid.

1 pound = 16 ounces

1 kilogram (kg) = 1000 grams (g)

Note: cups have different equivalents for different ingredients – these are not all the same. Information can be found about this on the pages that follow.

Remember, cooking/baking/working with food is an imperfect art, so you do not have to be too exact when it comes to measuring out your ingredients. A lot of people I know do it by eye, especially if they work in the catering industry, and it usually never makes a difference. As a general rule, there should be minimal differences in measurements – if a recipe says 50 grams but you have measured 52, that won't matter. It will matter, however, if you have measured out 60 grams, so try to keep the differences to a minimum.

Other things to keep in mind: a medium-sized egg, for example, is usually around 50 grams. (That's about 1.7 ounces.) Robin Van Creveld also recommends increasing the amount of liquid-based ingredients you use if you are working with gluten-free flour, as it absorbs more. Again, this is an imperfect art, after all.

The Scale of Spoons

Some things are just casually implied when it comes to cooking/baking/working with food. Chances are, unless you're upfront about it, autistic people are not going to catch the implication of language, which is why instructions need to be explicitly clear. However, there are some things that still need to be made a bit more obvious – for example, when it comes to weighing things.

When it comes to understanding the construction of making a meal or a sweet dish, understanding the science behind them can be really useful. Understanding the so-called 'obvious' details – such as weights and how they work together – is also useful. This was requested a lot by people on Twitter, in interviews or through private conversations. The common reason was that not understanding would throw up issues later on.

The spoons that most of us work with are on a scale, and knowing this can be really useful, especially when it comes to baking and cookery skills. In terms of liquid volume, a teaspoon is 5 ml, a dessert spoon is 10 ml and a tablespoon is 15 ml. Robin Van Creveld explained this further during a lesson involving baked muffins: 'When you're weighing things, liquids weigh the same as their metric volume.'

Some autistic people may struggle with weighing and measuring things out – for example, if they have interoceptive issues or a comorbidity such as dyscalculia. Some individuals use compensatory strategies – such as memorizing this type of thing – in order to get around potential issues.

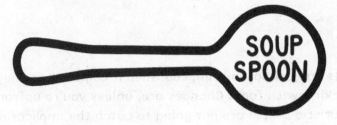
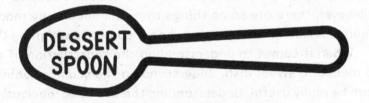

The Confusion over 'Cups'

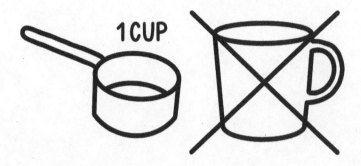

The measurement of cups seems to have caused a lot of confusion – and that is not just among autistic individuals. I have some neurotypical relatives who interpreted this measurement a bit literally – in measuring out quantities by using a mug – but they still do not want to change their own method, even years after I pointed this out to them!

A cup is a measurement that is typically used in the United States, but it also seems to be slowly gaining popularity here in the UK, as well as in other parts of Europe. However, the quantities are not fixed when it comes to different ingredients, which can be confusing – and Googling may be required. When this book talks about cups, it may either be in measurements or meaning an actual cup – this will be made clear throughout. If there is ever an oddly specific number, always round up or down to make things easier when weighing out.

Some basics to keep in mind, in terms of conversions:

- Half a cup of liquid is equivalent to 125 ml. Therefore, 1 cup is 250 ml.

- 1 cup of butter is 227 grams. (To make this easier, add 3 extra grams for an even number.)
- 1 cup of plain flour (all-purpose flour) is 140 grams.
- 1 cup of self-raising flour is 150 grams.
- 1 cup of granulated sugar is 200 grams.
- 1 cup of caster sugar is 190 grams.
- 1 cup of brown sugar is 220 grams.

Recipes

The following recipes have been collated from a range of autistic individuals. To make it easier, I have divided the recipes into four parts:

- Breakfast
- Lunch
- Dinner
- Desserts, Snacks and Miscellaneous.

For readers who may want to expand their knowledge, there are also hints at the bottom of each recipe as to how to adapt the recipe, as well as how to add more to it. People who have contributed recipes have a small biography and their name is beside each; any recipe that is not credited is written by the author. The recipes are designed to encompass all abilities, differences in budgets and kitchens, and other such factors.

The recipes do not follow a traditional format; I believe that, to be accessible, we need to rewrite the rulebook on cooking, so that it is as inclusive as possible. This has been designed to aid executive functioning, as well as time taken. To be as accommodating as possible, extra time for the duration of the recipes has also been factored in, as comorbidities are also very common when it comes to autism. Finally, please round up or down when it comes to the ounce amount shown.

Key to the Following Recipes

What needs to be remembered is that cooking and baking do not have to be exact. Being 5 grams outside a measurement is okay, but more than that is usually not. It does not have to be exact, and you can use alternative ingredients to meet your dietary needs. Where possible, I have tried to list alternatives that you could use, and there is a list at the end of the book that is more definitive. To make this book easier to navigate, the following recipes have been catalogued by different needs:

 Vegetarian-friendly

 Vegan-friendly

 Gluten-free

 Free from dairy

 Sensory seeker friendly (that the recipe in original form is suitable for)

 Sensory avoider friendly (that the recipe in original form is suitable for)

 Adaptable for either a sensory seeker or a sensory avoider. (Most of the recipes here can be adapted into being for a seeker or avoider, so you may see both symbols in use.)

The recipes in this book are catalogued to be more accessible to as many autistic people as possible. Each recipe will have:

- a duration, so that you can plan how long a task will take – with extra time added on, just in case
- an energy rating
- a skill level.

Cooking takes a lot of energy. As autistic individuals will know, we often have more limited energy levels. We often have to do more, just to cope in a world that is inaccessible. Prior to reading this, you may have found yourself relying a lot on pre-prepared snacks, simply as a way of getting round having to cook. (I know I did; I also relied on a lot of pre-prepared food, such as pre-chopped vegetables, and things like that.) Each recipe in this book has an energy rating, so that if you have little energy, you can still make yourself something. The boundaries on this scale are designed to be flexible, owing to the fluctuating nature of autism.

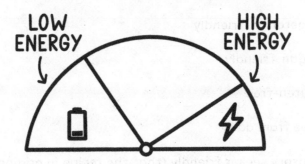

You will notice that the scale is divided into three sections; this should be taken, left to right, as low, moderate and high energy. When it comes to the recipes, that means:

Low energy
A simple meal that won't require a lot of skill or executive functioning skills.

1. Less than half an hour (30 minutes) or no more than 45 minutes preparation time. Some recipes may list a longer duration, but this is just to allow for time in the freezer or oven.
2. Only one thing will only be cooking at a time.
3. Minimal skills are needed.
4. Fewer than five steps.
5. Conserves the most energy.

Moderate energy

For those who may already feel confident in the kitchen and for days when you feel like you can handle more than one thing at a time.

1. Longer than 45 minutes.
2. Three or fewer items cooking simultaneously.
3. More than three skills needed.

High energy

These are the most challenging meals in this book that will take the most energy.

1. Longer than 75 minutes.
2. More than three items need to be cooked, baked or prepared at the same time.
3. Multiple skills are needed.

Breakfast Recipes

PART 1

Breakfast Recipes

AVOCADO ON TOAST

Duration: 10 minutes

Energy rating: Low

Skill level: Easy

To make when: you need more of a substantial breakfast than usual; you are in a rush; there is an exam you're worried about.

This recipe is suitable for sensory seekers but can also be adapted for people who consider themselves to be avoiders. There is an element of needing to interact with the food, too – so just be warned. There is a hint about this at the bottom, too.

EQUIPMENT YOU WILL NEED

1 paring knife

1 tablespoon

1 bowl

1 toaster

1 butter knife

1 plate for serving

INGREDIENTS

1 ripe avocado

1 bottle of sweet chilli sauce (we will not be using the whole bottle)

2 slices of bread (**note:** some types are vegan-friendly, while others are not)

HOW TO MAKE
Pre-preparation

Use the paring knife to cut the avocado in half. Scoop out all of the green guts into the bowl with the spoon. Get rid of the centre stone.

Method

1. Take the bowl of avocado and, using the back of the spoon, mash it until it becomes a smooth paste. Add a dash of the sweet chilli sauce on top; this will add a little extra flavour. Mix them together to create more of a sauce; if they aren't 'gelling' together, add more sweet chilli sauce in small quantities.

2. Put two slices of the bread into the toaster and toast for four minutes.

3. Spread the mix thickly on top with the butter knife. Enjoy.

EXPAND YOUR REPERTOIRE

This recipe is for sensory seekers but is quite easy to adapt to meet a wide variety of needs. All you need to be is a bit creative. For sensory seekers, adding flavourings and/or other herbs may add the extra 'input' that is needed. For example, this could be salt, pepper or even a pinch of smoky paprika. More 'leafy' additions could also work, such as coriander leaves (cilantro), chopped finely. You could even try changing up your bread; a trend on the internet a few years ago involved slicing up sweet potatoes and toasting. Sensory avoiders, take out all additions and stick with just the avocado on the toasted bread. (No chilli sauce!)

FRUIT SALAD KEBABS

Duration: 15 minutes
Energy rating: Low
Skill level: Medium
To make when: you need a pick-me-up if you have had a hard time recently
                    and like to have extra 'input'; you are having to grapple with
                    changes such as a new job or a new college.

This is easy to adapt from leftovers or just things you have in the kitchen; it is also extremely portable and a good recipe to use to 'meal plan' with. (Please note, this recipe was given a skill level of medium, due to the amount of cutting up of fruit involved. This is outside of the key but was adapted due to some individuals having dexterity issues.)

One of my earliest memories is of the fruit salad bowls my mum would make for me and my sister. It is summer, just before the oppressive heat kicks in. We are on a swing in a garden; my grandfather is showing me a false tooth he has, much to my horrified fascination. My mother kind of glides across the grass, holding two plastic bowls stuffed to the brim. Fruit salads are something autistic individuals have mentioned to me a lot. This is a breakfast recipe based on that time, with a bit of an upgrade.

EQUIPMENT YOU WILL NEED

1 chopping knife   1 colander

1 chopping board   2 kebab sticks

INGREDIENTS

1 small bunch of green   1 handful of strawberries
grapes
                                1 kiwi fruit
1 mango
                                1 orange
2 plums

HOW TO MAKE

Pre-preparation

Before you do anything, cut all of the fruit up on the chopping board and set aside for later. If you are a sensory avoider, cut into the smallest pieces possible, and if you prefer plainer flavours, only use plums, strawberries and grapes, for example. Wash all of the fruit and drain it in a colander over the sink. When it comes to the grapes, cut them in half. Peel the oranges and take off as much of the pith as possible.

Method

1. Using the kebab sticks, spear the halved grapes on to them.

2. Do this with all of the fruit pieces until you have filled up both of the sticks to create a 'kebab'. Enjoy!

EXPAND YOUR REPERTOIRE

When making the kebab sticks, try mixing and matching fruit combinations. Strawberries and grapes are a great duo; the tang of the strawberries contrasts with the plain flavour of the grapes. Using specific combinations could be a great way to add in extra sensory input. This can also be converted into a dessert very easily – and there is a recipe for fruit salad next. You could always upgrade that by serving with a small scoop of vanilla ice cream.

MEIR-LY (PRONOUNCED 'MERELY') FRUIT SALAD FOR THREE

Duration:	15–20 minutes
Energy rating:	Low
Skill level:	Medium
To make when:	it's the morning after a night out and you and your friends need a quick and easy breakfast; you can't decide what to eat for breakfast (happens to us all – sometimes having too many options is incompatible with executive functioning); you have a 'big day' at work, such as a presentation, and need to eat something inoffensive.

I (finally!) got to meet Deeivya 'Dee' Meir and her sister Chameli over snacks in Brighton while writing this book; that resulted in riotous mischief by all accounts. They are both so strikingly beautiful, as well as being immensely talented. It was as if we'd known each other a lifetime instead of just a handful of snatched hours. They were both very respectful of my support needs; we bonded over food and ideas for projects. They were both so sweet about the concept of an autism-specific cookbook – and they both should have a recipe in this book for this reason.

EQUIPMENT YOU WILL NEED

1 chopping board	1 colander
1 peeler	1 mixing bowl
1 chopping knife	3 dessert bowls
1 corer	3 dessert spoons to eat with

INGREDIENTS

3 satsumas	Half a box (125 grams, 4 ounces) of raspberries
2 kiwi fruit	
1 box (227 grams, 8 ounces) of strawberries	1 medium bunch of green grapes

| 2 small red apples | A dash of orange juice from a carton (**note**: check the brand is vegan-friendly) |

HOW TO MAKE

Pre-preparation

Peel the satsumas by hand and the kiwi fruit with a peeler. Wash all of the fruit and drain with a colander over the sink when needed. Chop the tops off the strawberries to remove the leaves and stalks.

Method

1. Cut up the apples into small, bite-sized pieces. Do the same for the kiwi fruit and strawberries. Put them in the mixing bowl and swish to combine all of them together.

2. Optional step for sensory seekers: Add a dash of orange juice to the mixing bowl; this will keep it fresh for longer and bring out the flavour. If you have leftovers, cover the mixing bowl with clingfilm and consume within two days.

3. Serve in the bowls with the spoons. Enjoy.

EXPAND YOUR REPERTOIRE

If you wanted to make this into a dessert, you could drizzle melted chocolate or chocolate sauce over the fruit pieces; just don't add the orange juice before you do! You could also serve with a scoop of vanilla ice cream. Sometimes a pinch of sugar can take away the tang of strawberries and raspberries if they are too sharp, which may be useful for sensory avoiders.

FROZEN YOGURT FRUIT POPS

Duration: 6 hours for freezing, and 15 minutes prep

Energy rating: Low

Skill level: Easy

To make when: you need something 'extra' for your breakfast the next day; you need to make a meal plan and use up food instead of wasting it; you have to entertain younger family members; you have some leftover ingredients and need an easy solution to get rid of them.

I was always very familiar with yogurt-based ice lollies when growing up; they were cheap and budget-friendly, and would keep us entertained as small children for a while.

EQUIPMENT YOU WILL NEED

1 chopping knife

1 chopping board

2 tablespoons

1 smoothie maker

1 set of ice lolly moulds with spaces for 4 lollies

INGREDIENTS

9 strawberries

1 handful of raspberries

5 tablespoons of strawberry yogurt

2 tablespoons of honey

HOW TO MAKE
Pre-preparation
Using the knife and chopping board, cut up the strawberries and raspberries; set aside for later.

Method

1. Combine all of the fruit, 5 tablespoons of yogurt and 2 of honey then pulverize in the smoothie maker.

2. Pour the mix into the moulds. If you are slightly short, add a tiny drop of water to help the mix set.

3. Freeze for 6 hours or overnight for your breakfast.

EXPAND YOUR REPERTOIRE

If you are a sensory avoider, consider using yogurt that is not strongly fla-voured – plain yogurt may be the best option. If you prefer, you could use a blender – such as when making a smoothie – to combine the fruit, yogurt and honey.

KEDGEREE FOR BREAKFAST FOR FOUR PEOPLE – BY LAURA JAMES

Duration: 25–30 minutes

Energy rating: Moderate

Skill level: Medium

To make when: you need something quick and easy – with minimal fuss – for four people, such as a late Sunday breakfast (this would be great for catering for relatives, for example); it's Boxing Day in the UK (the day after Christmas Day); you have friends round and they are staying overnight.

Laura James is a journalist and columnist. She is also the author of the memoir **Odd Girl Out**. You can find her on Twitter under the username @Girl_by_the_Aga.

EQUIPMENT YOU WILL NEED

1 measuring jug

1 chopping knife

1 chopping board

2 saucepans

1 frying pan

1 butter knife

1 teaspoon

1 set of digital scales

1 bowl (for measuring out your ingredients)

1 silicone spoon or wooden spoon

INGREDIENTS

25 grams of butter (1 ounce) (also at room temperature)

1 large onion

Optional: a sprinkle of fresh coriander/cilantro (from a plant, rather than the ground spice form)

3 large eggs

450 grams (16 ounces) of smoked haddock

150 millilitres of water (at room temperature)

175 grams (6 ounces) of basmati rice (pre-cooked 'microwave' rice)

¼ of a teaspoon of ground coriander

¼ of a teaspoon of ground cumin

¼ of a teaspoon of turmeric

A sprinkle of rock salt

2 limes

Editor's note: cooking is something of an imprecise science – so just use your eyes to guess how much a quarter (¼) of a teaspoon would be.

HOW TO MAKE
Pre-preparation

Take the butter out of the fridge and allow to warm up to room temperature; this will make it easier to work with. Use the measuring jug to measure out 150 millilitres of water and allow the same to happen again. Dice the onion with the chopping knife and the chopping board; if you are using the fresh coriander from a plant, chop it up with the knife and board again. Set all chopped ingredients aside for later. Measure out all other ingredients.

Method

1. Place the 3 large eggs in one of the saucepans, cover with water and begin to cook on the hob over a medium heat; we need them to be hard-boiled, which will take up to 10 minutes. Once you have finished doing that, lower the heat and allow to simmer gently, to keep them warm.

2. Put the haddock in the frying pan over a medium heat; cover with the water from the measuring jug and heat up for 6 minutes to cook. Once the fish is cooked, remove it from the pan and then flake the fish; this is to get rid of skin, scales and bones. Keep the liquid in the frying pan for later.

3. Melt the butter in the second saucepan and add the diced onion and the spices. Sweat out the onions; they should look soft and brown. Once that has happened, add the rice. Continue to stir with the silicone or wooden spoon to coat the rice with the spices and onions.

4. Next, add the water from the frying pan you used to prepare the fish in earlier to the saucepan with the rice. Add a sprinkle of rock salt and bring to the boil on the hob.

5. Simmer the rice by dropping to a low heat once it is boiling. Quarter the boiled eggs and add to the rice; flake the haddock into the rice and stir until combined.

6. Sprinkle the freshly chopped coriander on top of each portion on a plate. Cut the limes into wedges to serve.

EXPAND YOUR REPERTOIRE

In order to mix this dish up a bit, try using different combinations of fish. Salmon could be one such replacement – better still, go half and half with the haddock. While cooking the fish, you could also cook it in other herbs such as tarragon or any other favourite/preferred spices. Ground coriander and ground cumin is also a classic combination. Instead of serving with the chopped coriander, you could peel and grate ginger in with the rice; you could also add a small amount of crushed garlic for an extra sensory flavour. Curry powder is also another option if you prefer quite hot spices or heat for extra sensory feedback. If you are a sensory avoider, serve all components of this dish separately, and limit the number of different flavours used.

CHOCOLATE PANCAKE FRUIT DELIGHT

Duration: 15 minutes

Energy rating: Moderate

Skill level: Medium

To make when: you are in a 'treat yourself' mood, such as at the weekend and you're having a 'lazy day'; you need a dish for a date (just add chocolate-covered strawberries from the Desserts, Snacks and Miscellaneous Recipes part); when you need something to cheer you up.

Pancakes made up a significant part of my childhood, especially when it came to treats for celebrations such as birthdays. (Sugar and lemon toppings for breakfast on a school day? With golden syrup? Yes, please!) These are a thin type of pancake, owing to their structure and ingredients.

EQUIPMENT YOU WILL NEED

1 mixing bowl

1 measuring jug

1 chopping knife

1 chopping board

1 whisk

1 tablespoon

1 frying pan

1 butter knife

1 palette knife

INGREDIENTS

150 grams (5.5 ounces) of plain flour/all-purpose flour

150 millilitres of milk

2 bananas

8 strawberries

3 eggs

Cocoa powder (1–2 tablespoons, depending on taste)

1 pack of butter (you will only use a little for frying the pancakes)

Golden syrup (a bottle is easier than a tin)

HOW TO MAKE
Pre-preparation

Measure out the flour into the mixing bowl. Measure the milk into the measuring jug. Cut up the banana and strawberries and set aside for later. If you are a sensory avoider, keep them separate and cut them up into small pieces. (The strawberries should be in quarters at least.)

Method

1. Crack in the eggs into the bowl with the flour and then add the milk. Whisk to create a runny mixture; the egg should be dissolved. (If not, keep adding small amounts of milk to create a more liquid consistency.)

2. Add in a tablespoon of cocoa powder and whisk in. (If you prefer a more chocolately taste, repeat this step.)

3. Put the frying pan on the hob. Put a knob of butter (using the butter knife) in the pan and heat it up on the hottest temperature. Keep moving the pan so that the butter, once it begins to melt, covers the bottom.

4. Add a small amount of the pancake batter mix you just made to the middle of the pan. This mix should cover the bottom of the pan; keep moving the pan to spread out the mixture.

5. Wait for the wet look from around the edges to disappear; the pancake should look like a matt shade of chocolate. When this begins to happen, carefully use the palette knife to move the edges ever so slowly. Now, flip the pancake over! Cook the other side. Repeat until all the mix is used up.

6. Serve on a plate. Add the banana and strawberries into the middle; separate if you are a sensory avoider. Squeeze a small amount of golden syrup across the fruit. This will bring out the flavour of the chocolate in the pancake.

EXPAND YOUR REPERTOIRE

While constructing the batter of the pancake, consider adding mashed banana to the mix. This would make the pancakes thicker, more in the style of 'American pancakes'. The banana will add an extra texture to the pancake, too. If you are making pancakes to serve during a date, keep the pancake free of any toppings inside and serve with chocolate-covered strawberries on the side. See the recipe in the **Desserts, Snacks and Miscellaneous Recipes** part. If you have a job babysitting or need to look after younger members of your family, this can be adapted into a dessert. Cut a banana in half lengthways for a mouth and use two strawberries for eyes. That way, you can create a fun fruit face, without folding the pancake in half.

SCRAMBLED EGGS AND SMOKED SALMON FOR ONE

Duration: 15–20 minutes
Energy rating: Moderate
Skill level: Medium
To make when: you're up late on a Sunday morning and there is a 'lazy day' ahead; you need another option for a 'brunch' when the usual options don't always cater to someone; you need a low-maintenance breakfast – and relatively quickly.

While attending a course to aid the process of writing this book, some of the other 'students' – a merry band of rebels who'd assemble around rickety benches to devour our collective 'war spoils' – were discussing some of their favourite food combinations. Scrambled eggs and smoked salmon was a 'classic combination' espoused by at least two people – you could almost see them salivating over such a prospect! It was duly recreated in this book.

EQUIPMENT YOU WILL NEED

1 glass bowl

1 fork or 1 whisk

1 butter knife

1 saucepan

1 frying pan

INGREDIENTS

1 pack of butter (you will only need a 'dab' for this recipe)

2 eggs, medium size

3 slices of smoked salmon

Black pepper (to sprinkle when it comes to serving)

HOW TO MAKE
Pre-preparation

Take your butter out of the fridge and allow to come to room temperature. This will make it a lot easier to work with for the duration of this recipe. You will be working with two 'rings' on your hob for this recipe, which, although this recipe is fairly low maintenance, makes it more difficult in terms of executive functioning.

Method

1. Crack the two eggs into the glass bowl. Whisk briefly with the fork (or the whisk) in order to scramble in the next step.

2. Using the butter knife, put a dab of the butter in the middle of the saucepan and begin to heat it up on the hob. Add the egg mixture and keep whisking it in the saucepan; it will eventually begin to scramble. Once it has, reduce to a low heat to keep it warm.

3. Optional step: if you don't like mixing hot and cold textures, use the frying pan to heat up the smoked salmon while the egg is keeping warm. Follow the instructions on the back of the packet to do so.

4. Serve side by side. Sprinkle the black pepper on the scrambled egg to finish.w

FRUITY BREAKFAST ICE LOLLIES

Duration: Up to 12 hours for freezing
Energy rating: Moderate
Skill level: Medium
To make when: the weather outside is starting to become oppressive, such as when 'heatwave' warnings hit the UK headlines every summer; you need a change from your usual safe breakfast; you have been unwell and need to recoup lost energy and vitamin content.

As a pre-teen, I was obsessed with smoothies, and for the duration of one summer, my mum made me one every day. Looking back, that was probably a sensory-related issue as a result of being an undiagnosed pre-teen. This is an adaptation of fruit in another form, as changing how you serve food can help if there is an underlying sensory issue.

Editor's note: if you want this as your breakfast, make it the night before – most of the 12 hours will be spent sleeping!

EQUIPMENT YOU WILL NEED

1 mixing bowl

1 chopping knife

1 chopping board

1 blender

2 tablespoons

1 ice lolly mould with 3 spaces

INGREDIENTS

Half a bag of frozen fruit mix of your choice

1 banana

5 tablespoons of plain yogurt

1 small handful of raspberries

1 tablespoon of honey

HOW TO MAKE
Pre-preparation
If the fruit mix bag is already in your freezer, take it out. Measure out half the bag of frozen fruit and let it warm up a little for about 5 minutes. Use the chopping board and knife to cut the banana up.

Method

1. Plug in the blender and fill up half of it with the frozen fruit mix. Add 2 tablespoons of yogurt, then the raspberries and chopped banana, then 3 more tablespoons of yogurt. Top off with a tablespoon of honey and a dash of water. Put the lid on and blend to a liquid consistency.

2. Pour this mix into the ice lolly mould and then add the lid on top.

3. This should be frozen after about 12 hours, which makes it perfect if you would like it for breakfast. (Just freeze the night before, so you wake up to the ice lolly!) To release your ice lolly, run water on the outside of the mould to heat it up; the mix will begin to loosen and you can take your lolly out of its mould in one piece when it is set.

EXPAND YOUR REPERTOIRE
There are multiple options you could use and experiment with to make a breakfast ice lolly; keeping classic fruit combinations together could be a starting point, or you could try something more original. Just be warned that a lot of fruit is quite water-based, so you may need to build up the blended mix more with yogurt, to stop it being too runny. (Because no one likes a really runny smoothie, do they?) For bursts of flavour, you could try squeezing in juice from a lemon, replacing the water with juice from a carton (apple elderflower is a particular favourite of mine, in small doses), as well as switching up the flavour of the yogurt you use.

You could also practise layering up, which takes a lot more skill than this basic recipe needs. Make up one mix and pour this in to fill the mould up to halfway. Once this is frozen, pour in a contrasting mix to top it up. The first mix will not be affected. Freeze again to create a two-layer ice lolly. This takes a bit longer to plan, but it can be worth it if you get two combinations you like; you could also try creating a contrast between, say, more of a strawberry flavour and something more citrus-based.

CEREAL POT TO GO

Duration: 10 minutes
Energy rating: Low
Skill level: Easy
To make when: you'd like anything but standard cereals on a sleepy Saturday morning; you have guests over or perhaps you are meeting over breakfast; you need something that's summery in feel; you're running late but have had time to meal plan.

If you go to the States, you may find these 'pots' in shops that sell pretty much anything for breakfast. The first time I visited Manhattan, I was enamoured with the city – and, after a long flight (read: jet lagged the next morning!), these cereal pots were delicious. This is my healthier version. Cereal, fruit and yogurt are all included. It would most definitely be made better by eating it in Central Park, but that's just my opinion...

EQUIPMENT YOU WILL NEED

1 chopping knife

1 chopping board

1 colander

2 tablespoons

1 small pot to serve in (the sort you would serve mousse in)

INGREDIENTS

1 small handful of grapes

1 orange

8 strawberries

1 bowlful of cereal of your choice

1 tablespoon of plain yogurt

HOW TO MAKE
Pre-preparation

Chop up all the different pieces of fruit; if you are a sensory avoider, cut all pieces to be very small. Using the colander over the sink, wash the fruit, drain, then set aside in the fridge for later. If you prefer, keep all the different fruits separate – this is something sensory avoiders may prefer to do. Using the small pot for serving, fill with cereal; this is to measure out how much you will need.

Method

1. Once you have measured out the cereal in the pot, top with a tablespoon of yogurt.

2. Add the fruit on top to serve.

EXPAND YOUR REPERTOIRE

If there is a celebration underway – for example, if you need something for a birthday breakfast – you could use the process of bain-marie to melt chocolate to cover the cereal. (Sometimes this is used to make a quick and easy cake that has a chocolate flavour.) Melt the chocolate in a bowl over a saucepan of simmering water, add the cereal to the bowl, mix to coat the cereal and allow to set.

LOW-ENERGY BAKED OATMEAL TO GO – BY SARAH HACKERT

Duration: 55 minutes to 1 hour

Energy rating: Low

Skill level: Easy

To make when: you are working from home or have the morning off; you are stuck at home and are off work sick, such as with a cold, and need something easy to make that will have a low energy cost; you are entertaining younger family members – for example, if you are babysitting for a day – and need an activity to distract them.

Sarah Hackert is a physical therapist (physiotherapist) and is based in the United States.

Please note, this recipe will serve 6–8 people.

EQUIPMENT YOU WILL NEED

1 set of digital scales

1 measuring jug

1 serving bowl (for measuring with)

1 mixing bowl

1 teaspoon

1 medium-sized baking dish (for the oven)

1 silicone or wooden spoon

INGREDIENTS

(In order for this recipe to be suitable to sensory avoiders, do not make this with the cinnamon, chocolate chips, apple sauce or peanut butter.)

80 grams (3 ounces) of oatmeal (known as porridge in the UK)

350 millilitres of almond milk

1 teaspoon of baking powder

¼ of a teaspoon of salt

1 teaspoon of cinnamon

1 egg

55 grams (2 ounces) of chocolate chips

80 grams (3 ounces) of peanut butter

1 stick of butter (to grease your baking dish)

Optional for serving: 80 grams (3 ounces) of unsweetened apple sauce (to add moisture)

Optional for serving: 110 grams (4 ounces) of maple syrup for sweetness

HOW TO MAKE
Pre-preparation

Use the digital scales, measuring jug and the serving bowl to measure everything out, apart from the apple sauce and the maple syrup; put them all in the mixing bowl. We will come back to the sauce and syrup later on.

Method

1. Preheat the oven to 180°C/350°F and allow to heat up. While this is happening, use a little of the butter to grease the baking dish; this will prevent the oatmeal from sticking to it later on.

2. Combine all of the ingredients you measured out in the bowl; mix with the silicone or wooden spoon. Dribble a small amount of maple syrup and apple sauce on; mix in once more. Now, using the spoon, add to the greased tray and smooth out.

3. Bake the oatmeal for 40–45 minutes; it will look golden brown on the top and should be set in the middle – enough to not dent if pressed lightly. Allow to cool down for five minutes; serve while warm.

EXPAND YOUR REPERTOIRE

As a potential serving option, you could serve the oatmeal with milk dribbled across; a bowl or a plate with a deeper base than usual would be the best serving option for this. Or you could also add slices of your preferred fruit on top as another serving option – citrus fruits would add a contrasting tang, which would be suitable for sensory seekers.

STRAWBERRY PORRIDGE FOR ONE PERSON

Duration: 20–25 minutes
Energy rating: Moderate
Skill level: Easy
To make when: you have a late start to the day, more than usual; you are making breakfast at the weekend; there are some ingredients that you need to get rid of in your cupboards and your fridge.

In speaking to Sarah Hackert for the recipe prior to this one, we had to do a lot of what we called 'translating' – due to speaking to each other from across the pond! We explored various different ways to prepare oatmeal/porridge – so this recipe also had to be in the book.

EQUIPMENT YOU WILL NEED

1 chopping board

1 chopping knife

1 kettle

1 mixing bowl

1 silicone or wooden spoon

1 bowl for serving

INGREDIENTS

10 strawberries

35 grams (1.5 ounces) of porridge oats/oatmeal (gluten-free versions are available)

A sprinkle of sugar

Optional: maple syrup or honey for serving

HOW TO MAKE
Pre-preparation

Using the chopping board and knife, quarter all of the strawberries and set aside for later; they will be used when it comes to serving. Fill up your kettle so that it is half full and begin to boil.

Method

1. Mix the boiled water with the porridge oats in the mixing bowl and stir with the silicone spoon; it should start to feel thick and not watery, more like a paste than powdery oats.

2. Once that is the case, pour into the bowl you will be serving the porridge in. If you are a sensory seeker, stir in the strawberries to the paste; if you are an avoider, serve separately or on top. Sprinkle on a pinch of sugar; this will mean the oats won't have such a bitter taste. If you are going for the optional ingredients, dribble on a small quantity of the maple syrup or the honey on top of the ensemble to serve.

EXPAND YOUR REPERTOIRE

This is a really easy and budget-friendly recipe – and would be especially good for students. In terms of adding to this recipe, you could try a range of different fruit combinations – such as the 'classic' combinations – to add a different flavour. If you prefer a moreish flavour when it comes to breakfast, you could try sprinkling in different-sized pieces of nuts. Serving this with different milk options – such as whole milk or almond milk – could also be a way to expand this simple dish.

BOOKSHOP BACON BAP

Duration: 15–25 minutes

Energy rating: Moderate

Skill level: Medium

To make when: you need to serve something quickly for breakfast and yogurt will just not cut it; friends are round and you need a simple and low-energy breakfast meal to make, perhaps after a night out.

Whenever I used to visit one of my friends, Chelsea, we would always meet for a 'brunch'-style interaction at a local bookshop. Chelsea is one of those rare human beings who asks questions because she actually cares about people – by wanting to learn and do better – and over brunch we'd 'put the world to rights'. This is a healthier version of what I would always have.

Note: if you are a sensory avoider, you may prefer to keep the lettuce and tomato separate on a plate.

EQUIPMENT YOU WILL NEED

1 chopping board

1 chopping knife

1 bread knife

1 butter knife

1 frying pan

1 pair of tongs

1 plate for serving

INGREDIENTS

1 lettuce

1 large tomato

1 burger roll

Butter for the bread roll

A little oil (I use sunflower oil for this)

2 slices of bacon

HOW TO MAKE
Pre-preparation

Peel off approximately four leaves from the lettuce, wash and set aside for later. Cut three slices off the tomato and also set aside for later. Use the bread knife to cut open the burger roll; butter the insides with the butter knife and also set aside for later.

Method

1. On the back of the packet of bacon slices, there should be instructions for how long it will take to cook. This is usually around 15–20 minutes. Dribble a small amount of oil in the pan and heat up over the hob. Use the tongs to add in the two slices of bacon to the pan; it will make a crackling noise, but this is how you know it's cooking.

2. Add two lettuce leaves and one tomato slice to the bun.

3. Use the tongs to flip the bacon strips over every five minutes, to cook each side evenly. Once cooked – you will know this because steam will be coming off it and the texture will have changed to no longer be smooth – add to the bun. Top with the remaining lettuce and tomato to enjoy.

EXPAND YOUR REPERTOIRE

Most meat can be cooked with additional flavours; just cover the bacon with oil, sprinkle on whatever flavour you like and cook in the pan. This would add an extra dimension for sensory seekers. Sensory seekers can experiment with different meat flavours, such as smoked bacon, as this would add an extra dimension for them. And serve with sauces if you like them! I quite like ketchup to be evenly distributed throughout, but you can always 'dip'. Mayonnaise is also a potential option you could use. While preparing the lettuce and tomato, you could always add on a small amount of whatever salad dressing you like – such as traditional Caesar salad style or a squeezed lemon. Try changing up the bread style as well; I quite like brioche-style burger buns, which have a kind of glazed top to the bun.

CHEESE AND HAM TOASTIE

Duration: 15 minutes

Energy rating: Moderate

Skill level: Easy

To make when: you fancy something a bit more savoury; you and your friends have gone out for a drink the night before; you need quick and easy comfort food, such as the day after a meltdown.

Toasties are very simple and incredibly quick to make. Breakfast does not always have to be something sweet – such as with fruit or yogurt. As a child, I loved toasties, and that continued until I was a teenager. You can also adapt these quite easily depending on sensory preferences – plus, they also make a lovely snack for lunch. Just eat in moderation. Whenever we'd go away on family holidays, I'd make a beeline for a café in an airport or train station – and go for a classic ham and cheese toastie.

EQUIPMENT YOU WILL NEED

1 chopping knife

1 chopping board

1 butter knife

1 toasting grill (usually a plug-in device)

1 pair of tongs

1 plate to serve on

INGREDIENTS

6 small slices of cheddar cheese

2 slices of bread – it can either be brown or white

Butter to spread on the bread

2 small slices of packaged ham

HOW TO MAKE
Pre-preparation
Cut off six small slices of cheese from the end of the block and set aside for later. Peel off two slices of ham from the packet and also set aside for later.

Method

1. Using the butter knife, butter both sides of both slices of bread. This will stop it burning and sticking when you put it in the toastie machine/grill later.

2. On one slice, add half the cheese, ham and then the rest of the cheese. Then sandwich this all together with the other slice of bread.

3. Put your sandwich in the toastie machine, and toast for five minutes. The cheese should start to look stringy. If it needs toasting for longer – sometimes this can take 10 minutes – continue.

4. Using the tongs, remove the toastie and put on a plate. Cut into your preferred sandwich shape – square, triangle, etc. – with the chopping knife.

EXPAND YOUR REPERTOIRE
Try sprinkling a little pepper inside.

FRUIT AND YOGURT ON A BUDGET

Duration: 5–10 minutes
Energy rating: Low
Skill level: Easy
To make when: you're in a hurry and are running late for work; you need to save money before your next food shop; it's the day after a meltdown, and you haven't entirely regained all of your energy back.

This is a recipe that was sometimes used in my family, especially when we went away to places such as Greece when I was a child. This would be replicated for a few months afterwards, until lured away by another form of breakfast. This is adaptable for most sensory needs – seekers and avoiders – and is great if, for example, you're a student on a budget.

EQUIPMENT YOU WILL NEED

1 chopping board

1 chopping knife

1 colander

1 tablespoon

1 dessert bowl

INGREDIENTS

1 small handful of blueberries

1 small handful of raspberries

1 small bunch of red grapes

8 strawberries

1 large pot of strawberry yogurt

Note: if you're a sensory avoider, cut the fruit into the smallest pieces possible. If you cannot cope with any flavoured yogurt, go for a plain, non-flavoured option.

HOW TO MAKE
Pre-preparation
Wash the fruit in a colander over the sink and set aside so that it can drain; this is for hygiene reasons. Cut the strawberries into quarters and set aside for later. Cut the blueberries and grapes in half and also set aside for later.

Method

1. Put six tablespoons of the yogurt into the dessert bowl.
2. Add in all of the fruit so that is on top of the yogurt and use the tablespoon to mix around.

EXPAND YOUR REPERTOIRE
Sometimes fruit can be a little bit bitter, especially if it has yet to fully ripen. Sprinkle a little bit of sugar on top of the fruit after you wash it in the colander over the sink; this will bring the sweetness of the fruit out, making it more enjoyable to eat. Try switching up the fruit into classic combinations such as apples and pears, strawberries and bananas. You could also use seasonal combinations – such as blackberries around Halloween time. Peaches and nectarines are also another combination that is suitable for summertime, too.

BANANA AND PEANUT BUTTER TOAST

Duration:	10 minutes
Energy rating:	Low
Skill level:	Easy
To make when:	you need a little bit of a 'lift' to your mood; it's cold outside; you need a recovery snack after a meltdown (this can double as a breakfast option and an anytime snack); while you're recovering from a cold.

Peanut butter is a favourite food in my family, but it's something that I detest. I find it a bit too strong in terms of taste and smell, and the texture is a bit strange, too. However, some autistic individuals really like it – enough to make it a 'safe food' – so I have included this recipe, which I adapted from a breakfast my mother sometimes makes for herself on a Sunday. It's something you could try after experiencing a meltdown, as it's one of those foods that can bring you back, as well as making you feel a little bit better.

EQUIPMENT YOU WILL NEED

1 chopping board	1 butter knife
1 chopping knife	1 paring knife
1 toaster	

INGREDIENTS

1 banana	Peanut butter
2 slices of bread of your choice (white or brown)	

HOW TO MAKE
Pre-preparation

Using the chopping board and knife, slice the banana into circles and set aside for later; they will be the topping of your toast.

Method

1. Using the toaster, toast the two different slices of bread to your own preference. I would usually recommend 3–4 minutes for a golden brown colour, but a little bit longer if you prefer your toast crispy.

2. Using the butter knife, spread peanut butter on top of each slice.

3. Put on a plate and, using the paring knife, cut into triangles.

4. Top with the banana circles you set aside when preparing this recipe.

EXPAND YOUR REPERTOIRE

If you don't like peanut butter like me, you could consider replacing it with, well, conventional butter!

If you would like to make this a dessert, you could consider creating French toast! It's more of a sweet option if you have a sweet tooth.

DAILY GREEN JUICE FOR BREAKFAST – BY DAN JONES, THE ASPIE WORLD

Duration: 20 minutes

Energy rating: Low

Skill level: Easy

To make when: you wake up feeling sluggish with limited energy; you need a quick breakfast option without too much hassle; you're a sports fan.

Dan Jones is a social media influencer and content creator behind The Aspie World on YouTube, where he uploads weekly videos and has more than 189,000 subscribers. He also runs autism-related courses. You can visit his website at www.theaspieworld.com.

Editor's note: this recipe is in relation to body size, so may use unconventional methods of measuring. When this recipe makes reference to a 'handful of', we do literally mean this. This is a recipe that, in terms of flavour, is also best suited to sensory seekers.

EQUIPMENT YOU WILL NEED

1 chopping knife

1 chopping board

1 juicing machine

1 juice squeezer (this can be a small machine like a smoothie maker, but there is also a tiny kitchen implement you can buy where you can manually juice fruit by hand)

INGREDIENTS

1 cucumber (you will only need a chunk about 3 inches/7 cm long)

1 lemon quarter

3 medium-sized oranges

1 handful of spinach

1 handful of green grapes

1 handful of kale

1 green apple

Water

HOW TO MAKE
Pre-preparation
Cut 3 inches off a whole cucumber using the chopping knife and board. Dice it and set aside for later. Using the juice squeezer, juice the lemon and oranges separately; set the juice aside for later, and discard the pulp. Measure out the spinach, grapes and kale, and also set aside for later. Cut up the apple into small chunks and discard the core.

Method
1. In the juicing machine, add the cucumber, kale, spinach, grapes and apple. Juice all together.
2. Add the lemon juice and the orange juice to the green mix, fill the rest of the juicer with water, then screw the lid on. Next, juice!

EXPAND YOUR REPERTOIRE
There are a few different combinations of ingredients that you can add to this, to adjust the taste to your own preferences and sensory input needs. A small piece of fresh ginger root (peeled) can be added to add a bit of a 'zing' to the overall taste. Grated carrot can be added in the first step, alongside all the green ingredients. Blueberries are an alternative fruit that you could also add, for an extra 'kick'. This may be a juice, but it's quite easy to adapt to make more of a 'slushie'. Add ice to the juice mix and combine, freeze in your freezer and then defrost the mix. If you would like to make this into a smoothie, add in almond or coconut milk at the second step of the recipe. This will make it more of a creamy texture. Chia seeds add an extra element in terms of texture and also have nutritional benefits. Add in at step 2. Dandelion leaves can have a bitter taste, but if you add at step 1, this will largely be undetectable.

TOMATO, GUACAMOLE AND FETA CHEESE TOAST

Duration:	20 minutes
Energy rating:	Low
Skill level:	Easy
To make when:	you need something moreish when you have just woken up; it's a lazy Sunday; you need something to really 'set you up' for the rest of the day; you need to be on the go for hours – and lunch might not be a part of the day's agenda, due to a busy schedule.

I am not much of a 'breakfast' person; mornings are just not really my thing, and that is amplified by my sensory issues at this time of day. However, I have learned that my poor interoception is misleading and I need to eat, just like everyone else. Skipping meals is not a good idea. I was also converted to feta cheese through a delicious muffin I was taught to make in a class.

EQUIPMENT YOU WILL NEED

1 chopping board

1 chopping knife

1 toaster

1 baking tray

1 butter knife

INGREDIENTS

A pack of feta cheese (you will be using about half a pack)

1 large red tomato

2 slices of your favourite bread, white or brown

1 bottle of guacamole (you will need about 2½ tablespoons)

HOW TO MAKE
Pre-preparation
Using the chopping board and knife, cut off four slices of feta cheese from the block and then cut into smaller pieces; slice up half of the tomato as well, and set aside for later.

Method

1. Set the oven to 200°C/400°F and allow to heat up. Meanwhile, put the two slices of bread in the toaster and toast for two minutes.

2. Put the two slices of bread on the baking tray; squirt the guacamole on and spread out with the butter knife. Add the thin slices of tomato, and then the small pieces of feta cheese on top.

3. Grill in the oven for 15 minutes.

EXPAND YOUR REPERTOIRE
If you are a sensory avoider, you might want to avoid the guacamole; butter could be a potential replacement. Small amounts of salsa could be used if you are a sensory seeker, just in small doses.

TOMATO AND SPINACH TOAST

◊ ◊ ◊ ◊ ◊

Duration:	15 minutes
Energy rating:	Low
Skill level:	Easy
To make when:	you need something a bit more savoury in the morning – for example, if you have an early start to your day – and have more time to spend constructing your breakfast; you are going to need a maintained level of energy throughout your day.

Another toast recipe! Yep, you heard it. Toast is easy to adapt, as well as being very budget-friendly. This is the last toast-based recipe in this section as well. This can be suitable for sensory seekers and sensory avoiders, too – all you need to do is adapt, and how to do that is at the end of the recipe.

EQUIPMENT YOU WILL NEED

1 chopping board
1 chopping knife
2 medium-sized saucepans
1 silicone spoon

1 toaster
1 butter knife
1 plate to serve

INGREDIENTS

Butter for the toast
Half a large tomato
3 spinach leaves

1 capful of olive oil
2 slices of your preferred bread (brown or white)

HOW TO MAKE
Pre-preparation

Take the butter out of the fridge; this will allow it to warm up, meaning it will be a lot easier to work with later. Using the chopping board and the chopping knife, chop up half of the large tomato, and set aside for later. Cut three large slices of spinach; you will be working with this in a moment.

Method

1. Place a saucepan on top of the hob and turn up the heat to halfway. Take a capful of oil and spread out in the pan; you should hear it gently beginning to crackle. Put the spinach in the pan; it will begin to cook. After about 5 minutes, turn the heat down to the lowest setting possible. Turn it over once or twice with the silicone spoon so both sides are evenly cooked.

2. Do the same now for the tomato slices, in another pan. It will begin to look brown on the sides; make sure to flip over.

3. Use the toaster to toast your bread slices to your own preference; the longer you leave it in, the crunchier it will be. To be golden brown, toast for approximately 3 minutes.

4. Once the toast is done, take it out; butter one side on each slice. Top with the still warm tomatoes and spinach.

EXPAND YOUR REPERTOIRE

Sometimes my relatives like to add a small sprinkle of black pepper on top of this recipe; just be warned that this will create a very strong flavour and may not be to everyone's individual preference and sensory needs. Others like just a dash of sweet chilli sauce on the side, too.

BRIOCHE FRENCH TOAST – BY SIENA CASTELLON

Duration: 12 hours (the brioche needs to be left overnight)
Energy rating: High
Skill level: Complex
To make when: there is a late 'brunch' you need to cater for, such as when you have relatives visiting; for the period of 'Betwixtmas' in the UK (between Boxing Day and New Year's Eve, there tends to be a lot of food left over that we usually just 'pick at'); you need to pick yourself up, when you need cheering up.

Siena Castellon is an autism advocate. She is the author of **The Spectrum Girl's Survival Guide** and is the founder of Neurodiversity Celebration Week, an annual celebration.

This recipe can look complex – but the energy use on this is only moderate. There is some planning ahead required; the brioche needs to be left overnight and will not be suitable for eating right there and then as it will deflate. You can use shop-bought brioche for this by way of a shortcut, meaning this recipe will only take you around 20–25 minutes in total, rather than 12 hours. However, this book is about expanding your skills – and I would encourage you to try making the brioche for the French toast when you have enough time and patience to set aside to make it from start to finish.

Editor's note: this recipe is quite time-specific by nature – so the use of a timer is advisable, as it can either make or break this recipe.

EQUIPMENT YOU WILL NEED

1 timer (can be on your phone)

1 pair of disposable gloves

1 measuring jug for measuring out the 'wet' ingredients

1 set of digital scales

1 medium-sized bowl (for measuring the dry ingredients)

1 whisk

1 large mixing bowl

1 plastic bag

1 fork

1 loaf pan/tin

1 wire rack

1 teaspoon

1 tablespoon

1 frying pan

Optional: 1 baking tray and 1 pair of tongs

INGREDIENTS

To make the brioche, you will need:

80 millilitres of warm whole milk

500 grams (17.5 ounces) of plain flour/all-purpose flour (and a little extra for your work surface)

4 eggs

65 grams (2.5 ounces) of caster sugar

2 teaspoons of salt

A capful of olive oil

A little butter to grease the loaf pan/tin

7 grams (¼ ounce) packet of yeast

170 grams (6 ounces) of butter

To make 2 slices of French toast you will need:

2 slices of brioche (either shop-bought or what you will make by following this recipe)

1 large egg

40 grams (1.5 ounces) of heavy cream or double cream

½ teaspoon of nutmeg

½ teaspoon of cinnamon

2 tablespoons of granulated sugar

1 tablespoon of cinnamon

3 tablespoons of granulated sugar

1 capful of olive oil

Please note that you will be using some of the same ingredients twice, with different amounts – so you will need to measure them out separately, hence why they are separated in this list.

HOW TO MAKE
Pre-preparation

Make sure you allow the milk to warm up to room temperature. If you are making the brioche from scratch, measure out the flour, eggs, sugar, milk and salt. Make sure you prepare the bowl your dough will rest in; cover the insides with a capful of olive oil. This will stop the dough sticking to the bowl. Butter the inside of the loaf pan/tin.

Method

To make the brioche, the following will take around 12 hours, with a further 20–25 minutes to create the French toast. (The recipes have been separated to make this clearer.)

1. Add the packet of yeast to the milk, stir and wait for it to set. The yeast needs to get foamy in terms of appearance; when that happens, add 140 grams of the flour and 1 egg. Use the whisk to stir. Incorporate 140 grams more flour and allow to rest for 1 hour.

2. Add the sugar and salt, and mix. Next, add the remaining 3 eggs and the rest of the flour. Stir and allow to sit for 30 minutes.

3. Once the mix has risen, sprinkle some of the flour across your workspace, to prepare it for the dough. Tip out your dough and knead for 20 minutes; be warned: it will be sticky. (Use disposable gloves if this is something you feel uncomfortable with.)

4. After 20 minutes, add 170 grams of cold butter and knead it into the dough. Continue kneading until the dough is no longer sticky; this should take approximately 15 minutes.

5. Put the dough in the oiled bowl and leave it in a warm place for 2 hours; put in a plastic bag to allow it to rise.

6. Once this is done, use a fork to fold the dough in from the edge to the centre of the bowl; this will deflate it. Refrigerate overnight. Deflate the dough once again in the morning.

7. In the morning, put the dough in the buttered loaf pan to rise again for 2–3 hours, once again in a warm place. Bake at 190°C/375°F (no fan) for 30–40 minutes, or until golden brown. Allow to rest for 15–20 minutes; the brioche will still be hot and cutting it any sooner will mean it will lose its shape.

EXPAND YOUR REPERTOIRE

If you want to improve the appearance of your brioche, you could add an egg glaze on top. Separate an egg white from the yolk; add a pinch of salt to the egg white, and beat together with a fork. Brush on top of the brioche and bake it!

Method to make the brioche into 2 slices of 'French toast'

Please note, it is recommended that your brioche should be slightly stale, to not be soggy at the end of this recipe. If it's not, make sure you start from step 1; if it is stale, start from step 2.

1. Heat the oven to 180°C/350°F. Once it is hot, put the slices of brioche in the oven for 8 minutes; this will crisp them up.

2. In a frying pan that's over a hot hob, add the egg, cream, nutmeg and half a teaspoon of cinnamon; whisk to mix together.

3. Soak each side of the brioche for 30 seconds; make sure to flip over to cook the other side. (Use tongs to help you with this if needed.) Make sure it's golden brown on each side. Serve warm.

EXPAND YOUR REPERTOIRE

You could add a small sprinkle of sugar as a topping to serve.

ZESTY LEMON COUSCOUS BREAKFAST SALAD

Duration: 15 minutes
Energy rating: Low
Skill level: Easy
To make when: you need a quick and easy breakfast, with a hint of 'zest';
you need to make something that can be easily scaled up to
be shared with more than one other person; you have a long
day ahead of you but have not slept well – and need to wake
up quickly.

It may be slightly strange to have a more 'lunch'-like recipe in this section –
however, couscous has sometimes been the option on a breakfast menu when
I have been travelling. This is very easy to make and is easily adaptable – and
can fit pretty much all sensory needs and different preferences. This is also very
budget-friendly, and can also be used for meal prep – for example, for lunch
the next day. If you're using ounces, round up or down.

EQUIPMENT YOU WILL NEED

1 chopping board   1 measuring jug
1 chopping knife   1 mixing bowl
1 kettle   1 fork

INGREDIENTS

½ a green bell pepper   Optional: 1 stock cube in the
                               flavour of your choice
1 cucumber
                               60 grams (2 ounces) of
1 tiny bunch of coriander/   flavoured couscous (your
cilantro   choice)
50 millilitres of boiled water
                               ½ a lemon

Note: some types of couscous can contain dairy and gluten, but dairy-free and gluten-free types are readily available.

HOW TO MAKE
Pre-preparation
Using the chopping board and knife, cut the half of the pepper up into smaller chunks and set aside for later. Chop off three small 'rings' from the cucumber; quarter them and set aside for later. Roughly chop the leaves of the coriander and set aside.

Method

1. Boil the water using the kettle; pour into the measuring jug up to the 50 ml mark and crumble in the stock cube (if using). (Stir if necessary.) Add the couscous to the mixing bowl, then add the water/stock to the couscous; cover it for 5 minutes and wait for it to take its form. If needed, stir gently with a fork to make it fluffy; gently drain it if needed.

2. Add the pepper, cucumber and coriander to the couscous after 5 minutes is up; stir in. Squeeze the lemon juice over the mix and also stir it in until it's combined.

EXPAND YOUR REPERTOIRE
There are plenty of ways to adapt this dish – especially if you were to also eat this at lunch time. You could consider frying onions and shallots to mix in with, adding in small amounts of crushed garlic, even different types of beans; sprinkling spices on the top of the couscous, or stirring them through, also adds a unique flavour. This could be ground coriander, ground cumin – even something with more of a 'kick' to it, such as paprika. I quite like a small amount of black pepper, just to create a more smoky taste. You could also consider using a lime for contrast, too.

FISH AND PEPPER-INFLUENCED RICE

Duration: 45 minutes
Energy rating: Moderate
Skill level: Medium
To make when: you need a refreshing breakfast; you are hosting some kind of meeting – such as if you are freelance; it's a 'girls' day out' – and you have all your friends staying around (just scale up portion sizes); if you are travelling or just have a sense of holiday nostalgia.

When you travel through an airport sometimes – especially if you have had to be there early – you get to stop for breakfast. There are always sweet options – such as pancakes – which I would always go for. My mother is different in that she will almost always go for something savoury – especially if fish is on the menu. Granted, this is an unusual dish to have in the breakfast section of this book – but if you can eat it while travelling, why can't it be an option at home, too?

Note: this recipe is for one person – just scale up the amounts if you need to make it for more than one person.

EQUIPMENT YOU WILL NEED

1 chopping board   1 set of tongs

1 chopping knife   1 teaspoon

1 baking tray   1 tablespoon

1 roll of foil   1 saucepan

Optional: disposable gloves. (This is if you are a sensory avoider, as we will be handling raw fish.)

INGREDIENTS

1 red bell pepper   2 fillets of salmon

3 leaves of basil   2 capfuls of olive oil

1 lemon   2 teaspoons of ground cumin

2 teaspoons of ground coriander	1 pack of plain basmati rice (pre-cooked 'microwave' rice)

HOW TO MAKE
Pre-preparation

Use the chopping board and the chopping knife to cut up half of the red pepper into small pieces; set aside for later, as this will be cooked along with the rice. Do the same with the basil leaves – just make sure to remove the stalk as this does not taste very nice. You will be sprinkling this on top of the salmon before it goes in the oven. Cut the lemon in half – again, with the chopping board and knife. Conserve half and set the other half aside for later as a kind of garnish. While in its packet, make sure you separate the rice by breaking it up by gently squeezing; this will make it easier to cook with later on. And finally, set out the foil on the baking tray; it should cover the bottom, with a little extra to cover the fish.

Method

1. Set the oven to 200°C/400°F and allow to heat up. (There should be instructions on the back of the packaged salmon which will tell you the right temperature, but it's usually around this mark.)

2. Use the tongs to take the salmon out of the packaging and place on top of the foil on the baking tray. Dribble a capful of oil across the top and cover evenly with the cumin and ground coriander. Finally, top with the basil leaves, and gently squeeze the lemon over the top. Add a tablespoon of water and then cover the fish with the foil. Place in the oven to cook for up to 25 minutes; check in occasionally to check to see if the fish is cooked before then.

3. While this is happening, we will be cooking the rice. Add a capful of the olive oil to the pan over a medium heat on the hob and allow to heat up. Add the rice and begin to stir. After 5 minutes, add the red pepper to soften it up. After another 5–10 minutes, turn the heat down low and allow to cook gently.

4. Once the salmon is cooked, take it out of the oven and put it on the plate you will be using to serve. Add the rice next to it and squeeze the rest of the lemon gently over the top to finish.

EXPAND YOUR REPERTOIRE

It may be an unusual recipe – but, as I said, I have witnessed versions of this being eaten at various times of day, although this is just scaled down. Instead of peppers, you could just serve plain rice on a spinach leaf. When it comes to rice, instead of a lemon, you could flavour it with black pepper or paprika; this will add an extra fiery kick and would be ideal for sensory seekers. Changing up the rice could also be an adaptation, too – whole-grain rice with this would be delicious. You can also change the type of fish that is used, too – just make sure it is flaky if you decide to do that. You can also experiment with the spices that cover it as well. You could 'up' the spice level if that's your preference, too.

HACK YOUR EVERYDAY CEREAL

Duration: 10 minutes

Energy rating: Low

Skill level: Easy

To make when: your everyday 'safe food' at breakfast starts to become a bit too boring and you want to try experimenting; you'd like to add more fruit to your diet in a way that is not too overwhelming; you have a big day ahead of you, such as an exam, and you feel anxious.

Okay – this recipe is slightly cheating and it may come across to a few people as not being 'proper'. However, some autistic people struggle to eat enough fruit and vegetables – and this is just one way you can add more to your breakfast, even if it's more of a 'hack' than anything else. This serves one person.

EQUIPMENT YOU WILL NEED

1 bowl

1 dessertspoon to eat with

1 chopping board

1 chopping knife

INGREDIENTS

1 small bunch of grapes

1 apple

60 grams (2 ounces) of cereal of your choice (or 1 portion)

Milk of your choice (dairy or plant-based)

HOW TO MAKE
Pre-preparation
Using the chopping board and knife, cut the grapes in half; quarter the apple, remove the core and then cut the quarters into bite-sized pieces. Set aside for later.

Method

1. Pour out the cereal as you usually would do and add a splash of milk as usual. Stir with the spoon you will be using to eat this with.

2. Add the fruit on top of the cereal. Enjoy!

EXPAND YOUR REPERTOIRE

A lot can be said for the role of milk when it comes to humble cereal; put too much in and it becomes soggy, put too little in and the cereal is too crunchy. (Yep – these are the sort of debates I have heard between some autistic individuals over the years.) Add the cereal to the bowl first to try to strike a balance; add only a splash of milk at a time, until you get the desired amount. For alternative flavours, you could try different types of milk – such as those made from nuts. Sprinkling a little sugar – a tiny pinch – on the top of the fruit could bring out the sweetness. Try other fruits but not ones that are very water-based – so not strawberries or oranges.

APPLE AND BANANA SMOOTHIE

Duration: 15 minutes

Energy rating: Low

Skill level: Easy

To make when: you need to wake yourself up for the day ahead – such as if you know you have a lot of meetings to attend and are concerned about making it to the end of the day; you need to get rid of some extra fruit you have sitting around, to not let it go to waste; you're about to go travelling.

Smoothies are easy to make and are easily adaptable to most sensory needs and preferences; they can be changed according to dietary requirements, too. They are also suitable for a wide range of budgets and skill sets.

EQUIPMENT YOU WILL NEED

1 chopping board

1 chopping knife

1 corer

1 blender or smoothie maker

1 tablespoon

INGREDIENTS

3 bananas

1 red apple of your choice

2 tablespoons of plain yogurt

1 carton of orange juice (you won't need the whole carton)

HOW TO MAKE
Pre-preparation

Using the chopping board and knife, peel and cut the bananas into chunks; set aside for later. Use the corer to remove the centre of the apple, and use the chopping knife to cut into small chunks. You don't need to be too careful about the size and shape of the fruit chunks.

Method

1. Plug the blender or smoothie maker in.

2. Put half of the banana pieces into the blender or the smoothie maker. Add half the apples, then 2 tablespoons of the yogurt. Add the rest of the fruit, leaving enough space for the lid to be tightly screwed into place.

3. Pour the orange juice into the blender or smoothie maker, so it reaches about the halfway point; this is to help blend all of the ingredients smoothly. Blend for 30 seconds at a time to get your preferred consistency.

EXPAND YOUR REPERTOIRE

This is a very basic version of a smoothie and can be adapted in a multitude of ways. Sometimes I like to match the fruit used to the juice – so, if you add in apple pieces, replace the orange juice with apple juice. If you prefer a smoothie to be quite thick, add in more yogurt – and you can also change the flavour of that, too. You can always covert a smoothie to a milkshake as well. If you prefer to cut out the element of preparation of ingredients, you can always use frozen fruit of your choice; most supermarkets sell bags of pre-prepared fruit.

BACON, EGG AND GREENS BREAKFAST WRAP

Duration:	20–25 minutes
Energy rating:	Moderate
Skill level:	Complex
To make when:	you have woken up feeling exceptionally peckish – and need something that is very filling; if you are going out for the day – such as for cultural reasons – or if you are travelling to a new place and aren't too sure when lunch or dinner will be; when it's the first day of the holidays.

When we went on holiday as kids, my sibling was particularly taken with a specific type of breakfast wrap – and asked for it for a long time, even years, afterwards. Wraps are very easy to work with, especially if executive functioning is working well that day – this is just a more savoury version. This makes two wraps – that can be eaten by one individual or shared. Just be warned that you will be boiling the eggs and cooking the bacon simultaneously; if you need to, you can do one after the other, so you can learn how to sequence the recipe, if needed.

EQUIPMENT YOU WILL NEED

1 chopping board	1 frying pan
1 chopping knife	1 pair of tongs
1 saucepan	2 cocktail sticks

INGREDIENTS

1 small bunch of fresh coriander/cilantro	1 capful of olive oil
1 small bunch of fresh basil	3 slices of bacon
2 medium eggs	2 wraps
	Optional: black pepper

HOW TO MAKE
Pre-preparation

Using the chopping board and knife, chop the coriander and basil up finely into tiny pieces that can be sprinkled; set aside for later. Read the instructions on the back of the bacon packet – this should tell you how long to cook the bacon for.

Method

1. Place the 2 eggs into the saucepan and cover with water so they are fully immersed. Place on the hob with the heat at halfway; this should start to slowly boil them.

2. In the frying pan, drizzle a capful of oil across the bottom. Place the slices of bacon in the pan, and put on to the hob – again with the heat at about halfway. This will start to cook; follow the instructions on the back of the packet, as this will have the instructions specific to that bacon brand. Once the time that is on the packet is about halfway through, turn the rashers over by using the tongs and cook for the remaining time.

3. The eggs will be done in about 12 minutes; a tip would be to run water over them to prevent further cooking. Once that's done, take out the saucepan, peel, and chop up into small squares. (Just be careful as they will still be hot.)

4. Once the bacon is cooked – it will have a less shiny appearance and will have reduced in size, and you can also probably start to smell it – pick up with the tongs and put it on the chopping board. Chop one slice in half. Put one and a half rashers on each wrap.

5. Sprinkle the egg over each wrap, and then also sprinkle across a tiny amount of black pepper. Next, add the coriander and basil you cut up earlier. Roll up and use the cocktail sticks to keep each wrap closed for the purposes of presentation.

EXPAND YOUR REPERTOIRE

This is quite a simple recipe and it is easily adaptable; try experimenting with the flavours – you could even try a tiny amount of tarragon (slightly unconventional). The bacon can be replaced, of course – you could try cheese (dairy-free versions are available), or other 'greens' such as lettuce or salad leaves are available from most supermarkets. Try snipping the bacon into tiny pieces with kitchen scissors; this will provide a different sort of sensory input.

BREAKFAST BUN SALAD TRAY FOR ONE

Duration: 25 minutes
Energy rating: Moderate
Skill level: Medium
To make when: it's the weekend and you have woken up later than usual after a lie in; somebody – be it a partner or housemate – is in the final stages of recovering from an illness, such as a cold or the flu.

If you can be indecisive about what to eat – perhaps as a result of an executive function issue – then a potential breakfast solution would be to make a small piece of everything available! (Everything apart from cereals, that is, when it comes to this recipe.) This would also go really well with the next recipe, too – to be served side by side. This is the sort of thing family members may have had on holiday – well, an approximation. Please be aware that this mixes many different textures and flavours – and not all ingredients will be the same temperature. This is not an adaptable recipe for that reason.

EQUIPMENT YOU WILL NEED

1 chopping board	1 frying pan
1 chopping knife	1 pair of tongs
1 paring knife	1 toaster
1 fork	1 butter knife
1 bowl for serving	1 plate for serving
1 bread knife	

INGREDIENTS

1 small bunch of green grapes	1 pear (you will only use half)
1 small bunch of red grapes	1 apple (you will only use half)

1 avocado

1 breakfast bun

1 bottle of sweet chilli sauce
(you will only use a little
according to taste)

1 capful of olive oil

2 slices of bacon

1 slice of bread of your choice

HOW TO MAKE
Pre-preparation

Using the chopping board and knife, cut all of the grapes into halves, slice half of the pear into bite-sized chunks and then do the same for the apple. Using the paring knife, cut the avocado in half and gently ease out the stone in the middle. Use the fork to scoop out the innards into the bowl; set aside for later. If it has not come pre-prepared, use the bread knife to slice the breakfast bun in half.

Method

1. Pour a capful of olive oil into the frying pan and heat up over the hob with the gauge at the halfway point. Use the tongs to lower on the 2 slices of bacon; this will begin to cook. Follow the instructions on the back of the packet for an overall time this will take; turn over when that is halfway through.

2. Meanwhile, while the bacon is cooking, we are going to make the guacamole. Add a drizzle of the sweet chilli sauce to the ripe innards of the avocado and mash until nice and pulpy; this will take maybe 4–5 minutes.

3. Toast the two halves of the breakfast bun for 3 minutes; do the same with your bread slice. (If you want it to be more toasted, try for a further minute – this is to avoid burning.)

4. Arrange the fruit bites from earlier on the plate you will be using to serve however you like.

5. Assemble the buns! Take the (now cooked) bacon out of the frying pan and sandwich between the toasted buns; use the butter knife to cover your bread slice with the guacamole you made earlier. Arrange all the elements on your plate.

EXPAND YOUR REPERTOIRE

Hard-boiled eggs could also be included with this dish. When making the gua-camole, you could try adding fresh leaves of basil or coriander; growing your own inside is very cheap and adds extra greenery to your diet in a very subtle way. Try flavouring the guacamole also with a small pinch of black pepper; this could add extra sensory feedback. You could even try adding in oregano, tarragon or ground coriander. Buttering your breakfast buns will also produce more of a 'bap' type feel.

STRAWBERRY PARADISE SMOOTHIE

🔥 🌱 ⚗️ 👁 ✋ ⚙️

Duration: 10–15 minutes

Energy rating: Low

Skill level: Easy

To make when: you need to start the day off on the right note – such as if you are nervous about a social gathering later on that day; it's exam season and you're nervous; you need just that little bit more self-regulation to be provided.

One of my favourite things to have for breakfast is a strawberry smoothie; it has just a pleasantness about it – and can be made pretty much all year round, too. Smoothies are also very budget-friendly – and tick a range of sensory needs, too. It is like a small slice of paradise to me – something that I can just kind of drift away with, to my happy place, far, far away...

EQUIPMENT YOU WILL NEED

1 chopping board

1 chopping knife

1 paring knife

1 smoothie maker

1 tablespoon

INGREDIENTS

5–7 fresh strawberries

1 banana

6–7 tablespoons of straw-berry yogurt

4 frozen strawberries (from a packet of frozen fruits, available at most supermarkets)

1 carton of orange juice (some brands are vegan-friendly)*

*It's always worth having a look to check if any product fits with your dietary requirements; some orange juices may contain products such as fish oil or gelatin.

HOW TO MAKE
Pre-preparation
Using the chopping board and knife, cut the fresh strawberries into halves. Peel the banana and use the paring knife to cut all of the banana into small circles. Set all aside for later.

Method

1. Plug in the smoothie maker to a power socket. Take out the cup that you will put the ingredients in to blend and unscrew the lid.

2. First, add in the banana, then 3 tablespoons of the strawberry yogurt. Next, add the frozen strawberries, then the fresh strawberries.

3. Add the remaining yogurt. Top the cup up with orange juice, making sure to leave enough room for the smoothie maker's blade when you screw it back on to the cup. Screw the lid back on tightly and make sure it is secure.

4. Blend for 30 seconds, and undo. Make sure that all the ingredients are fully blended; if you prefer a thicker smoothie, add more yogurt, but slowly. If you prefer a runnier smoothie – which you may do if you are a sensory seeker – add more of the orange juice, but do so gradually. Keep blending until you get your desired consistency.

EXPAND YOUR REPERTOIRE
A pinch of turmeric could be blended into the smoothie; this, some suggest, has other benefits in terms of health. If you quite like to wake up to food/drink that has a zest, try juicing a lemon and adding that in, with only half of the orange juice you would usually use. If you also would like to bring out a bit more of the strawberry flavour, sometimes I like to add in a capful of undiluted elderflower cordial; only do this sparingly as it has a high sugar content. If you would prefer your smoothie to be thicker but with more of a 'froth' to it, try doubling or tripling your banana use, while taking away from the amount of orange juice or frozen strawberries that you will be using. (This is just to scale up the proportions of the smoothie.)

PART 2

Lunch Recipes

LYDIA'S RANDOM PASTA

Duration: 20–30 minutes
Energy rating: Moderate
Skill level: Medium
To make when: you need something to 'fill you up'.

This recipe came about because I was hungry one day and put together random ingredients! This is suitable for sensory seekers, and for individuals who are perhaps more in touch with their interoception.

EQUIPMENT YOU WILL NEED

1 colander

1 saucepan

1 teaspoon

1 chopping board

2 chopping knives

1 tablespoon

1 garlic crusher

1 cheese grater

INGREDIENTS

25 grams (1 ounce) of cheddar cheese

2 cloves of garlic

1 onion

6 cherry tomatoes

60 grams (2.5 ounces) of pasta

4 teaspoons of salsa from a jar

Salt and pepper

HOW TO MAKE
Pre-preparation

Before you do anything, grate the cheese, prepare the garlic for the crusher by peeling it, dice the onion and chop up the tomatoes. Set all of them to one side; we will come back to them later.

Method

1. Pour the pasta into the saucepan. In either a kettle or separate pan, boil enough water to cook your pasta in. Pour the boiled water in with the pasta; now, set that on a hob with a high heat to boil the pasta. Crush the garlic into the saucepan and stir through.

2. The pasta will be cooked once it's squishy; this will take around 15 minutes. Drain with the colander over the sink and mix through the salsa.

3. Layer up your pasta and toppings, and then repeat until your bowl is full. Add a sprinkle of pepper on top.

EXPAND YOUR REPERTOIRE

If there is one particular flavour you like in this – such as the onion or the salsa – you may want to add more of that and less of the other ingredients. This would bring out the flavour you like more than the others. To make this suitable for sensory avoiders, keep the flavours to a minimum – perhaps just use grated cheese and possibly chopped-up tomatoes as one topping. Serve the different ingredients separately.

BEANS ON TOAST A GO GO

Duration: 15 minutes

Energy rating: Low

Skill level: Medium

To make when: you're low on ingredients in the house and have no energy to go shopping.

This recipe is something I'm aware of some autistic individuals eating after a stressful day – such as to recharge. This took me a while to 'get the hang of' – so I'd suggest this is for someone who has more of a background in cooking, who has more of a moderate skill level and already has some knowledge.

EQUIPMENT YOU WILL NEED

1 colander (for washing the optional salad)

1 bowl to serve

1 cheese grater

1 can opener

1 saucepan

1 wooden or silicone spoon to stir with

1 toaster

INGREDIENTS

Optional: salad leaves – you can buy a pre-prepared bag of salad leaves, or make your own by chopping up things such as tomatoes, cucumber and carrots

1 pack of cheese (you will need enough to grate a handful)

1 can of beans

2 slices of bread of your choice, brown or white

A pinch of pepper

HOW TO MAKE
Pre-preparation
If you are using the option of salad leaves, make sure you wash them in a colander over the sink, drain and set aside to dry. If you decide to make your own salad, chop up all the vegetables you will be using – for example, a cucumber, cherry tomatoes, lettuce – and set aside for later. Get out the cheese grater and grate about a handful of cheese (judge the amount by eye).

Method
1. Pour your can of beans into a saucepan and place on a medium heat on the hob, in order to heat them up. Keep stirring periodically so the beans do not stick to the bottom of the pan. The longer you stir, the thicker the bean mix will be. Set aside on the lowest possible heat just to keep warm.

2. Toast two pieces of bread in the toaster for up to 4 minutes. They should look light, golden brown and with a soft(ish) texture.

3. Once cooked, pour the beans over the two pieces of toast. Add the grated cheese on top of the two pieces of toast and beans. Sprinkle the pepper on top.

4. Add the salad you have prepared (it was an option) on the side to serve. Enjoy!

EXPAND YOUR REPERTOIRE
Sensory avoiders may prefer to keep two main elements, the toast and the beans, separate. If you want 'more' as a sensory seeker, try experimenting with different herbs, such as paprika. Different cheeses would also change the flavour and texture.

SENSORY SUMMER TIME SALAD – BY EMILY AT @21ANDSENSORY

Duration:	15 minutes
Energy rating:	Low
Skill level:	Easy
To make when:	you need a 'quick' meal to rustle up for lunch, if you feel like the world is 'too much' and are feeling overloaded or have just experienced a meltdown.

Emily is the 'brains' behind 21andsensory, an Instagram page and blog documenting her life on the autistic spectrum with sensory issues. Emily is an illustrator by trade and has a first-class BA (Hons) degree in Graphic Design. She is also the person who illustrated this very book! Emily also hosts the podcast of the same name, as well as creating colouring-in sheets available to download. Emily also has sensory processing disorder (SPD), and this is one of her 'staple' meals.

This recipe can be adapted for sensory seekers, and more details about that can be found under 'Expand your repertoire'. Sensory Summer Time Salad requires minimal skills; this meal is also easily adaptable and is ideal if you struggle with motor skills. You will only need one fork to eat it with.

EQUIPMENT YOU WILL NEED

1 mixing bowl	1 fork
1 colander	1 kettle
1 chopping board	For serving: either 1 standard
1 chopping knife	bowl or 1 plate

INGREDIENTS

1 packet of couscous	1 small bunch of grapes
1 bag of mixed salad leaves	1 carrot
1 cucumber	

HOW TO MAKE
Pre-preparation

First of all, decide how much salad and couscous you would like; this can either be a generous plate, or a small(ish) bowl, and measure ingredients according to the size. Measure the couscous into the bowl. Wash the mixed salad leaves, cucumber, grapes and carrot in the colander over the sink, and allow to drain. Cut the cucumber into circles, the grapes in half and the carrot into small pieces. Or, if you struggle with textures, or consider yourself to be a sensory avoider, cut up the cucumber, grapes and carrot into even smaller pieces.

Note: if you make too much, this can be used for leftovers the next day.

Method

1. Follow the instructions on the back of the couscous packet; add the water and set it aside for later on. The couscous will begin to form while you create the salad.

2. Mix up the cucumber, salad leaves, grapes and carrot. If you are a sensory avoider, set aside on the plate. If you are a sensory seeker, set the salad aside, and wait for the couscous.

3. Once the couscous has finished forming, make sure you fluff it up a bit – mix it with a fork.

If you are a sensory seeker, mix the salad with the couscous on your plate. If you are an avoider, keep the salad and couscous separate on the plate.

Tip: people who are sensory avoiders often like to have different foods separate from one another on the plate, so the textures do not mix. If this is the case, consider using food separators. They are available to buy cheaply on Amazon and elsewhere.

EXPAND YOUR REPERTOIRE

This recipe is for sensory avoiders and is suitable for those who have sensory processing disorder; it is also ideal if you have particular challenges when it comes to textures and the 'feel' of particular foods. If you are a sensory seeker, however, it may be worth using different sauces to flavour the salad. Use a small amount of olive oil and drizzle it across the salad leaves. Peri-peri sauce as an extra flavouring is also a good option; if you can stand it, sweet chilli sauce is also an option. You can also consider adding extra ingredients to the dish. Try adding small pieces of cheese to the salad, crumbled up as a way of adding a little extra 'flair'. Walnuts would create a moreish feel to the dish. To make the salad and couscous more substantial, try heating up a can of baked beans and adding them on the side. Shredded carrots are also something that taste great in a salad.

'SOCIAL JUSTICE' STUFFED SANDWICHES

Duration: 10 minutes

Energy rating: Low

Skill level: Easy

To make when: you need a hug for whatever reason, such as if angry at the state of the world.

Autistic individuals have a strong and innate sense of justice. This is also great if you have had a hard day at work, for example. These are quick to make and you can easily take them in to work. This recipe was made for me on an occasion for this exact reason!

EQUIPMENT YOU WILL NEED

1 chopping board

1 paring knife

1 butter knife

1 bread knife

1 plate or foil if you are transporting your sandwich elsewhere

---

INGREDIENTS

Butter for spreading

6 slices of cold cooked chicken

1 packet of cheddar cheese (you will not need the whole pack – see below)

1 cucumber (you won't need a whole cucumber)

1 orange bell pepper (you will be using about a half)

2 slices of white bread

Note: if you are a sensory avoider, you may wish to only use the cold chicken or cheese for the contents of your sandwich. This will limit the many different flavours tangling up and becoming potentially overwhelming.

HOW TO MAKE
Pre-preparation

Make sure you leave the butter out so it can warm up to room temperature; this will mean it will be easier to spread. Cut the chicken into smaller pieces. Cut 4 slices of cheese from the end of the packet. Cut off the end of the cucumber and get rid of it; cut a further 6 circles off the end. Quarter the pepper and remove the centre. Use the paring knife to cut half of the pepper into smaller slices. Set all aside for later.

Method

1. Butter the two slices of white bread with a thin layer by using the butter knife. This will create a kind of 'seal' for the contents of your sandwich later on.

2. Choose one slice of bread to 'build on'. Add a thin layer of the cold chicken. Next, add a thin layer of cheese slices, then the pepper and cucumber.

3. Add the second slice of bread on top. With the bread knife, cut diagonally from the top left to bottom right corner. This will create two triangles of sandwiches.

EXPAND YOUR REPERTOIRE

If you are a sensory seeker, you might want to experiment with spices you can add to your sandwich. For example, you could add a small sprinkle of pepper to the inside contents of the sandwich, in order to create another flavour, as well as to add a little 'kick'. Cheese and tomato are great combinations to experiment with, too. You could make a heartier meal by adding these sandwiches to a salad on a plate.

HAND-BLENDED RED PEPPER VEGETABLE SOUP

Duration: 1 hour and 15 minutes

Energy rating: Moderate

Skill level: Medium

To make when: the seasons are just starting to turn to winter, and it is horribly blustery and cold outside; you finish an exam or an assessment, and need time to just sit and collect yourself in the aftermath; when you are going out with friends later in the evening; you're about to go travelling and need something light before setting off; when there are too many options to decide from.

Everyone loves a soup, right? (Well, most of us do.) Generally speaking, if you own a blender of some sort, you will be able to make a huge range of soups – you do not necessarily need a specific soup maker. One of the people interviewed for this book also showed me how to make a two-minute pea soup! This is adaptable to a range of sensory needs and specific diets. It is also a way of adding more vegetables to your diet, if you struggle with texture and the shape of particular types.

EQUIPMENT YOU WILL NEED

1 chopping board

1 chopping knife

1 garlic crusher

1 baking tray

1 handheld blender (sometimes called a stick blender)

1 tablespoon

1 saucepan

INGREDIENTS

1 courgette/zucchini

2 red bell peppers

1 garlic clove

1 red onion

1 tablespoon of crème fraîche (dairy-free/vegan options are available)

1 carton (500 grams/17.5 ounces) of passata (sieved tomatoes – known in some countries as tomato purée)

Olive oil to drizzle on the vegetables

1 basil leaf

Optional for sensory seekers: a pinch of black pepper

HOW TO MAKE
Pre-preparation
Using the chopping board and knife, chop up the courgette into medium-sized chunks. Gut the peppers and discard the innards as well as the top of them; once again, use the chopping board and knife to cut into rough chunks. Skin the garlic clove and crush in the garlic crusher. Peel and dice the onion. And finally, if, like me, you struggle with motor skills, open the crème fraîche and the passata; set aside for now, as we will come back to them later on.

Method

1. Set your oven to 180°C/350°F and allow to heat up.

2. Scatter the pieces of courgette, red peppers, onion and garlic across the baking tray. Drizzle them with a dash of olive oil, enough so that they are all well covered; shake the baking tray from side to side to do this if needed. Roast in the oven for up to 20 minutes, or until the vegetables start to have a dull, matte appearance.

3. Once out of the oven, add all of the vegetables to the blender. Add the passata into the blender and then add a tablespoon of the crème fraîche; this is to stop the overall soup being too watery. In the blender, pulverize for up to 30 seconds at a time; repeat to achieve the texture (i.e. smooth or chunky) of your own preference.

4. In the saucepan, heat the mixture up again so it's warm; in a serving bowl, serve with a sprinkle of black pepper and a basil leaf on top.

EXPAND YOUR REPERTOIRE

It is always worthwhile experimenting with soups, as they are very adaptable to a wide range of different sensory needs as well as diets; it takes some practice, as this recipe uses various different motor skills as well as calling upon executive functioning a lot of the time. If you prefer, you can replace the crème fraîche with double cream. You could also serve with garlic bread or other types of bread.

ROASTED TOMATO AND AUBERGINE PASTA – BY GAVIN DAVEY

Duration: 45 minutes
Energy rating: Moderate
Skill level: Medium
To make when: you need something quick and easy before an early night; you need a comfort or a 'safe' food.

Gavin Davey is an engineer with a self-diagnosis of autism; he is currently waiting for an ASD assessment. He also has ARFID (avoidant restrictive food intake disorder). This recipe was created while Gavin was undergoing treatment for ARFID; texture for him is the biggest hurdle, meaning roasting and blending evened it out.

EQUIPMENT YOU WILL NEED

1 chopping board
1 chopping knife
1 garlic crusher
1 baking tray
1 wooden spoon

1 kettle
1 saucepan
1 fork
1 colander
1 blender

INGREDIENTS

1 aubergine/eggplant
2 courgettes/zucchini
2 carrots, medium-sized
2 bell peppers, colour of your own choosing
1 red onion
4 garlic cloves

3 sprigs of thyme
Olive oil to drizzle over the vegetables
200 grams (7 ounces) of cherry tomatoes
60 grams (2.5 ounces) of pasta in any shape that you like

HOW TO MAKE
Pre-preparation

There is some pre-preparation needed for this recipe, which will save a large amount of time when it comes to working with this recipe later on. Using the chopping board and knife, cut up the aubergine, courgettes, carrots and peppers into chunks. Set all of these ingredients aside for later. Do the same for the red onion, but this time cut up into wedges. Peel the cloves of garlic, then, using the garlic crusher, crush them. Also set aside for later.

Method

1. Preheat your oven to 180°C/350°F and allow it around 10 minutes to heat up.

2. Add all the ingredients you prepared earlier to the baking tray, along with the thyme. Cover with a drizzle of the olive oil, then mix up all the different ingredients on the tray with the wooden spoon.

3. Roast for approximately 20 minutes. (Make sure you check every so often to prevent burning.) Take out the tray, add the tomatoes, then roast again for up to another 20 minutes, all the while checking.

4. While the roasting is happening, you will need to cook your pasta. Boil water in the kettle; add to the saucepan over a medium heat on the hob. Add the pasta in and boil until soft and squishy. (This will take around 15 minutes, and you can test it using a fork.) Drain the pasta in the colander over the sink and set aside for later.

5. Once the roasted vegetables have cooled, blend until the consistency you want has been achieved. Reheat this by adding to the pasta and stirring over a medium heat on the hob for up to 7 minutes.

EXPAND YOUR REPERTOIRE

Cheese can be used to serve this with – just sprinkle on top to make a topping. If you need to make the blending of the vegetables more manageable – as well as to create a richer flavour – add a carton of passata. If you are a sensory seeker, consider adding some fresh chilli peppers when it comes to the blending stage of this recipe; it will add a little extra kick to the overall flavour of this dish.

HACK YOUR OWN SENSORY SOUP

Duration: 10 minutes

Energy rating: Low

Skill level: Easy

To make when: you need something quick and have not eaten for hours due to back-to-back Zoom meetings; when the weather outside is cold and you need to warm up ASAP, complete with 'rosy pink cheeks'.

Soup as a ready-made meal is available from all supermarkets – but there are options to 'hack' it, to create a more moreish, sensory-seeking meal, with extra feedback for sensory seekers. It can be more than just heating up soup and buttering warm bread to eat. This is a really basic meal to make and takes less than ten minutes. It is also really cheap and can be used when you need to budget drastically.

EQUIPMENT YOU WILL NEED

1 chopping board

1 butter knife

1 garlic crusher

1 jar opener

1 bowl for serving

1 large saucepan

1 ladle

1 grater

INGREDIENTS

1 garlic clove

1 tablespoon of salsa from a jar

1 can of plain soup (I like to use 'cream of tomato' soup by any brand going)

Salt and pepper

1 packet of cheese, flavour of your choice (you will only need a little to grate on top of your soup)

HOW TO MAKE
Pre-preparation
Put the garlic clove on its side on the chopping board and use the butter knife's blade to crush it slightly. This will make the skin easier to remove; once this happens, put it in the garlic crusher to crush it.

Method

1. Put a tablespoon of salsa at the bottom of the bowl. Following the instructions on the tin, bring the soup to a high temperature over the hob to cook in the saucepan.

2. Once it's finished – it should be making a cackling sound – pour into the bowl with the salsa at the bottom.

3. Sprinkle the salt and pepper on the top. Add the crushed garlic, too, and stir around.

4. Grate a small amount of cheese on top to finish.

EXPAND YOUR REPERTOIRE
When it comes to serving, consider adding buttered slices of bread on the side or brioche rolls. This also tastes nice with salad, too.

WINTER RICE BOWL

Duration: 10 minutes

Energy rating: Low

Skill level: Easy

To make when: you feel 'under the weather' and need something to clear away your hideous cold; you need something quick and easy to make, such as if you are right in the middle of exam season. Please bear in mind that this is suitable for sensory seekers but not sensory avoiders.

While studying for my NCTJ qualification, we'd have a lunch break in the kitchen; a TV monitor was in the corner, always broadcasting the news. All of my classmates watched, for example, the wedding of Harry and Meghan. We'd have our Naan Hut wrap – more on that soon – or we would sometimes bring packets of rice, and some of us experimented with (sometimes whacky) flavours. I spent a lot of that winter studying eating rice, a memorable student experience if ever there was one.

EQUIPMENT YOU WILL NEED

1 chopping board

1 chopping knife

Optional: 1 garlic crusher

1 saucepan

1 silicone or wooden spoon

1 bowl for serving

INGREDIENTS

¼ cucumber

¼ red bell pepper

Garlic paste or 2 garlic cloves

Olive oil

1 packet of plain rice (pre-cooked 'microwave' rice)

1 jar of a spice of your choice (a sprinkle for cooking with the rice)

Sweet chilli sauce (you will only need a dash)

Pepper (as in the shaker kind)

HOW TO MAKE
Pre-preparation
Cut up the cucumber and red pepper and set aside for later. If you are using the garlic cloves, crush them in the garlic crusher.

Method

1. Put a tiny drop of oil in the saucepan, and then add in the rice. Add the spice of your choice; bring to a medium heat on the hob to begin cooking. Stir with the silicone or wooden spoon to evenly distribute the spice into the rice.

2. Add the red pepper, cucumber and a squirt of garlic paste or the crushed garlic. Add a dash of the sweet chilli sauce; stir all together.

3. Once cooked, add the rice to your bowl and sprinkle pepper on top to serve.

VEGETABLE AND HAM OMELETTE – BY KELLY GRAINGER

Duration: 10 minutes

Energy rating: Low

Skill level: Medium

To make when: you need to make something easy for your lunch, such as if you are experiencing a low-energy day; you need something moreish; you need to recover from a lot of sensory input.

Kelly Grainger is an autism speaker and advocate. He is the co-founder of Perfectly Autistic, a website providing support for parents, partners and autistic people. Diagnosed as autistic at the age of 44, Kelly joined forces with his wife Hester to help businesses grow. He is also the father of India Grainger, whose recipe appears in the next part.

Omelettes are easy and budget-friendly; they are also incredibly easy to adapt, such as if you are a vegetarian or if you need to get rid of ingredients in your fridge before your next 'big shop'. If you would like to make them for more than one person, all you need to do is double the ingredients. (Twice as many for two, three times as much for three people, etc.)

EQUIPMENT YOU WILL NEED

1 frying pan

1 chopping board

1 chopping knife

Knife and fork

1 plate for serving

1 palette knife, spatula or another implement to flip your omelette with

1 mixing bowl

1 fork

INGREDIENTS

¼ of a red onion

¼ of a red bell pepper

¼ of a yellow bell pepper

2 mushrooms

1 jar of olives (we will be using 5 olives)

1 packet of pre-prepared ham (we will be using about half a packet)

2 large eggs

A little olive oil or butter

1 pack of cheese (we will grate a sprinkle of cheese into the omelette)

Pepper (the sort that you sprinkle)

HOW TO MAKE
Pre-preparation
Finely chop the onions, peppers and mushrooms. Set all aside separately for later use. Cut the olives into two, remove any stones, and also set aside for later. Shred half of the ham in the packet into strips and also set aside for later. Crack the eggs into the mixing bowl and beat with a fork.

Method

1. Turn the hob on to a medium heat. (In other words, turn the hob to the halfway point.) Add in the oil or a dab of butter, so it slowly begins to heat up, in order to cook your omelette.

2. Put the red onion and mushrooms into the pan to cook. They should look soft in their texture, and you will hear the oil crackle as they begin to cook.

3. Pour in the eggs to form the batter of the omelette. Make sure the egg covers the whole pan to form the structure. As the eggs begin to cook, use the spatula or other type of implement to lift from the sides of the pan; the runny eggs can flow underneath.

4. When the eggs are nearly 'set', add the ham, olives and peppers, and grate a sprinkle of cheese over the top with the grater. Cook for 1 extra minute.

5. Use the spatula or other implement to fold the omelette in half. Serve on the plate with a sprinkle of pepper on top.

EXPAND YOUR REPERTOIRE
The thing about this recipe is that it is easy to adapt – and can be adapted for sensory seekers and avoiders. As a rule of thumb, if you are a sensory avoider, consider limiting the number of flavours that you use. A green pepper instead

of red or yellow will add a slightly different taste. You could also consider replacing the red onion with spring onions, to create a fresher taste. When cracking the egg, you could also add a spice of your choice. Paprika creates more of a smoky flavour, for example.

STUFFED PEPPER AND RICE BONANZA

Duration: 20 minutes
Energy rating: Moderate
Skill level: Medium
To make when: the weather outside is awful, but your cupboards have nothing left and you cannot bear the idea of going outside; you need something that is quick and easy to make.

Peppers are incredibly versatile to cook with – whether you prefer to have sandwiches, want a salad or include them as a part of your daily hot meal come dinner time. Vegetables have never been my favourite thing – but adapting the form they come in, or even just using a little bit of seasoning, can go a long way. This is a recipe that is very budget-friendly, as well as being adaptable if you are a sensory seeker or avoider. If you are a student, this is easy to make, and also very healthy. The use of the word 'Bonanza' in the title of this recipe is because there are several different flavours involved, but you can limit them if this is too much.

A version of this recipe was included in **BBC Good Food Magazine**.

EQUIPMENT YOU WILL NEED

1 chopping board

1 chopping knife

Optional: 1 garlic crusher

1 baking tray

1 saucepan

1 tablespoon

1 plate (to serve with)

INGREDIENTS

1 large bell pepper (I usually prefer the red sort for sweetness reasons)

1 carrot

Optional: 1 garlic clove or paste

1 packet of basmati rice (pre-cooked 'microwave' rice)

1 bottle of olive oil (we will be using just a drizzle of oil)

Optional: spice of your choice (if you are a sensory avoider, use salt instead)

Optional: sweet chilli sauce for serving

HOW TO MAKE
Pre-preparation

Chop the pepper in half and hollow it out. Set aside for later and get rid of the stalk as well as the insides. Chop the carrot up into the smallest pieces you possibly can. If you are using the garlic in the form of a clove, crush it up ready. Squish the packet of rice to separate the grains into smaller chunks; this will make it easier to cook with.

Method

1. Set the oven to 200°C/400°F and wait for it to heat up. This is the temperature you need it to cook the quickest.

2. Put the bottom half of the pepper you just saved on the baking tray. Drizzle the oil across evenly and sprinkle your preferred choice of spice across it as well. (Use salt if you are a sensory avoider.) Put in the oven to cook; it will begin to look squishy, as well as slightly losing its structure.

3. With the pan on a medium heat (hob at halfway point), drizzle the oil over the base, then add in the garlic, rice and carrot. Over the medium heat, cook the rice – it will begin to sizzle.

4. Once the pepper looks squishy enough to your own preference, take it out and let it cool down slightly on the plate. Fill the inside of the pepper with the rice mix once it's cooked. Add the (optional) sweet chilli sauce to serve.

EXPAND YOUR REPERTOIRE

Investing in a small selection of spices is always worthwhile. You can create a smoky flavour or something spicy – there is a huge amount that you can do with spices. Having a play around is always worthwhile; this can also provide additional sensory input that sensory seekers may want. You also do not have to just chop the head off the pepper; you could try chopping it in half. You could experiment by just topping its head off, hollowing out, stuffing the insides with the rice mix, and then baking all at once. You could even try adding a little passata to the rice mix, then stuffing the pepper, too. Growing herbs is budget-friendly and adds to your ultimate vegetable count; consider experimenting with herbs such as chives and parsley to serve on top.

SOHO HALLOUMI FRIES AND SALAD

Duration: 35–45 minutes
Energy rating: High
Skill level: Complex
To make when: you've woken up a bit groggy and still feel grumpy later on; you need a pick-me-up for lunch; you need to entertain friends, such as if they have travelled a long way to meet you; there's some sort of reunion on.

Soho is one of my favourite places – and it's also where I got to meet the film director Jacqui Morris, a friend who is the 'voice of reason'. Her flat is utterly magical – crammed with books, posters, photography, history, stories just waiting to be uncovered. A large poster of Congresswoman Alexandria Ocasio-Cortez (AOC) caught my imagination in particular; it was a promotion for the Netflix documentary **Knock Down the House**. To me, that was hope in a single photograph – something to aspire to one day.

This recipe is based on two meals I had while visiting Soho previously; it evokes the area for me.

EQUIPMENT YOU WILL NEED:

1 paring knife

1 chopping board

1 colander

1 small bowl

1 chopping knife

1 plate

1 frying pan

1 pair of tongs

INGREDIENTS

1 small handful of cherry tomatoes

¼ of a cucumber

1 small handful of lettuce leaves

1 small handful of rocket (arugula) leaves (you can buy pre-prepared bags in most supermarkets)

¼ of a red bell pepper

¼ of a yellow bell pepper

1 bottle of sweet chilli sauce (only a dash is needed)

1 pack of halloumi (usually 225 grams or 8 ounces)

1 bottle of olive oil (you will only need a drizzle for the frying pan)

1 lemon (optional)

HOW TO MAKE
Pre-preparation

Using the paring knife and chopping board, you need to prepare the cherry tomatoes, cucumber, lettuce and rocket. Wash and drain using the colander over the sink; chop the tomatoes in half; and slice up half the cucumber into smaller chunks. Gut each of the peppers and dispose of their tops; chop into small slices and also set aside for later. Put a dash of sweet chilli sauce in the small bowl; finally, use the chopping knife to cut the halloumi into strips. These will be the 'fries' later on.

Method

1. On a plate arrange all the different elements of the salad once you are done preparing, washing and chopping; if you are a sensory avoider, keep the elements separate and the pieces as small as you can, as this will make them all easier to cope with overall. Add the small pot of sweet chilli sauce on the side; this is for dipping.

2. Put the frying pan on a high heat on the hob and dribble oil across the bottom of the pan. Allow it to heat up. Each strip of halloumi is going to be added to the pan to crisp up on either side, to create the fries; keep pressing them gently into the oil, and flipping round every so often to prevent burning. (Use your tongs!) If you struggle with motor skills, you can do this one at a time as well.

3. This can take some time; once they have all been cooked, add to the plate, and serve alongside the salad.

4. Optional step: by way of 'dressing', squeeze lemon juice over the salad for a zesty tang.

EXPAND YOUR REPERTOIRE

This is the basic version of this meal; you can always add different dressings to the salad, or even try incorporating small pieces of blue cheese. You could also serve small pieces of flatbread with this, too – it's more like a 'platter'-style recipe that way.

SISTER'S APPLE SURPRISE

Duration: 5 minutes

Energy rating: Low

Skill level: Easy

To make when: you need a quick and easy snack at lunch time that is easy to prepare in minutes, before being called back to a jam-packed schedule. This can be put in a small plastic tub, and taken with you on the go, too.

In terms of our tastes when it comes to food, my sister and I diverge quite widely. We both go through phases of what we like, as well as our preferred snacks – and this recipe, based on a previous habit, deserves a place here as none of us can forget eating the apple and peanut butter.

EQUIPMENT YOU WILL NEED

1 chopping board

1 chopping knife

Optional: 1 elastic band (if you are putting this in a small plastic tub, the band will stop the apple oxidizing, meaning it will not go brown in a few hours, and will retain its taste)

1 potato peeler

1 grater

1 teaspoon

INGREDIENTS

1 green apple

1 carrot

1 jar of peanut butter (you will only need a few spoonfuls)

HOW TO MAKE
Pre-preparation

Cut the green apple into quarters and take out the core. If you are taking this in a small plastic tub, make sure to wrap the band round all four quarters so it looks like a whole apple. Make sure this stays in a sealed box, so that it doesn't go brown. Peel and grate the carrot and set aside for later.

Method

1. Spoon the peanut butter on to whatever surface you are serving this on, such as a plate – or, if using the tub, put it in the corner of the box.

2. Set the apple and carrot separately next to the butter.

3. Coat each quarter in butter and carrot to enjoy. Make sure you use a spoon, as this can be messy at times.

EXPAND YOUR REPERTOIRE

Caramelized apple takes a little while to make but could be great as a dessert with the peanut butter. Melt butter in a saucepan; add the apple to brown up. Add a sprinkle of brown sugar to bring out the zany taste. This should take maybe two minutes total.

TOMATO CHICKEN PASTA POT

Duration: 45 minutes

Energy rating: Moderate

Skill level: Medium

To make when: the world is getting on your case, and you need something just a little bit moreish than usual; you need to get rid of a lot of ingredients in your fridge all in one go; you are at home and need to revise.

EQUIPMENT YOU WILL NEED

1 chopping board

2 chopping knives

1 garlic crusher

1 saucepan

1 baking tray

1 wooden or silicone spoon

1 colander

1 mixing bowl

INGREDIENTS

3 chicken sausages (if you are a vegetarian, this recipe still works with vegetarian alternatives)

1 medium carrot

Optional: 1 garlic clove

60 grams (2.5 ounces) of penne pasta

1 bottle of olive oil (we will be

using just a little oil on the baking tray)

1 spice of your choice for flavour (you will only need a pinch)

250 grams (9 ounces – approximately half a carton) of passata (sieved tomatoes – known in some countries as tomato purée)

HOW TO MAKE
Pre-preparation

Read the instructions on the back of the sausages packaging; usually they take around 20 minutes to cook, meaning we will start to boil the pasta first. You just need to be aware of the time difference of around 10 minutes between starting to cook the pasta and the sausages. To make the pasta really soft, this will take around 25–30 minutes, if you do not have a kettle to boil the water first. Make sure the sausages are defrosted and ready to go. Chop the carrots into tiny chunks and crush the garlic clove if you are using that.

Method

1. Pour the pasta into your saucepan and add the crushed garlic if using. Add boiling water so the pasta and garlic are fully submerged; put the heat of the hob on to a medium temperature, so this begins boiling away. Wait 10 minutes.

2. Having read the instructions on the back of the packet of sausages, drizzle a small amount of oil across the baking tray. Add the sausages, covering them evenly all over in the oil. Sprinkle a pinch of your chosen spice on top. Follow the instructions on the back of the packet to begin cooking, making sure to check in every so often.

3. Keep stirring the pasta. Once cooked – which you can check by testing the taste or by seeing if the pasta tubes are soft – drain away the water through the colander over the sink. Add the pasta back into the saucepan and keep on the lowest heat possible. This is just to keep the pasta warm while the sausages cook.

4. Once the sausages are cooked, take out of the oven. Chop them into small pieces and add to the pasta. Add the pieces of carrots and half a carton of passata. Stir and serve warm.

Note: not everyone has a kettle. Pouring water in from the tap, and then bringing to boil on the hob, is another option for cooking. This will take longer, however, and the overall duration can depend on your hob.

EXPAND YOUR REPERTOIRE

Sensory avoiders may prefer to replace the garlic with a pinch of salt; this will bring out the flavour of the pasta without being too overwhelming. As a serving option, they may prefer to keep all the different elements separate, or to limit the amount of passata a lot more. Sensory seekers may prefer to add more tangy ingredients such as red onion slices or other vegetables and spices – a small pinch of tarragon or black pepper could add extra sensory feedback to this recipe.

KATSU SAUSAGE VEGETABLE MIX

Duration: 35 minutes

Energy rating: Moderate

Skill level: Medium

To make when: you need a quick and easy meal for yourself like when you have had several remote meetings back to back; you have young children (or are looking after younger relatives) and need a quick meal to rustle up; you're waiting for pay day to stock your freezer back up.

Some days are just horrible, and this is essentially a hug in the form of food. Sometimes friends say that to be my friend is a danger to their waistlines – but this is a quick and easy dish, one that is very simple, as well as being incredibly adaptable. I absolutely love the flavour of katsu. This can be made for sensory seekers and avoiders, and can be constructed from a limited budget.

EQUIPMENT YOU WILL NEED

1 chopping board

2 chopping knives

1 colander

1 baking tray

1 saucepan

1 non-stick spoon or spatula

1 grater

1 plate for serving

1 pair of tongs

1 pair of oven gloves (for when you take out anything from the oven)

INGREDIENTS

8 cherry tomatoes

1 small handful of salad leaves

1 lemon (you will use half for a little juice at the end)

1 carrot

1 pouch of katsu sauce (you will use approximately ½ a tablespoon)*

5 sausages of your choice (can also be vegetarian sausages for this recipe)

Sunflower or olive oil

1 packet of katsu spice (you will use approximately 1½ tablespoons)*

1 packet of basmati rice (pre-cooked 'microwave' rice)

*Sensory seekers may prefer stronger flavours; they can try increasing the amount of katsu spice used in the recipe.

HOW TO MAKE
Pre-preparation
Cut the tomatoes into quarters and set them aside. Wash the salad leaves, drain in the colander over the sink and also set aside. Cut the lemon and carrot in half and also set aside for later. Open the pouch of katsu sauce. If your sausages are frozen, make sure they are defrosted if required before cooking.

Method

1. Look at the directions on the back of the packet of sausages. Drizzle a small amount of oil across the baking tray. Roll the sausages across the tray to coat in a thin layer of oil. Sprinkle with the katsu spice and cook for the duration specified on the back of the packet.

2. While your sausages are cooking, start to construct the rice. Separate in the packet, and add to the saucepan. Grate in a few pieces of carrot, too. Once it begins to sizzle on the hob, bring the heat down to the lowest setting. It will simmer and be kept warm until the sausages are ready.

3. Arrange the tomatoes and salad leaves as a 'side' on your serving plate. Squeeze out a little lemon juice manually with your hands on top.

4. Once the rice and sausages are cooked, chop the latter up into small pieces. Add a dollop of the katsu sauce and mix all together. Squeeze a tiny amount of lemon on top to finish, to add just a hint of a tang.

Note: if you are a sensory seeker, keep the rice completely plain and free of flavour. Cut the salad elements up as small as possible and do not use any lemon. Only use the katsu sauce. Add on top of the rice and top with the sausages in pieces. If necessary, keep all elements separate and try a meal separator, too.

EXPAND YOUR REPERTOIRE

Instead of katsu as the flavouring for this recipe, you could use other flavours such as peri-peri. Just add it to the sausages before you cook them or sprinkle across the rice. Consider using a lime instead of a lemon. You could also use your preferred salad dressing options, too.

QUICK AND MILD TACOS FOR THREE PEOPLE

Duration: 25–30 minutes
Energy rating: Moderate
Skill level: Medium
To make when: you are having a day out with friends – but need something quick and easy to make, such as if you are going out later on that evening; you need to cater to a bigger gathering – such as if there is a bridal party (this recipe is adaptable to larger gatherings with minimal energy); you are having a night in with your housemates/roommates, such as when the weather outside begins to become colder and a lot more frosty.

Tacos are an easy dish to work with; the fillings can be adapted in pretty much anyway possible, for a wide range of sensory needs, and there is minimal input for maximum output. This recipe was inspired by my visit to New York in March 2020. This recipe assumes that each person will have two tacos each, meaning that there will be six tacos. This recipe uses a range of ingredients, and some are not suitable for sensory avoiders, due to their spicy flavour or texture. If you are a sensory avoider and you would still like to have a go at making this recipe, I would suggest limiting the ingredients to just the mince, and maybe sour cream if you dislike spice and other strong flavours.

EQUIPMENT YOU WILL NEED

1 chopping board

1 chopping knife

Optional: frying pan (if you choose to cook the peppers separately)

1 large saucepan (you will also need a lid – as there is about 10 minutes when this recipe will need to 'sit')

1 wooden or silicone spoon

1 kettle

1 measuring jug

1 colander

INGREDIENTS

1 pack of beef mince/ground
beef (500 grams, 17.5 ounces)
(or vegetarian/vegan
alternative)

2 bell peppers in the colour of
your choice

6 taco shells

Olive oil

1 stock cube

Salt

1 bottle of spice of your
choice (you will only need a
sprinkle of this)

HOW TO MAKE
Pre-preparation

Depending on how you have stored your mince, you may need to take this out
of your freezer the night before, in order for it to defrost in time. (Just make
sure to put a plate underneath if you do – it stops the defrosting from going
absolutely everywhere.) If possible, try to break up the mince when it is time
to start working with it; I have previously seen my mother gently whack it on
our family kitchen's counter top or even use a rolling pin to break it into smaller
pieces. The method you choose is entirely up to you. This will make the mince
easier to work with when it comes to cooking it. Using the chopping board and
knife, cut the top off each pepper and then cut in half in order to remove the
middle seedy part. Chop up into smaller pieces and set aside for later on. For
convenience – and this might be a good idea if you have another condition
such as dyspraxia – it might also be a wise idea to open up the pack of tacos,
just to make serving a little bit easier.

When it comes to the two peppers – the colour of your choosing – there
are two options for serving. You can sweat them separately while the mince is
sitting, which is while step 3 is happening; you will need a frying pan to do this.
Add a capful of oil to the frying pan over a medium heat on the hob, add the
peppers and keep stirring until they begin to feel squishy. Alternatively, once
step 4 is complete, you could serve them raw in the taco for a crunchier texture.

Method

1. Put the saucepan over the hob. Drop in a capful of the olive oil, and turn the hob to a medium heat, lining it up to halfway on the dial. (This will heat up the oil for when you begin to cook and work with the mince.)

2. Put in all of the mince; you should hear a gentle sizzle as it comes into contact with the oil. Using the wooden spoon, keep stirring the mince around so it begins to 'brown'; the colour will change to a darker and more matte brown, which will show it is cooking. Make sure all of the mince is this colour before proceeding to the next step.

3. Boil the kettle. Check the back of the stock cube packet for the amount of water you will need. Measure the amount of water out in the measuring jug, then add the stock cube to dissolve. Add to the saucepan; it will hiss, so do this gently. Once you have added in all the liquid, turn the hob heat down to a lower temperature. Put the saucepan lid on and allow to sit for around 5–10 minutes; this will bring out the flavour of the mince.

4. Drain any excess liquid by using the colander held over the sink. Add a pinch of salt and a sprinkle of your preferred spice. Stir it; now, put it in the tacos.

EXPAND YOUR REPERTOIRE

There are a host of different sauces you could try adding to a taco – that could include guacamole or even salsa. Sour cream is typically used to take away the 'heat' of the spice – but it also adds an alternative texture.

NAAN HUT CHICKEN WRAP

Duration: 20 minutes
Energy rating: Medium
Skill level: Easy
To make when: you have half an hour before your next Zoom meeting; you need something substantial, such as when you have had a day out or a trip somewhere; you return to university or college.

When training for my journalism qualification, Naan Hut was a place where we spent so many lunch times. Pete Taylor introduced this place to us in a classroom conversation while all of us reminisced about particular favourite foods. This is my favourite chicken wrap from Naan Hut reconstructed with my own variations; it's quite easy to make, as well as being adaptable. This can be for the sensory seekers and avoiders – just don't use the sweet chilli sauce if you are the latter!

EQUIPMENT YOU WILL NEED

1 chopping board

2 chopping knives

1 colander

1 baking tray

1 digital timer

1 pair of oven gloves

1 pair of tongs

INGREDIENTS

1 lettuce (you will be using 4 leaves)

½ a large tomato

1 cucumber (you will be using 4 slices)

Olive oil (a drizzle to oil the baking tray)

2 breaded chicken fillets

1 large wrap

Optional: 1 bottle of sweet chilli sauce (you will only need a small amount)

HOW TO MAKE
Pre-preparation
Wash all the different salad items and drain in the colander over the sink. Peel off four lettuce leaves and set aside; cut the half of tomato up into circular slices and also set aside. Cut four circles off the cucumber and also set aside for later.

Method

1. Check how long your chicken fillets take to cook; this should be around 25 minutes. Follow the instructions on the packet and set your oven to the temperature it says you need. Cover your baking tray with a drizzle of oil and place the chicken fillets on the tray. Put the tray in the oven. Set a timer for the duration it says on the packet.

2. Open up the wrap packet and put one on your plate. On the wrap, lay down two lettuce leaves and some of the tomato slices. This will be the 'base' of the wrap.

3. Having cooked the chicken fillets, use the oven gloves to take the baking tray out of the oven. Use the tongs to put the chicken in the centre of the wrap. Top with the rest of the vegetables, and – if you decided to use it – add a squeeze of sweet chilli sauce on top. Serve while warm.

EXPAND YOUR REPERTOIRE
If you are a sensory avoider, you may prefer to use mayonnaise instead of sweet chilli sauce. Hate spicy food but want something to top your Naan Hut wrap off with? Try sour cream in small quantities to cool down the spice. You can always cook your chicken in a different spice for just another layer of flavour; I quite like peri-peri. Just drizzle a little bit of oil on the baking tray, cover the chicken fillets in it, and then sprinkle your preferred spice over the top. You can always sprinkle a little extra in the wrap, too. If you have trouble rolling up wraps to seal them 'shut' – so the contents do not fall out – you could use a cocktail stick to do this. Just remember, when eating, to avoid spiking yourself!

GUACAMOLE ON TOAST FOR ONE

Duration: 15 minutes
Energy rating: Low
Skill level: Medium
To make when: you need a lunch break if you work from home; you need to make your budget stretch a little bit further, such as if you are a student.

Toast is usually seen as a breakfast option – however, I know of many students who repurpose it into something for lunch, as it's quite budget-friendly and adaptable into several meals. Avocados seem to be a 'safe food' that is often cited in terms of autistic popular culture – so it made sense to put both together for a lunch time meal in this book.

EQUIPMENT YOU WILL NEED

1 chopping board   1 toaster
1 chopping knife   1 butter knife
1 mixing bowl   1 plate for serving
1 fork

INGREDIENTS

1 small handful of coriander/ cilantro leaves (ground coriander can also be used as an alternative)

1 avocado

2 capfuls of sweet chilli sauce

2 slices of bread – doesn't matter what sort it is, as long as it fits in a toaster

HOW TO MAKE
Pre-preparation
If you are using fresh coriander, cut into the smallest pieces you possibly can, and set aside for later on the chopping board. Cut the avocado in half and remove the stone; scoop out the insides and put in the mixing bowl for later.

Method

1. Using the fork, mash up the avocado. Add in 2 capfuls of the sweet chilli sauce and combine to get a sauce consistency. (This should not be liquid – but if it's still too thick, add more sweet chilli sauce.) Add the coriander in and mix.

2. Toast the slices of bread for your preferred amount of time in the toaster.

3. Put the slices of toast on the serving plate.

4. Using the butter knife, cover the bread with the guacamole. Enjoy!

EXPAND YOUR REPERTOIRE
If you want a little extra, try seasoning with a sprinkle of black pepper when it comes to serving. Sensory avoiders – just mash up the avocado and put on the toast; avoid making the guacamole entirely.

PERI-PERI SWEET POTATO WEDGES

Duration: 35 minutes
Energy rating: Low
Skill level: Easy
To make when: you are in a rush in the middle of a work day and you might not have enough time to stop for a fuller lunch; you are only in need of something bite-sized; you're not sure what you'd like to eat – too many choices can be a hindrance when it comes to executive functioning.

I am a big fan of simple meals – ones that can be made on a budget, with limited energy output, too. 'Wedges' – sweet potato or otherwise – are a budget-friendly, bite-sized dish, and I sometimes make this when it comes to a pitstop between appointments. (This is, however, not a substitute for a 'proper' meal – it's just for the in-between moments.) If you are a sensory avoider, do not use peri-peri – go without or try with a small amount of salt for a 'ready salted' flavour.

EQUIPMENT YOU WILL NEED

1 chopping board

1 chopping knife

1 baking tray

1 spatula

INGREDIENTS

1 large sweet potato

1 capful of olive oil

Optional: peri-peri spice

HOW TO MAKE
Pre-preparation
Wash and then roughly cut the sweet potato into circles to a thickness of your own preference. Set aside for later.

Method

1. Set your oven to 200°C fan/425°F and allow to heat up.

2. Spread a capful of the oil across the baking tray. Put the potatoes on the baking tray. Using the spatula, make sure all the circles are covered in oil. Sprinkle the spice liberally all over.

3. Cook for 30 minutes or until golden brown. Enjoy!

EXPAND YOUR REPERTOIRE

If you prefer crunchy textures, cook for longer – the wedges will become crispier, and more like a crisp! It should satisfy your sensory preference – just check in on the wedges periodically, as they are very easy to burn this way. If you are a sensory seeker, you could try different spices – even to the point of combining them. If you're feeling brave, you could even try chilli flakes.

TOMATO GARLIC PASTA – BY ANONYMOUS

Duration: 35 minutes

Energy rating: Moderate

Skill level: Medium

To make when: you have had a busy day and are really hungry; you need an additional element of sensory regulation.

Anonymous was diagnosed as autistic and with ADHD at the age of 14. They are currently into digital art and photography.

This recipe is largely designed for sensory seekers but can be adapted for needs that are more sensory-avoidant. Cream, for example, has a plainer taste than the cream cheese.

EQUIPMENT YOU WILL NEED

1 chopping board

1 chopping knife

1 frying pan

2 saucepans

1 kettle

1 colander

1 serving bowl

1 tablespoon

1 ladle

INGREDIENTS

250 grams (9 ounces) of cherry tomatoes

100 millilitres of cream or 100 grams of cream cheese

Optional: garlic cloves (for the most sensory input, go for 6)

1 capful of olive oil

Salt and pepper shakers

60 grams (2 ounces) of your preferred dried pasta

HOW TO MAKE
Pre-preparation
Using the chopping board and knife, chop the tomatoes in half and set aside for later. Take out the cream or the cream cheese out of the fridge.

Method

1. Optional step: Put a capful of the olive oil in the frying pan and put on the hob over a medium heat (dial to halfway). Allow to heat up for 2 minutes, then add the garlic to begin cooking. (This is also known as 'sweating'.)

2. Add the tomatoes to the saucepan to begin sweating them as well. Turn down slightly; this will keep them warm while we prepare the pasta.

3. Boil the water in the kettle; once that has finished, add the water to the other saucepan along with the pasta, over the hob. Turn the heat on the dial to halfway to begin boiling the pasta. Keep checking in every so often. This should take about 15 minutes until this is cooked; check the pasta is soft with a fork. (Once this happens, drain with a colander over the sink, then add back to the saucepan. Turn the heat down to the lowest possible setting; this will keep it heated for the next step.)

4. While the tomatoes are soft – check for a golden colour – add the cream cheese or the cream. Keep on the hob for up to 10 minutes, or until the pasta is finished cooking. Add the pasta and tomato mixes together. Flavour with salt and pepper to serve.

EXPAND YOUR REPERTOIRE
If you are a sensory avoider, consider blending the tomato/garlic mixture in order to create a sauce. This will eradicate potential challenges around the texture. If you prefer different shapes of pasta, use whatever you are comfortable with – this could be rigatoni, spaghetti, etc. The flavouring of the cream cheese could also be experimented with, especially if you are a sensory seeker – for example, garlic-flavoured. Other herbs could also be used, along with chilli flakes. If you need an alternative version, Anonymous also has a suggested oven version for this recipe. Prepare all the ingredients and put them into an ovenproof pot; mix all of them well together. This will take 1 hour to cook at 200°C/400°F.

THREE BEAN PEPPER MIX – BY AOIFE BEAR CASSON

Duration: 1 hour
Energy rating: High
Skill level: Complex
To make when: you have a high amount of energy and enough time on your hands in order to make more than just one portion for the here and now; you fancy something that has several different flavours to it, along with different textures; you need to get rid of a few key ingredients that have been left in your fridge and cupboards.

Aoife Bear Casson is the internal communications manager for Alzheimer's Research UK. In her spare time, she likes to craft items to sell on her Etsy shop, KumaRooma. Her two dogs are called Alfie and Stanley, and her weekends are spent happily curled up with them on the sofa or playing computer games. Aoife has a diagnosis of autism, dyslexia, dyspraxia and dysgraphia. She advocates for greater awareness and understanding of disabilities, as well as mental health.

Note: this recipe makes around eight portions, which can be frozen for lower-energy days. The recipe involves a lot of stirring and waiting, but it is written on the presumption of frozen ingredients being used. Preparation of ingredients may add to the overall preparation time of this recipe. The recipe relies heavily on beans and is therefore only suitable for sensory seekers; the 'membrane' textures of the beans may be challenging for sensory avoiders.

EQUIPMENT YOU WILL NEED

1 chopping board	1 wooden spoon
1 chopping knife	1 teaspoon (to measure out the herbs)
1 garlic crusher*	
1 large frying pan	1 tablespoon (to measure out the spices)

*This is not needed if you decide to use pre-crushed garlic to save time and energy.

INGREDIENTS

1 large onion

1 bell pepper

3 medium carrots

300 grams (10.5 ounces or 1 punnet) of white button mushrooms

½ a celery plant

2 garlic cloves

1 tin of kidney beans (400 grams/15 ounces)

1 tin of black-eyed beans (400 grams/15 ounces)

1 tin of cannellini beans (400 grams/15 ounces)

A capful of olive oil

1 tin of chopped tomatoes (400 grams/15 ounces)

1 carton (500 grams/17.5 ounces) of passata (sieved tomatoes – known in some countries as tomato purée)

1½ teaspoons of oregano

1½ teaspoons of Italian herbs

1 tablespoon of cumin

1 tablespoon of chilli powder

1 small tin of sweetcorn (198 grams/7 ounces)

HOW TO MAKE
Pre-preparation

Using the chopping board and knife, you need to prepare the ingredients that are not in any tins. Dice the onion and pepper, quarter the carrots, slice the mushrooms and chop up the celery. Set all aside for later on. Peel the cloves of garlic and crush in the garlic crusher; set aside for later. Drain two tins of beans and, once again, set aside for later. Open the third can of beans but do not drain it.

Method

1. Using the large frying pan, add a capful of olive oil over a medium heat. Fry the onions, garlic and mushrooms with the spices until the mushrooms begin to shrivel and shrink in size.

2. Add the carrots and celery. Stir for 5–10 minutes with the wooden spoon; this preserves the flavour of the spices before adding the wet ingredients.

3. Next, add the chopped tomatoes and one of the drained tins of beans. Continue stirring.

4. Once the mixture is bubbling, add the next tin of drained beans and the passata.

5. Add the last tin of beans that has not been drained; this will thicken the mixture up. Keep stirring for up to another 30 minutes; this ensures the carrots and celery will be fully cooked, and the sauce will also reduce. Put on a low heat while you do this; stir at periodic intervals.

6. Add the peppers and sweetcorn; leave to simmer for a further 10 minutes in total. Serve and enjoy!

EXPAND YOUR REPERTOIRE

If you would like other serving options, you could serve with rice, tortilla chips, add it to a burrito or centre it in a quesadilla. You could even use it as a topping on a jacket (baked) potato. You could also top the mixture with grated cheese and/or sour cream.

QUICK AND EASY SWEET CHILLI CHICKEN SALAD

Duration: 30 minutes

Energy rating: Moderate

Skill level: Easy

To make when: you need a quick and easy lunch – such as when you are in between meetings, if you work from home; you need a way to add extra vegetables to your diet; if you need to keep doing other tasks – this is quite a 'hands-off' recipe.

Let's be honest about this; I really do not like vegetables – and yes, ostensibly I qualify as an 'adult' in the grand scheme of things. The fact of the matter is we all need at least some goodness in our diet; it just took me a while to find forms of vegetables that I am happy with, in order to get around related sensory issues. Salads are quite easy to prepare – and this recipe also uses minimal energy, which is a bonus. The chicken may not be accessible to everyone – but you can swap for an alternative of your own preference, such as if you are vegan. Please note that this recipe does not use quantities, as it is designed to be adaptable in terms of size – it can easily feed more people. The way I have written it would be more than enough for one person, however.

EQUIPMENT YOU WILL NEED

1 colander

1 baking tray

1 plate for serving

1 pair of tongs

INGREDIENTS

1 packet of your favourite salad leaves (I use roughly half a packet for one person)

2 frozen breaded chicken fillets

1 jar of ground coriander (you will only need a little for sprinkling)

Optional: 1 bottle of sweet chilli sauce (you will only need a small amount)

HOW TO MAKE
Pre-preparation
Use the colander held over the sink to wash your salad leaves; allow to dry. Make sure your chicken is defrosted if it needs to be.

Method

1. Set the oven to the correct temperature according to the instructions on the back of the packet of chicken, and allow to heat up. Put 2 of the fillets on the baking tray, sprinkle on a pinch of coriander, and cook at the temperature for the allotted amount of time on the back of the packet.

2. Arrange your salad leaves on the plate.

3. Take out your chicken from the oven; to avoid touching the tray, I use a pair of tongs to take the chicken out. Put on top of the salad – or, if you are a sensory avoider, keep these two elements separate from each other.

4. Optional step: dribble a small amount of sweet chilli sauce across your chicken and salad leaves. Enjoy!

EXPAND YOUR REPERTOIRE
If you have the time and patience – or even just the inclination – this recipe can be easily adapted to become more elaborate; in this book it has been included in its simplest form, by way of conserving energy for some individuals with limited supplies.

For example, you could try making your own salad from scratch. This could be done by cutting up peppers, a cucumber, carrot, ripping up lettuce leaves – even sprinkling with a few pine nuts to serve. This will add more to the amount of energy it will cost you to make this recipe, however. Some supermarkets also sell pre-prepared vegetables – such as carrots that have already been chopped up – which may be worth investing in. Try experimenting with different sauces or spices; some salads also taste great with small amounts of grated cheese.

'SAME FOOD' BUTTER PASTA – BY KIERAN ROSE

Duration: 20 minutes
Energy rating: Low
Skill level: Easy
To make when: you need a 'safe food' – such as just after a meltdown, or
if you have a big day ahead of you – such as with a presentation at work or a big exam while studying; you are low
on energy and need a boost, but quickly; you have low or
little energy left at the end of the day – and you're in need of
something to feel just that little bit better about yourself.

Kieran Rose is a consultant, writer, trainer, public speaker and researcher in
autistic burnout and autistic masking. You can find out more about him and
his work at www.theautisticadvocate.com.

Editor's note: this recipe is only for one person, but the portion sizes can easily
be scaled up in order to make this for multiple people at any given time.

EQUIPMENT YOU WILL NEED

1 pair of digital scales   1 butter knife

1 saucepan   1 bowl for serving

1 kettle   1 silicone spoon

1 colander

INGREDIENTS

70–80 grams (2.5 or 3 ounces)   1 salt shaker
of pasta in the shape of your
preference   1 pack of butter (you will
                                  only need a small amount)

HOW TO MAKE
Pre-preparation
Use the digital scales to measure out the portion of pasta and add to the saucepan. Bring the butter out of your fridge and bring to room temperature; this will make it easier to work with later.

Method

1. Use the kettle to boil enough water to fill the saucepan you are using. Pour on top of the pasta in the pan and begin to heat up over a heat that is about halfway on the dial of the hob you are using. This will take 10–15 minutes to boil to an edible stage; just make sure it's soft before eating.

2. Pour the pasta into the colander held over the sink and shake it off to dry.

3. Tip the pasta back into the saucepan. Slice off a small amount of the butter from the end of the pack with the butter knife and add to the pasta to begin melting. Stir through with the silicone spoon.

4. Sprinkle a pinch of salt over and stir through to evenly melt and cover all of the pasta.

EXPAND YOUR REPERTOIRE
To expand this version of a safe food, you could try experimenting with different herbs to sprinkle on top. For people who eat meat, you could consider adding different types of cooked meat throughout – if you are a sensory avoider, just make sure you cut them up into small pieces. Chorizo and/or pepperoni add more of a 'kick' to the dish. Different cheeses create different flavours, too – it's always worth experimenting with your own preferences.

MOTHER'S SUNDAY AFTERNOON NACHOS

Duration: 20 minutes

Energy rating: Moderate

Skill level: Medium

To make when: you have friends visiting and need something easy to create without having to go shopping (it takes so much energy!); your family visits you in your first independent living space for the first time; you are celebrating a minor achievement.

It is an ongoing joke in the family about how much I adore salsa; I adore it so much, enough that I went through two and a half bottles the first month I lived independently. As a Sunday tradition, my family and I would take our dog, Bailey, on an extended walk, but then a quick pitstop on the way back home would take place. We'd all share a plate of nachos, and my choice of drink was always a (slightly warm) pint of lemonade. This is a fairly healthy version of nachos, based on what my mother sometimes makes us. This is definitely one for the sensory seekers – but separation of the sauces into distinct categories may help sensory avoiders. To make this suitable for non-dairy eaters and others, just take out the cheese.

EQUIPMENT YOU WILL NEED

2 small bowls

2 baking trays

1 grater

1 chopping board

2 chopping knives

1 fork

2 tablespoons (for stirring the guacamole and the salsa)

1 plate for serving

INGREDIENTS

1 avocado

1 red onion

1 packet of tortilla chips

1 packet of cheese (enough to grate a handful)

1 small bunch of coriander/
cilantro

1 small bunch of basil

2 small handfuls of cherry
tomatoes

1 bottle of sweet chilli sauce
(just a little is needed for the
guacamole)

1 bottle of tomato sauce (just
a small amount is used)

Optional: 1 jar of smoked
paprika (only a pinch is
needed)

HOW TO MAKE
Pre-preparation
Scoop the insides of the avocado into a small bowl and set aside. Chop the onion up thinly and set aside in a separate bowl. Spread the tortilla chips out across the 2 baking trays. Grate a handful of cheese. Finely chop the coriander and the basil, and set aside for later. And, finally, chop up the tomatoes.

Method

1. Set your oven to 180°C/350° F and allow it to heat up. After about 5 minutes, put in the trays with the nacho crisps on them; this is just to warm them up.

2. While this is happening, we will be making guacamole and salsa, to add on top of the nacho crisps – rather than using a pre-prepared sauce. First up, the guacamole. Mash the avocado with the fork, and add a dash of the sweet chilli sauce to the bowl. Stir until combined to create a sauce-like texture.

3. For the salsa, combine the onion and half of the chopped-up tomatoes, and add a small amount of tomato sauce. Stir until combined. Add the coriander and basil and stir again. (As an option here, I sometimes like to add a pinch of smoked paprika.)

4. Take the nacho crisps out of the oven briefly. Spread the guacamole and the salsa on top; sprinkle the handful of cheese across both trays, and top with the remaining cherry tomatoes. Put back in the oven until the cheese melts.

EXPAND YOUR REPERTOIRE
If you feel brave, you could consider adding a small amount of finely chopped fresh chillies to the salsa; make sure you remove the seeds. Any packaging

will provide guidance on how hot the chillies are; be cautious. If onions make you cry, or you want less of the burning tang while eating, sometimes soaking them in room-temperature water is said to help take out the sting. Just factor this in when you make the recipe, and be warned that the feel of the onion may not be pleasant when handling it while making the salsa. Spices are always worth experimenting with as well, and personal preference can be formulated by individual sensory profiles. For example, you could try using black pepper to flavour the nachos – or, if you are a sensory avoider, using only salt may be the way to go.

STUFFED TOMATOES AND SALAD FOR THREE

Duration: 25 minutes
Energy rating: Moderate
Skill level: Medium
To make when: you need something quick and easy for your friends, just before a night out; it's a quiet Sunday afternoon and you need to feed other people in the house (it's the sort of thing I could see my mum making for me, her and her partner); when friends come to visit for the day and they may be staying overnight.

Things that can be stuffed are really easy to make, they are budget-friendly, and they are also incredibly healthy as well. This is something I would make for other people – it's quick and easy.

For those who are sensory avoiders, try to keep as many elements as separate as possible; you may prefer just to have the rice in the tomato, and everything else separate on the plate, for example. Do not use the optional ingredients, either.

EQUIPMENT YOU WILL NEED

1 chopping board

1 chopping knife

1 paring knife

1 large saucepan

1 silicone or wooden spoon

1 teaspoon (to measure the spice)

1 baking tray

1 pair of tongs

1 silicone brush

1 digital timer

1 colander

INGREDIENTS

1 bottle of olive oil (only a dash is needed)

3 large tomatoes

1 packet of rice in the flavour of your choice (pre-cooked 'microwave' rice)

1 cucumber

Optional: 1 jar of spice of your choice (we will only be using a pinch)

1 lettuce

1 packet of rocket (arugula) leaves

Optional: 1 lemon

HOW TO MAKE

Pre-preparation

Cut up the cucumber, rocket leaves and lettuce; set them all aside for later on. If you're a sensory avoider, cut all of the salad elements apart from the tomatoes into the smallest pieces possible.

Separate the rice in the packet by squishing it around and also set aside for later. Cut the top off all three large tomatoes and remove the insides, making them hollow. Keep the 'lids' for later and discard the 'guts'.

Method

1. Set your oven to 200°C fan/425°F and allow to heat up. Meanwhile, add a dash of oil to the saucepan and begin heating up over a medium heat on the hob. Add the rice to the saucepan to begin heating up; keep stirring with the wooden or silicone spoon for 5 minutes on the same heat.

2. To the rice, add the (optional) spice of your choice and continue stirring. The rice should start to take on the colour of the spice you use. In total, this should take roughly another 5 minutes. If it begins to spit or heats up too quickly, reduce the temperature to the lowest heat possible.

3. Once the rice has been heated up, spoon into each of the tomatoes. Put the lid of each tomato on top, brush each with oil and then add to the baking tray. Put in the oven and bake for 15–20 minutes; they should start to look glazed on top, slightly losing their structure. Make sure to check in on them often.

4. Use the tongs to put each tomato on to a plate. Add a selection of the cucumber, rocket leaves and lettuce on the side, and squeeze a little lemon juice on top of the salad.

EXPAND YOUR REPERTOIRE

One of the things I quite like to do is to add a little dash of my favourite sauce inside the tomato; you could also add a little of this on the edge of the tomato, in order to seal it shut while it's cooking, too. Sweet chilli sauce can be combined while cooking the rice in order to create sticky spicy rice! You could also cook mint leaves or salad leaves into the rice, too.

RED KIDNEY BEAN RICE FOR ONE

Duration: 25 minutes

Energy rating: Moderate

Skill level: Medium

To make when: it's cold outside and you need a hot meal – such as after you have come in out of the blustery weather; you have a cold.

At the first secondary school I attended, an approximation of this was on the menu every single day at lunch time. It's quick to make, and it still is a firm favourite of mine.

EQUIPMENT YOU WILL NEED

2 saucepans

2 silicone spoons

1 kettle

1 measuring jug

INGREDIENTS

1 packet of basmati rice (pre-cooked 'microwave' rice)

250 grams (9 ounces) of beef mince/ground beef (or a vegetarian alternative)

2 capfuls of olive oil

1 chicken-flavoured stock cube

1 can of kidney beans (215 grams/7.5 ounces)

Optional: 1 pinch of smoked paprika

HOW TO MAKE
Pre-preparation

Shuffle the rice inside the packet in order to break it up into smaller chunks. If you can, try breaking the mince up into smaller pieces, too.

Method

1. Put one of the saucepans over the hob and heat up with the gauge at the halfway point (to a medium heat). Add in a capful of oil and put the mince in the saucepan. This will begin to cook, and you should hear a crackling sound; keep stirring with one of the silicone spoons.

2. Boil your kettle and fill up quarter of the measuring jug; add the stock cube so it begins to dissolve. Once the mince has taken on more of a grey colour, which indicates it's cooking, add half the stock in, and stir until it dissolves. Do the same again. Next, add the can of kidney beans and a pinch of the (optional) paprika and keep stirring until fully cooked.

3. Repeat step 1 again, but this time with the rice in the second saucepan.

4. Once the rice is fully cooked – to the point of looking fluffy – put out on the serving plate. Make sure the mince is cooked and make sure the liquid has evaporated. Put the mince atop the rice.

EXPAND YOUR REPERTOIRE

Try adding in frozen vegetables – such as carrots or some spinach. Black pepper could also replace the paprika.

STUFFED MUSHROOMS FOR ONE

Duration: 25–30 minutes
Energy rating: Moderate
Skill level: Medium
To make when: you have time between lectures and need to recharge – such as if you have a test or exam later on; you need to revise but need to 'power up' first; it's been a 'long day' already.

If you can make stuffed tomatoes, you can make stuffed mushrooms – it's almost wholly vegetable based and very budget-friendly, too. It is basically the same method, just with different ingredients.

EQUIPMENT YOU WILL NEED

1 chopping knife

1 chopping board

1 saucepan

1 silicone spoon

1 baking tray

1 paring knife

INGREDIENTS

1 packet of your preferred rice (this recipe uses pre-cooked 'microwave' rice)

2 large mushrooms

5 cherry tomatoes

½ a carrot

1 small bunch of coriander/cilantro

1 packet of mangetout (you will need 4–6 pieces)

Olive oil

HOW TO MAKE
Pre-preparation

Separate the rice while inside the packet; this will make it easier to work with. Use the chopping board and knife to cut off the stems of the mushrooms and discard them. Cut the cherry tomatoes up, as well as the carrot. Chop the coriander into tiny pieces; do the same for the mangetout.

Method

1. Heat the oven up to 200°C/400°F first and allow to heat up for a few minutes.

2. Put the saucepan over the hob and turn the gauge to the halfway point. Add in a capful of olive oil to begin heating up. Add in the rice and begin to stir with the silicone spoon, so it will cook. Add the tomatoes, the carrot and the mangetout to the rice and allow to heat up.

3. Put the mushrooms on to the baking tray with each mushroom head face down – so you can see the site where you chopped off the stem. Using the silicone spoon, ladle on the rice across both the mushrooms. Sprinkle the coriander on top and drizzle a capful of the oil across the tray once more. Bake until the mushrooms begin to look squishy – this should take around 15–20 minutes. It may be longer, however, as everyone's oven is different.

EXPAND YOUR REPERTOIRE

Rice can virtually always be flavoured to suit most sensory needs – it's just about experimenting to find your preference. You could try different pre-packaged sauces, for example – or even more herbal spices, such as ground cumin and ground coriander, for a more aromatic taste. Try adding in different frozen vegetables, too.

PART 3

Dinner Recipes

STIR FRY FOR TWO – BY INDIA GRAINGER

Duration:	45 minutes
Energy rating:	Moderate
Skill level:	Medium
To make when:	you are having a night in or when you have friends around, or to share with housemates.

India Grainger is a secondary school student; she was diagnosed as autistic in 2019. Her mother and father are also neurodivergent, and run Perfectly Autistic, a website of useful resources about autism. Her father, Kelly, also works with companies on raising awareness and understanding of autism in the workplace. India loves cooking, and this is her recipe.

This dish is more elaborate than most, so will require you to have 'more' energy when starting. If you would like to make it for more people, adjust the quantity of ingredients. If you are vegetarian, you can change the chicken for an alternative. Stir fries are a little bit complex but can have a variety of flavours and textures. They are ideal for sensory seekers.

EQUIPMENT YOU WILL NEED

2 chopping knives (one for the chicken, the other for the vegetables)

2 chopping boards

2 frying pans

1 teaspoon (to measure the ginger paste)

1 tablespoon (to measure the soy sauce)

1 spatula

1 bowl

1 pair of tongs

INGREDIENTS

2 chicken breasts

½ a red bell pepper

½ a yellow bell pepper

4 spring onions/scallions

6 mushrooms

½ a packet of baby corn

½ a courgette/zucchini	1 small handful of peanuts
2 teaspoons of olive oil	1 packet of 'straight to wok' noodles
2 teaspoons of ginger paste	
4 tablespoons of soy sauce	1 pack of pak choi

HOW TO MAKE
Pre-preparation

Dice all of the following ingredients separately from each other: chicken breasts, red and yellow pepper. Chop the following ingredients separately from each other: spring onions, mushrooms, baby corn, courgette. If you struggle with interoception and sizing, it may be worth measuring out the oil, ginger paste, soy sauce and peanuts. Use your hands to crumble up the peanuts into small pieces.

Editor's note: if you are a vegetarian or vegan, you can go without the chicken. This recipe is for sensory seekers.

Method

1. Heat the olive oil in a frying pan. Once you have done that, add the diced chicken to the oil. The chicken should start to have a white/grey texture on top when it is beginning to cook.

2. Add the soy sauce to the chicken, then add the ginger paste. Cook the chicken until it is brown, having been coated evenly all over; make sure you test it by cutting the chicken in half, to check the insides are cooked.

3. Add the vegetables to the pan with the chicken in it. Stir with the spatula.

4. Using a separate pan, heat the noodles up for three minutes until cooked. Add two tablespoons of soy sauce to the noodles.

5. Put the noodles in a bowl with the vegetables and chicken mix on top. Add the crushed nuts on top.

EXPAND YOUR REPERTOIRE

If you are a sensory seeker, try eight tablespoons of soy sauce instead of four – it's India's favourite part of this dish. Try serving with sweet chilli sauce, too. For sensory avoiders, take out the soy sauce and don't add sweet chilli sauce. You can always experiment with different flavours – such as changing the ginger paste for tomato paste.

WINTER'S JACKET POTATO

Duration:	3 hours
Energy rating:	Low
Skill level:	Easy
To make when:	you need something easy to cook without worrying; when the world is cold outside and the weather is horrible (that almost sounded like a Michael Bublé song!); when your executive functioning is not 'up to par'. It is also nice after a meltdown, too.

EQUIPMENT YOU WILL NEED

1 grater

1 chopping knife

1 chopping board

1 garlic crusher

1 colander

1 baking tray

1 plate for serving

1 fork

1 paring knife

INGREDIENTS

1 packet of cheese (you will need a handful of grated cheese)

1 red onion

Optional: 1 garlic clove

1 small handful of salad leaves

Olive oil (about 1 tablespoon)

1 packet of rock salt (you will only need a small amount)

1 large baking potato

HOW TO MAKE
Pre-preparation

Use the grater to grate a handful of cheese and set aside for later. Use the chopping board and knife to dice the red onion into small pieces. Crush the (optional) garlic clove in the garlic crusher, ready for later. Finally, wash the salad leaves in the colander over the sink, drain and set aside for later.

Method

1. Set the oven to 120°C/250°F and allow to heat up. Put the potato over the baking tray, and cover it with a dribble of oil all over. Add a sprinkle of rock salt and stab the centre of the potato with a fork.

2. Bake the potato for 2 hours and 30 minutes; check to make sure it is cooked. There should be steam and the centre should also be hot.

3. Slice in half so you have two pieces of the 'jacket potato'. Scrape the garlic from the crusher and scatter over the potato. Layer the cheese and then all the onion pieces. Add the handful of salad leaves on the side to serve.

EXPAND YOUR REPERTOIRE

Sensory seekers may have a preference for different textures than a sensory avoider would do. You can make the skin of the potato crispy; you just need to stab it a few times with a fork, cover it in salt and oil, and then bake. In terms of textures, you can add herbs you can grow yourself on a budget, such as cress; it is always worth experimenting with flavours. I hear that mint is a good option, although the jury is out on that. And, for the sensory seekers, take out all of the toppings; if you can bear it, cheese may be a good one to keep.

BEEF HOTPOT FOR FOUR PEOPLE
– BY VICTORIA ELLEN

Duration: 3 hours 20 minutes
Energy rating: Moderate
Skill level: Complex
To make when: you need a quick and easy meal for your household and
                     need something to 'rustle up' as soon as possible; when
                     you need something hearty having been outside for a while
                     or after a long day at work.

Victoria Ellen is the brains behind the Actually Aspling blog and is often active on Instagram. She is currently a PhD student exploring the different presentations of autism in adults.

A beef hotpot is fairly easy to make and can be adapted for a wide variety of needs; it is also fairly cheap to produce, and can be frozen and saved for another time, too. Victoria also pointed out that pre-prepared food can be bought to make this easier to construct; this has been noted in the ingredients. Victoria is a sensory seeker by nature, and adaptations for seekers and avoiders are also noted below.

EQUIPMENT YOU WILL NEED

2 chopping knives (1 for the potatoes, one for the beef)

2 chopping boards

1 large frying pan or a skillet

1 silicone or wooden spoon for stirring

1 casserole dish or slow cooker

1 kettle

1 measuring jug

INGREDIENTS

3 large baking potatoes

500 grams (17.5 ounces) of pre-prepared diced beef

Salt and pepper

1 bag of pre-chopped casserole mix (carrots, celery, onions, leeks, swede, etc.)	1 beef stockpot (sometimes known as cubes) Cornflour/corn starch

HOW TO MAKE
Pre-preparation
Chop up the potatoes into very thin slices so they can sit on top of the casserole. Set them aside for later. Make sure the beef is properly diced up; if you decided to cook from scratch, make sure you dice it up into more manageable chunks. This will help especially if you struggle with your motor skills.

Method
Note: there are two different ways to cook this depending on the facilities you have access to.

If you have access to an oven:

1. Switch on your oven to 180°C fan/400°F and allow to heat up.

2. Over a hob, add the oil to the frying pan and heat up. It should start to sizzle audibly when it is warm enough. Add in the beef to fry it up. Mix around to separate the pieces of beef.

3. Add a sprinkle of salt and pepper to bring out the flavour. If you are a sensory avoider, go without this.

4. Add the bag of pre-chopped casserole mix. Stir to cook with the beef.

5. Turn the heat down in the pan to its lowest setting before switching off; this is just to give you time while preparing the stock. Follow the instructions on the back of the stockpot packet; this usually involves adding water to dissolve. If you need to thicken it up – which it will also do while cooking – add a little cornflour. Once complete, add to the beef mix.

6. Stir all of this and allow to simmer for a while to make sure it is all cooked.

7. Add the mix to a casserole dish. Put in the oven for three hours.

8. After one and a half hours, add the potatoes on top. Cook for the remaining hour and a half.

If you plan to use a slow cooker, follow steps 1–7. Then follow the settings on your slow cooker to slowly simmer the recipe; this usually means cooking it overnight on the lowest setting.

To tell if the hotpot is fully cooked, the potatoes should look brown and the gravy will be thick. The meat will also have a 'fall apart easily' quality.

EXPAND YOUR REPERTOIRE

Sensory seekers may like to add spices to the hotpot; for a smoky flavour, add paprika before you put it in the oven. It would be worthwhile experimenting with other spices, too; sensory avoiders should avoid this. If you prefer to have a brown look to your meat, try using a brush to cover the beef with the rapeseed oil. Fry as usual. For extra flavour, when it comes to step 7, seal with a lid and allow to sit for up to seven or eight minutes on a low temperature.

FISH AND RICE IN A BOWL FOR ONE

Duration: 30 minutes

Energy rating: Moderate

Skill level: Medium

To make when: you've had a 'meh' day and need a pick-me-up – such as when it's a blue Monday or the month of January seems to be dragging on; you are not in the mood to faff around with fancy ingredients and don't want to spend too long cooking; there are too many options and you can't decide what to eat.

This dish in innately adaptable for both sensory seekers and avoiders – which makes it suitable for a wide variety of people. To make this clear, ingredients that can be swapped around to be accommodating have been marked out.

EQUIPMENT YOU WILL NEED

1 colander

1 chopping board

1 chopping knife

1 baking tray

1 microwave or a saucepan

1 bowl

1 silicone or wooden spoon

INGREDIENTS

1 handful of salad leaves

¼ of a cucumber

1 carrot

Olive oil (a little for the baking tray)

1 piece of breaded fish of your choice

1 packet of rice (plain if you are a sensory avoider) (this recipe uses pre-cooked 'microwave' rice)

Optional: sweet chilli sauce to serve

HOW TO MAKE
Pre-preparation
Wash the salad leaves in the colander over the sink so they are clean; let them drain, dry and set aside. Cut the cucumber and carrot into tiny pieces; set them both aside for later.

Method

1. Set the oven to the temperature stated on the back of the fish packaging. Dribble the oil across the baking tray and put the fish on top. Usually, these need to cook in the oven for around 20–25 minutes; cook for the amount of time the packaging tells you to.

2. While this is happening, we will be making the rice. Follow the instructions on the back of the rice packet; this should say how long to heat up in the microwave or in the pan. Once you have done that, turn the heat to the lowest setting possible to keep the rice warm.

3. Put the rice into a bowl for serving. Next, add the salad leaves, cucumber and carrot pieces to the rice. Mix all together with the silicone or wooden spoon. If you are a sensory avoider, you may prefer to keep all of the different textures separate. If that is the case, put the rice on a plate, and use meal separators to divide all the different ingredients. Now you're ready to serve.

4. If you are a sensory seeker, add a drizzle of sweet chilli sauce over the rice to serve.

EXPAND YOUR REPERTOIRE
If you think you might enjoy it, sensory avoiders may wish to add a tiny drop of olive oil as dressing to the salad leaves when using meal separators. It's a small hint of flavour – but is worthwhile experimenting with. Sensory seekers may want to try to expand this dish into more of a meal for one person, which can be done very easily; this is the sort of dish you can craft from the last few ingredients in your kitchen before you need to go shopping. Consider frying up a mackerel or salmon fillet and mixing in the pieces of fish with the rice and salad mix. Small pieces of blue cheese or other types may add the extra sensory input you might be after, too.

FLYING SALMON TO GO FOR TWO

Duration: 1 hour and 30 minutes
Energy rating: Moderate
Skill level: Medium
To make when: you need a 'grown-up meal', such as if someone is coming round for dinner and you feel like showing off a little bit; you want a dish you could make for a date night.

This is not a dish for everyone, not least because it contains fish, but it is easily adaptable to sensory needs. This recipe has worked like magic when I have made it for friends, enough so that even my friend Lalaine has had no complaints!

Salmon takes practice to cook well, and flipping it can be a nightmare if you struggle with your motor skills.

EQUIPMENT YOU WILL NEED

1 colander

1 chopping knife

1 chopping board

1 saucepan

1 frying pan

1 plate for serving

INGREDIENTS

1 pack of butter (you will only need a small amount)

1 handful of salad leaves

2 large leeks

1 bottle of olive oil (a little for cooking the rice and salmon)

1 packet of rice (pre-cooked 'microwave' rice)

2 small fillets of salmon

Salt and pepper

HOW TO MAKE
Pre-preparation

Make sure the butter has had time to warm up, to bring it to room temperature; this will make it malleable and easier to use. Wash the salad leaves in the colander over the sink; drain, allow them to dry and set aside for now. Cut off both ends of the leeks; there should be no leaves and no root. Wash the leeks and roughly cut them at a 45° angle; the size does not really matter.

Method

1. Follow the instructions on the back of the packet of rice and heat up in a saucepan with oil. Set aside for later.

2. Put the frying pan over a low heat on the hob and melt a small knob of butter in the pan. (This will allow you to cook the leeks more easily; it also adds a slight creamy taste.) Add a capful of olive oil to the pan and add in the leeks. Bring to a higher temperature slowly; you will hear the oil begin to make a crackling sound as it gets hot.

3. Keep flipping the leeks around so both sides are cooked. Once they start to look cooked – they should have a glazed appearance and be more floppy – turn the heat off and allow to rest.

4. Follow the instructions on the back of the packet of salmon. This will usually involve putting on a pan with olive oil and flipping over once to cook the other side. Once it is at that point, turn the heat down to the lowest possible setting. It will be resting for a short time and this will keep it warm. (Instructions might also suggest sealing the fish in foil and cooking in an oven – put the fillets on a sheet of foil, drizzle over a little oil, add a tablespoon of water, seal up the foil into a 'parcel' and cook at the temperature on the instructions for up to 25 minutes or until browny pink and flaky. Make sure to test that it is cooked in the middle.)

5. Heat up the rice and leeks again; this should take maybe 6 minutes in total.

For serving: if you are a sensory avoider who hates textures to touch, use meal separators to separate the leeks, fish and rice. Add in the salad leaves separately, too. If you are a sensory seeker, mix the rice and salad leaves up, and sprinkle salt and pepper on your leeks.

EXPAND YOUR REPERTOIRE

If you want to develop your skills a bit more, it could be worth trying out different toppings – most of which can be found in your kitchen as leftovers. Try cooking in foil alongside small pieces of tomato and a drizzle of oil on the top. Or try adding a splash of lemon juice (from a bottle or a fresh lemon) just before serving.

ROASTED VEGETABLE POTATO BAKE FOR TWO

Duration: 1 hour

Energy rating: Low

Skill level: Easy

To make when: you are low on energy and need something simple to make, but you also have to provide something for someone else; there are too many potatoes in your house (it happens!); you have to entertain a guest who is staying over.

Roasting most things can be wonderful when you have little to no energy to spare. Added to that, this meal is also very adaptable, it's accessible to most sensory needs and is also extremely budget-friendly. This is based on part of a recipe I made for my friend Lalaine when she visited me a few years ago.

EQUIPMENT YOU WILL NEED

1 chopping board

1 chopping knife

1 baking tray

1 silicone brush

INGREDIENTS

1 green bell pepper

1 red bell pepper

1 yellow bell pepper

1 bag (500 grams/17.5 ounces) of baby potatoes

1 capful of olive oil

1 packet of rock salt (you will only need a small amount)

1 bag of salad leaves

Optional for sensory seekers: oregano and black pepper

HOW TO MAKE

Pre-preparation

Using the chopping board and knife, cut the tops off the peppers, cut out the centres and discard, then chop into medium-sized pieces. Set them aside for later. Chop the potatoes in half and also set aside for later.

Method

1. Set the oven to 200°C/400°F and allow it to heat up.

2. Put a capful of olive oil over the baking tray. Then put all of the peppers and potatoes on top. Roughly cover them all with the oil by using the brush; sprinkle with a tiny amount of rock salt.

3. Optional step: if you want to use the oregano and black pepper, sprinkle a little bit on top now.

4. Bake until golden brown; this should be for approximately 45 minutes, but make sure to keep checking, as everyone's oven is different. Serve with a handful of the salad leaves on the side.

EXPAND YOUR REPERTOIRE

If you would like to make this dish a little bit more moreish, you could try adding in small cubes of feta cheese. They will bake along with the vegetables and peppers and melt to create more of a creamy texture. When it comes to potatoes, try switching them up; you could add in sweet potatoes instead of just using baby potatoes. Experiment with different herbs and spices. Finally, you could also add in diced red onion pieces for more of a tang; this would be ideal for a sensory seeker. Crushed garlic cloves sprinkled throughout the tray will also add to the dish; use a garlic crusher and spread across.

SLOW COOKED POTATOES AND VEGGIES – BY LOZ YOUNG

Duration: 3 hours

Energy rating: Low

Skill level: Easy

To make when: you know you have a busy and/or stressful week, because this is ideal to keep in your freezer; you are experiencing a low-energy day.

Loz Young is the community manager at Sensooli, formerly known as Chew-igem, a brand of products for a wide range of sensory needs across all ages for autistic individuals. She is also a co-host of the brand's podcast, Sensory Matters. Lorraine was recently diagnosed as autistic, and is currently awaiting a referral for ADHD.

Recipes that use a slow cooker are ideal for autistic individuals, as there is little risk; they also do not require a lot of complex skills, and executive functioning is not needed to be on top form. A slow cooker, in my view, should be given to every single autistic individual.

There are no quantities with this recipe, because it can be adapted to the number of people who would eat it. The ingredients in the recipe are also pre-prepared when bought. This is also suitable for sensory avoiders and avoids meat due to the texture.

EQUIPMENT YOU WILL NEED

1 slow cooker (if you haven't got one, see the note about expanding your repertoire for suggestions)

1 measuring jug

1 kettle or saucepan (the kettle is for the stock cube; a saucepan is an alternative)

3 bowls (for serving)

1 silicone or wooden spoon for stirring

INGREDIENTS

1 bag of vegetarian mince

2 stock cubes of your choosing

1 bag of pre-prepared vegetables

1 can of tinned new potatoes

Salt and pepper

HOW TO MAKE
Method

1. Heat up your slow cooker to a high temperature. Allow it to wait to ensure it is fully hot. Add the vegetarian mince to the slow cooker.

2. Fill up your measuring jug with boiling water from the kettle and dissolve the stock cubes in it by stirring. (The saucepan can be used to heat the water if you do not have a kettle.) Add to the slow cooker; this will act as a 'gravy' bond to bring the meal together.

3. Add all of the potatoes and vegetables. Stir around. Leave for roughly 3 hours to cook in total on a high temperature.

4. Serve with a light sprinkle of salt and pepper on top. You may want to serve with bread and butter, as this recipe has a lot of gravy.

EXPAND YOUR REPERTOIRE

Supermarkets often have pre-prepared food, and this can be an asset if you have challenges surrounding your motor skills, or if you have any other disability. However, this can quickly become quite expensive. This is worth always having in the back of your mind, particularly if you need to be aware of your budget. If you feel you can, you could always try making this with fresh ingredients – so vegetables such as carrots and potatoes. It may be significantly harder, due to the skill needed to chop and peel. Small pieces of food are also suitable for sensory avoiders and will make food more manageable. Sensory seekers may wish to experiment with flavour. There are many different spices or sauces you could add, as well as other things including tinned chopped tomatoes.

BUDGET SAVOURY PANCAKES

◊ 👁 ✋ ⚙

Duration: 10–20 minutes
Energy rating: Moderate
Skill level: Medium
To make when: you need to get rid of several ingredients in your fridge before
                            going shopping for more; when you're in a snack(ish) mood
                            but need to wait for dinner; when you need to budget.

During my teenage years, my household held a **Come Dine with Me**-style week – complete with main courses, 'afters' and a prize at the end for those who were voted the best over the five days. My mother made savoury pancakes and we also had pancakes for dessert; all rules about nutrition, vegetables, etc. were temporarily put on hold for a week, as an experiment. This is a healthier version of my mum's savoury pancakes.

EQUIPMENT YOU WILL NEED

1 chopping board   1 whisk

1 chopping knife   1 frying pan

1 set of digital scales   1 ladle

1 mixing bowl   1 palette knife

1 teaspoon (to measure the   1 plate
baking powder)

INGREDIENTS

4 spring onions/scallions   3 eggs

2 bell peppers (yellow and   1 teaspoon of baking powder
orange are my favourite
– you will use half of each   150 millilitres of milk
pepper)
                                                      Butter for frying the
150 grams (5.5 ounces) of   pancakes
plain flour/all-purpose flour
                                                      Optional: salsa to serve

HOW TO MAKE
Pre-preparation
Cut the top and bottom off the spring onions and put in the bin. Cut the stalks at a 45° angle into rounds, and set aside for later. Hollow out the peppers and then cut into quarters. Using half of each pepper, chop up into long sticks.

Method

1. Weigh the flour and put it into the mixing bowl. Crack the eggs and add the eggs to the flour. Add a teaspoon of baking powder and add all of the milk gradually, while stirring. Whisk so it's a runny mix. This is the pancake batter.

2. Take the frying pan and put it on the hob. Put a knob of butter in the middle; this will stop the batter from sticking. Use the ladle to add some of the mix to the middle of the pan. Move the pan around so it spreads out to cover the bottom. The edges will begin to have a matt appearance; when the centre looks the same, carefully flip it over by using the palette knife.

3. Repeat until all the mix has been used up to create a stack of pancakes. Put them all on the plate to serve.

4. Add the spring onion and pepper to the middle of the pancake when serving; the salsa is optional.

EXPAND YOUR REPERTOIRE
There are specific salts that you can buy from supermarkets to change the flavour. Try just using things such as lettuce and cucumber if you are a sensory avoider, without any additional flavouring. Sweet chilli sauce is a favourite of mine, to dip the pancake in while eating. You can also cook the vegetables before including the pancakes – this recipe just has an extra 'crunch' element.

GRAMPS' FISH AND CHIPS

Duration: 1 hour
Energy rating: High
Skill level: Complex
To make when: you are in a 'treat yourself' mood, such as on pay day; you're
                     entertaining family members and need something a bit out
                     of the ordinary; you have recently had a meltdown.

Sometimes people say to me things like 'tell me about growing up and how you began writing'. From the get-go, my grandfather 'got it' – even deliberately taking his time to talk to me, in detail, about whatever book I was reading. He expanded my inner world, instructing me how I could travel through time and space through the simple act of reading a book. Long before I was ever diagnosed, he foretold I should be writing for newspapers – and that I should write as myself, rather than emulating the style or the syntax of anyone else. Some of my oldest, earliest memories are of the home of my grandparents; the room is safe, the smell homey. And my grandfather cooked chips. This is a recipe I created off the basis of this – a sort of memory replication – as he deserves a place in this book. He stepped up to the plate when he was needed, far more than most.

EQUIPMENT YOU WILL NEED

1 scrubbing brush   1 large mixing bowl

1 potato peeler   2 baking trays

1 chopping knife   1 plate for serving

1 chopping board

INGREDIENTS

1 breaded fish fillet of your choice (some brands have gluten- and dairy-free varieties)

3 sweet potatoes

1 cucumber

Olive oil (just a dribble is needed)

Optional: 1 jar of paprika (enough to cover 3 potatoes)

1 packet of rock salt (you will only need a sprinkle)

1 handful of salad leaves

HOW TO MAKE
Pre-preparation

Read the instructions on the back of the fish packet to find out how long it takes to cook; keep this in mind for later. Scrub the sweet potatoes with the scrubbing brush under running water; this is just as a basic hygiene measure to clean the potatoes. Peel all the potatoes, then chop into the shapes you would like your chips to be. Cut up the cucumber into small discs.

Method

1. Heat the oven up to 200°C/400°F.

2. Dribble some olive oil into the bowl and add the (optional) paprika. Put the pieces of potato in and cover them in the oil/spice mix with your hands. This will give the chips some flavour for later; the oil will help them cook. Put the chips on the baking tray. Add a sprinkle of rock salt for a little bit of crunch.

3. Put in the oven. This usually takes around 40 minutes to cook, but may be done sooner; the potato pieces will look golden brown, so make sure to keep checking in. You can test if they are cooked by taking one out and cutting it open. If steam comes out, they are ready to eat. I usually check them every ten minutes, just to prevent them from burning.

4. Put the fish in the oven when the chips have the same time left as the fish takes to cook.

5. On your serving plate, add the cucumber slices and a few salad leaves.

6. Once the fish and chips are ready, add them to the plate. If you are a sensory avoider, use separators to keep all the elements of the meal apart.

EXPAND YOUR REPERTOIRE

Potato wedges can be tricky to master; you can disguise any mistakes by creating a sauce to put them in if needed. As a sensory seeker, I like salsa or a sweet chilli sauce. Fish can be difficult to cook, which is why I sometimes go for breaded options. However, you could try cod without breadcrumbs, and cook with a topping on top. All you would need to do is put the fish on foil, add a knob of butter and sprinkle with your choice of herbs – such as basil or mint. You could even include tomatoes as an added bonus.

FAT HEAD PIZZA DOUGH FOR TWO
– BY SAMANTHA STEIN

Duration: 1 hour
Energy rating: Moderate
Skill level: Medium
To make when: you are having a night in with your best friend; you need an easy date night meal to make; you are entertaining a guest of the family and need something quick and easy to make.

Samantha Stein is a YouTuber who creates under the username YoSamdySam. Diagnosed later in life as being on the autistic spectrum, Samantha set the channel up and now has over 100,000 subscribers. She can be found periodically on social media, and lives in the Netherlands with her husband and two children.

A fat head dough is basically a dough that can be adapted into all sorts of other recipes. This recipe is gluten-free and is also keto-friendly. (Please always consult your doctor before commencing any diet.) You can use this recipe for meal planning as well; all you would need to do would be to pre-bake the bases and freeze for another day.

EQUIPMENT YOU WILL NEED

1 set of digital scales	1 pair of scissors
1 tablespoon	1 rolling pin
1 standard bowl	1 pizza tray
1 microwave	1 paring knife
1 roll of baking paper	1 butter knife

INGREDIENTS

200 grams (7 ounces) of shredded mozzarella*

100 grams (3.5 ounces) of almond flour

2 tablespoons of cream cheese (dairy-free options are available)

1 egg

1 carton (500 grams/17.5 ounces) of passata (sieved tomatoes – known in some countries as tomato purée)

Optional for sensory seekers: slices of salami and chorizo for serving

Optional for sensory seekers: a selection of herbs, such as parsley and oregano, to your taste

Optional for sensory seekers: jalapeño peppers

*You will need extra for pizza toppings, and this recipe will not work with dairy-free alternatives.

HOW TO MAKE
Pre-preparation
Use the digital scales and standard bowl to weigh out the mozzarella, almond flour and cream cheese; set aside for later.

Method

1. Heat your oven to 200°C/400°F.

2. In a microwave, melt the flour and mozzarella together – for approximately 30 seconds. It will look sticky; leave to cool enough so that it's just bearable to touch. You can also do this on the hob, over a medium heat. Add the egg and mix together. This will begin to look more like a dough – and should start to form into a solid ball. If it is still sticky, add a pinch of almond flour. Knead until the ball forms.

3. Cut the dough in half. Cut out two pieces of baking paper per ball, and put the ball between the two pieces. Roll out until thin, to match the size of a pizza baking tray. Pull the top layer of paper off and put the pizza base on the tray. Bake for 7 minutes.

4. Take the base out of the oven. Add the passata (as the tomato sauce base), then the cheese. Add the optional toppings if you are a sensory seeker.

5. Bake again for 5–7 minutes, until the cheese has started to melt to become gooey and is turning to a brown colour.

EXPAND YOUR REPERTOIRE

A fat head dough is an all-purpose dough, says Sam – meaning that you can adapt it to be the base of other recipes, including garlic bread. This could also include sweeter options, such as cinnamon rolls. All you need is a little creativity to adapt it, by combining this recipe with whatever you would like to make. Toppings are a matter of personal preference, which is why those recommended are marked as optional. Toppings are something sensory seekers will love – but if you are an avoider, you may wish to keep these to a minimum. Experiment with the herbs you use, as this can add to and enhance overall flavour – and anything green is (usually) good for you. Chives could be a great addition, as well as small sprigs of mint or basil leaves.

VEGETARIAN SAUSAGES AND MASH

Duration: 30 minutes
Energy rating: Moderate
Skill level: Medium
To make when: you are spending the night in by yourself and need minimal sensory input; you have to entertain younger members of your family and are after a meal that suits a variety of needs; you have had a meltdown earlier in the day and need heart-warming food.

This takes a little more energy than most, so having someone make it for you might be a good idea, too. Sausages and mash is a very easy meal to make – something that you can budget into your weekly shop at a very small cost. As someone who rarely eats meat, I found this quite easy to adapt. The sensory flavours are also really pleasing – and keeping them separate, and limiting the use of butter and pepper, will also help sensory avoiders.

EQUIPMENT YOU WILL NEED

2 saucepans

1 chopping knife

1 chopping board

1 baking tray

1 potato masher

1 silicone or wooden spoon

1 colander

1 peeler

INGREDIENTS

1 packet of butter (you will only be using a little)

6 small baking potatoes

1 small can of baked beans (200 grams/7 ounces) (**note:** some brands are not gluten-free)

1 carrot

4 vegetarian sausages of your choice

Salt and pepper

1 small handful of salad leaves

HOW TO MAKE
Pre-preparation

Put a knob of butter in a saucepan. Set it aside for later. Open up the can of beans. Peel and cut the carrots into small pieces, chop the potatoes into rough quaters. In a pan add water and salt, set the hob to a medium heat and bring water to the boil. Add the potatoes and carrots, boil for 10 minutes or until soft. Drain with a colander and set aside. If you have the sausages in your freezer, make sure to take them out in time for them to defrost.

Method

1. Check the instructions for the temperature and cooking time of the sausages. This is usually about 15–20 minutes; cook the sausages on the oven tray at the temperature shown on the packaging. Once done, turn down the oven to a low heat. This will keep them warm until serving time.

2. Put the potatoes into the saucepan and heat over a medium heat, this will melt the butter. Add in the carrots, and, using the masher, begin to pound to create the 'mash'. It will eventually have a slight orange colour. Sprinkle a small (optional) amount of salt and pepper on top, too.

3. Once the sausages have been cooking for 10 minutes in total, heat up the baked beans on the hob in a separate pan. The gauge should be at halfway, to create a medium heat. Stir periodically to make sure the beans do not stick to the pan.

4. Once the potato is ready to eat – it will have a small amount of steam rising and will be soft – put it out on a plate to serve. Add the finished beans, which will look thick in texture, on the side. Once the sausages are complete – they will look brown and will sizzle – add to the plate as well. (Cut one in half to check if cooked. Steam will rise out if it's safe to eat.) Add salad leaves to the plate as well to serve.

EXPAND YOUR REPERTOIRE

If you have any spice preference, you can always cook your sausages in the spice. Add oil to the baking tray and swish the sausages around. Sprinkle them with the spice before cooking. You could also add herbs on top of your mash, too.

VEGETARIAN SPAGHETTI BOLOGNESE FOR TWO PEOPLE

Duration: 30 minutes

Energy rating: Moderate

Skill level: Medium

To make when: you need an easy meal to serve to friends when it has been an overwhelming day; you need to sit quietly, by yourself, to process your day; you have family visiting. (If you do have family visiting, adjust the quantities according to the number of people that you need to make this for. This recipe is for two people, so halving is for one person, doubling makes four, etc.)

Spaghetti bolognese is one of my favourite meals; everyone has a different interpretation of how to create such a dish, ranging from very basic to very complex. (Notice the use of 'very' twice, there.) Creating a very basic, budget-style version in the style my mother makes this dish was one of my favourite moments in creating recipes for this book. Plus, you can easily adapt for virtually all sensory needs, too.

EQUIPMENT YOU WILL NEED

1 chopping board

1 chopping knife

Optional: garlic crusher

2 saucepans

1 colander

Optional: cheese grater

INGREDIENTS

½ a red onion

1 bag of vegetarian mince (300 grams/10.5 ounces)

Optional: 1 garlic clove

Olive oil (just a dash to cook the mince)

1 carton (500 grams/17.5 ounces) of passata (sieved tomatoes – known in some countries as tomato purée)

60 grams (2 ounces) of penne pasta (gluten-free alternatives are available)

Salt

2 small sprigs of parsley

Optional: cheese of your choice (enough to grate on top of the finished dish)

HOW TO MAKE
Pre-preparation
Use the chopping board and knife to dice the red onion into small pieces. If you need to, make sure the vegetarian mince is defrosted. Crush the garlic clove up in the garlic crusher.

Method

1. In a saucepan, pour in a dash of oil and begin to heat up over a medium heat; add in the vegetarian mince and begin to heat it up. Once brown all over, turn the heat down to its lowest setting possible, just to keep it warm.

2. In a separate pan, combine the pasta, crushed garlic and a pinch of salt. Pour in boiling water so that the pasta is submerged. Bring the heat up to a medium setting to begin cooking. Keep stirring both the mince and pasta to avoid the mixes sticking to the bottom of the pan.

3. Add the onion to the mince mix and begin to heat up.

4. Drain the pasta using a colander over the sink. Now, add the pasta to your serving plate.

5. Once the mince mix has finished cooking, mix in the passata. Heat up and stir together. Pour on top of the pasta. Optional: grate the cheese over the top. Serve with two parsley sprigs on top for decoration.

Note: not everyone has a kettle. Heating up water in a kettle to begin boiling pasta is a great shortcut and will save you a significant amount of time; however, you can just heat water in the pan before you add the pasta if you do not own a kettle. This will take longer, however.

EXPAND YOUR REPERTOIRE

Generally speaking, we could all be doing with eating more vegetables. I know I need to. (Hear that? My mother has just died from shock.) But you can easily add in frozen peas and sweetcorn to the sauce; I am not a fan of the feel of popping membrane foods in my mouth, however. This is not one for the sensory avoiders. Other alternatives could be to include more salad-based elements as a side salad, such as lettuce leaves. There are branded sauces that are tomato based that are designed specifically for these sorts of dishes. If you're feeling brave, these can often be picked up quite cheaply.

SPAGHETTI BOLOGNESE FOR THREE PEOPLE – BY REBEKAH GILLIAN

Duration: 40 minutes to 1 hour

Energy rating: Moderate

Skill level: Medium

To make when: there are too many options and you aren't sure what to cook. (It has been suggested to me that this is something very common when it comes to executive functioning and related challenges.) This is also a great meal that can be repurposed for a number of social occasions, such as for a date night, or even when you need to entertain a key professional contact.

Rebekah Gillian received an autism diagnosis at the age of 17. Now in her 20s, she is a blogger who shares many of her experiences to promote a wider understanding and acceptance of autism.

EQUIPMENT YOU WILL NEED

1 chopping board

1 chopping knife

1 kettle

1 garlic crusher

2 medium-sized saucepans

1 teaspoon

1 measuring jug

1 silicone spoon or a wooden spoon

1 colander

INGREDIENTS

1 large onion

2 garlic cloves

1 carton (500 grams/17.5 ounces) of passata (sieved tomatoes – known in some countries as tomato purée)

250 grams (9 ounces) of soya mince

2 teaspoons of Marmite

1 vegan stock cube

Optional: mixed herbs for serving

| Salt | 180 grams (6.5 ounces) of uncooked spaghetti or pasta in the shape of your choosing (gluten-free alternatives are available) |

HOW TO MAKE
Pre-preparation
Using the chopping board and knife, chop up the onion into small pieces and set aside for later. Take the time now to boil your kettle. Peel and then crush the garlic cloves for later.

Method

1. In one of the saucepans, sweat the onion for a few minutes on a high temperate on the hob. (The onion will begin to look brown around the edges of the slices.) Add the crushed garlic as soon as you notice this start to happen.

2. Next, add in the passata, mince and 2 teaspoons of Marmite. Stir everything together to create the bolognese.

3. Measure out 250 millilitres of the boiled water to dissolve the stock cube, and add to the pan. Optional: add the mixed herbs and salt after you add the water.

4. Reduce to a low medium heat and simmer for 15–20 minutes.

5. Boil the spaghetti or pasta in another pan for 15–20 minutes until done. Drain in a colander over the sink and put on the serving plates. Top with the bolognese and serve.

EXPAND YOUR REPERTOIRE
Worcestershire sauce can be added, in order to create an extra meaty flavour; however, it is not vegetarian. Lentils can be sprinkled on top when serving, which will add another texture. At the point of working with the mince, you can add in mixed peppers (frozen or otherwise), to add more vegetables. Mushrooms or carrots can also do the same thing – and grating them can solve potential issues with texture.

AUNTY'S LAMB KOFTA AND SALSA

Duration: 1 hour and 30 minutes
Energy rating: High
Skill level: Complex
To make when: you need a dish to share with people who come around that
                   is sophisticated just enough to impress without being too
                   obnoxious; you want to celebrate an achievement and need
                   a hearty dish in response; it's your last night living at home.

Back when I had just graduated from my training as a journalist, a contact
used to take me to a particular restaurant in London – where we would put
the 'world to rights' over good food and white wine. The lamb kofta dish from
this restaurant – which this recipe is based on – is one of my absolute favour-
ites. The staff at this restaurant are also wonderful, and the proprietor always
has a naughty spark in his eye, too! It's something of a 'safe food' – one that's
also delicious.

EQUIPMENT YOU WILL NEED

1 chopping board

2 chopping knives

1 colander

1 small bowl

1 sheet of kitchen roll paper

1 mixing bowl

2 teaspoons

1 garlic crusher

2 skewers

1 silicone brush

1 frying pan or 1 baking tray

1 saucepan

INGREDIENTS

A few sprigs of parsley

1 small handful of mint leaves

1 small red onion

Sunflower oil

1 pack of minced/ground lamb (usually 500 grams/17.6 ounces)*

1 teaspoon of ground cumin

1 teaspoon of ground coriander

1 garlic clove

1 avocado

1 bottle of sweet chilli sauce (just a dash is needed)

1 packet of plain basmati rice (pre-cooked 'microwave' rice)

1 small handful of salad leaves

1 lemon

*This will not work with a vegetarian alternative.

HOW TO MAKE
Pre-preparation

Snip the parsley into very small pieces and set aside. Do the same for the mint. Wash the salad leaves in the colander over the sink and set aside to dry. If you hate the tang of onions, soak the onion in a bowl of water for at least one hour beforehand. Just be warned that it will be soggy; make sure they're dry when cutting. Dice half of the onion and set aside for later. Gently soak a sheet of kitchen roll paper with the oil; rub that around the inside of the bowl, setting it aside for later.

Method

1. In an oiled bowl combine the mince, chopped parsley and mint, cumin and coriander. Crush in the garlic, and make sure the mince is well mixed. Firmly squish the mince to create the patties; repeat until all the mince is used up.

2. Put on the skewers gently and coat in a layer of oil with a silicone brush. Start to cook the patties in the frying pan or grill them until cooked.

3. While this is happening, cut open the avocado, remove the stone and scoop

out the guts into the bowl. Add a dash of sweet chilli sauce and combine to create guacamole.

4. Put a drop of oil in the saucepan, squish the rice in the packet, and then put in the saucepan. Cook the rice until cooked.

5. On your serving plate, arrange the salad leaves, then add the kofta patties, guacamole and rice alongside. Squeeze the lemon over the rice for a citrus flavour.

EXPAND YOUR REPERTOIRE

If you need a bit more sensory input, adding some chilli flakes in the kofta is always a good way to go – but exercise caution while doing so! Salad leaves can be grown inside and out – and fresh ingredients add a little 'pop' to any recipe.

TUNA PASTA BAKE FOR THREE

Duration: 45 minutes
Energy rating: Moderate
Skill level: Medium
To make when: you haven't got the energy or the executive function to go shopping and your cupboards are a bit bare; you live with two other housemates and everyone is having a night in; you have a big event – professional or otherwise – the following day and need to be prepared.

Tuna Pasta Bake is a really simple meal to construct, as well as being very easily adaptable. This was a staple meal of my childhood, and for that reason it needed to be included here. This is a delicious meal and should be served with steamed or boiled vegetables on the side, too. To make this vegetarian, replace the tuna with cheese or other alternatives. If you are a sensory avoider, do not use the pepper or salt.

EQUIPMENT YOU WILL NEED

1 set of digital scales

2 saucepans (more if you prefer vegetables to be separated)

1 chopping board

1 chopping knife

1 kettle

1 colander

1 baking dish

1 cheese grater

INGREDIENTS

60 grams (2.1 ounces) of penne pasta

½ a head of broccoli

1 tin of tuna (145 grams)

Salt and pepper

1 packet of cheese (enough to grate over the pasta bake)

1 individual bag of crisps/ potato chips of your choice

2 carrots

¼ of a bag of frozen peas

¼ of a bag of frozen sweetcorn

HOW TO MAKE
Pre-preparation
Measure out the pasta; put in one saucepan and set aside for later. Chop up the broccoli and carrots and also set aside for later. Drain the tuna.

Method

1. Set the oven to 200°C/400°F to start heating it up.

2. Boil some water in the kettle. Once boiled, add to the pasta in the saucepan and put on a medium heat to begin cooking the pasta. Sprinkle in the salt and pepper to add a little flavour to the pasta. It should take about 15 minutes for the pasta to be squishy and edible.

3. Drain the pasta with the colander over the sink and add to the baking dish.

4. Add the tuna to the pasta and stir through. Grate enough cheese over the top to cover it. Arrange the crisps on top and bake until it looks golden brown; the cheese will be gooey and stretchy.

5. While your pasta bake is in the oven, boil more water in the kettle. Add the vegetables to another saucepan, put in the water from the kettle, and boil over a medium heat on the hob. This will take about 15 minutes total; drain with the colander over the sink. Serve the vegetables and pasta bake side by side.

EXPAND YOUR REPERTOIRE
While boiling the pasta, crush up a clove of garlic with a garlic crusher and add to the water. Chives could also be a good addition, too.

TARRAGON CHICKEN BREAST AND FLUFFY POTATOES

Duration: 1 hour
Energy rating: High
Skill level: Complex
To make when: it's cold and wintry outside, and you've come home with rosy cheeks; you're reconnecting with an old friend over a meal; you need to impress your parents – such as if they come to visit you for the first time when you begin to live independently.

During the lockdowns my family and I would play a game: 'What would you like to do after?' My answer was that I'd love to go on a 'train experience' – where you have in-house dining on a train from the 1960s. I'd been entranced by seeing one where I lived at the time, due to having no idea what this was – everyone was bedecked in pearls and tweed! For my second lockdown birthday, I was granted that wish. This is an adapted version of what I was served; the chicken was so good, I was just disappointed there were no 'seconds'.

The recipe is for one person. Just multiply the ingredients for more than one person.

EQUIPMENT YOU WILL NEED

1 chopping board

2 chopping knives

1 potato peeler

1 kettle

1 large saucepan with a lid

1 butter knife

2 smaller saucepans

1 colander

1 potato masher

2 silicone spoons or a pair of tongs

INGREDIENTS

1 carrot

1 leek

1 chicken breast

1 jar of dried tarragon
(to sprinkle on top of the
chicken while it cooks)

Butter (you will need a dab
and an extra 5 grams, which
is 0.1 ounces)

7 small potatoes (they will be
mashed up later)

Salt

Black pepper

HOW TO MAKE
Pre-preparation

Peel the carrot and chop up into small circles; set aside for later. Prepare the leek, chop up roughly at a 45° angle, and also set aside for later. Wash the potatoes using a colander over the sink and allow to dry. Peel, chop up and set aside for later.

Method

This recipe uses just the hob – so you don't need to worry about putting things in an oven. However, this will mean it is more complex – and may be a challenge if you struggle with executive functioning. While dealing with one element of this recipe – say, the potatoes – make sure to keep an eye on everything else; check back in periodically.

1. Boil the kettle. Put the larger saucepan on the hob over a low heat; put a dab of butter in the pan. Put in the chicken breast, sprinkle a small amount of tarragon on top, then add the water to immerse it halfway. Put the lid over the top and allow to simmer. This is called broiling.

2. To make the potato, you are going to need to boil the potatoes in a separate saucepan. Do this over a high heat on the hob by adding in water, so the potatoes are all fully immersed; drain once the potatoes begin to feel soft. Add a dab of butter, then use the masher to mash all until nice and fluffy.

3. Using the final saucepan, repeat the same process to boil the carrots and leeks. This will take maybe 5 minutes. Make sure you season with a pinch of salt and a pinch of black pepper.

4. Take the chicken out and put on the serving plate; sprinkle extra tarragon on top to add just that little bit of extra flavour. Add the potatoes, leeks and carrots alongside. Enjoy!

EXPAND YOUR REPERTOIRE

Personally, I like to add grated cheese to any potato – but that is not accessible to everyone for dietary reasons. You could use sweet potatoes, too – just use the same method. If you also prefer them to be thicker, add a small dash of cream. You could also experiment with stock instead of water to cook the chicken, and different spices.

MACARONI AND CHEESE GRATIN – BY LEONIA CZERNYSZ

Duration: 1 hour and 15 minutes
Energy rating: Moderate
Skill level: Medium
To make when: you need to entertain your friends who are staying over; it's the end of exam season and you need to celebrate; the weather is cold and you want something hearty to eat for dinner, such as around Christmas time.

Leonia Czernysz is a high school senior/student-to-be from Poland who wishes to pursue a degree in Finnish. She was diagnosed as being on the autistic spectrum in August 2020.

EQUIPMENT YOU WILL NEED

2 chopping boards

2 chopping knives

1 garlic crusher

1 cheese grater

2 medium-sized pots/saucepans

1 frying pan

2 colanders

1 ceramic oven baking dish

INGREDIENTS

½ of a large red onion

3 cloves of garlic

250 grams (8.5 ounces) of chicken breasts

500 grams (17.5 ounces) of broccoli florets

1 bottle of olive oil (you will need about a tablespoon)

1 jar of oregano (for seasoning)

500 grams (17.5 ounces) of penne pasta

Salt and pepper

250 grams (8.5 ounces) of cheese of your choice

Editor's note: there are two ways you can prepare this dish, but this is the way Leonia likes to make it. However, keep in mind that this will use a degree of executive functioning as it involves multitasking while at least two pots boil separately. This recipe is ideal for sensory avoiders, says Leonia, as the overall flavour is very mild compared with other dishes. However, it can also be adapted for a multitude of other different dietary and sensory needs; notes on how to do that are at the end of this recipe.

HOW TO MAKE
Pre-preparation
Chop the onion into slices and crush the cloves of garlic. Dice up the chicken and set aside for later. Grate the cheese with the grater and also set aside for later.

Method

1. Set your oven to 180°C/350°F. Boil the water for the penne and the broccoli in the two different saucepans. Add the penne to one pan and the broccoli to the other, and begin to boil both.

2. Heat up the oil in the frying pan. Once hot, add the onions and garlic from earlier to begin cooking, and season with oregano.

3. When the broccoli and penne pasta begin to boil, add in a sprinkle of salt. Cook until they are both squishy and edible. Use a colander to strain them over the sink and leave to dry.

4. Once the onions and garlic look golden brown, add the diced chicken to the pan, and sprinkle on salt and pepper to add flavour. Keep mixing the chicken until it's cooked.

5. Get out a baking dish and layer up the ingredients using this pattern: penne pasta, vegetables and chicken, cheese. Repeat until you have used everything.

6. Cook in the oven for approximately 25 minutes. The cheese on the top of the gratin should be gold and melted. Take the dish out and allow to cool down for 5 minutes prior to eating.

EXPAND YOUR REPERTOIRE

Leave out the chicken if you are a vegetarian and, instead, add different vegetables such as sweetcorn, peas and cauliflower. Just make sure to boil in the same way. Paprika sprinkled in with the pasta while boiling or on top before the baking stage will add a smoky flavour. Other spices to experiment with could be other types of pepper, more oregano, basil, rosemary, thyme, etc. Take out the onions and garlic if you are a sensory avoider; some sensory avoiders can cope with them, but not all can do.

EASY FLIP QUESADILLA

Duration: 20 minutes
Energy rating: High
Skill level: Complex
To make when: you're in the mood for something savoury; it has been a good
                     day and you have a lot of energy; it's a Friday night.

Quesadillas in my family are a particular favourite – the sort of thing we
often have such as when there is a particular event, or when there are a lot of
us assembled all in one place. (Happens a lot less than it should do.) This is
enough for one person – but can be easily increased for more portions. Just
multiply the ingredients up (so double for two people, etc.). This recipe is also
easily adaptable to virtually all sensory needs and food access requirements.
Just make sure that cheese is used liberally to stick the quesadilla together.
(Please note that non-dairy alternatives will not work very well.)

EQUIPMENT YOU WILL NEED

1 colander   1 large frying pan

1 chopping board   1 pair of tongs

1 chopping knife   1 spatula

1 cheese grater

INGREDIENTS

5 cherry tomatoes   1 capful of olive oil

¼ of a cucumber   2 wraps (gluten-free versions
                            are available)
A few leaves of lettuce
                            1 jar of salsa (you will need
1 packet of cheese (enough about 2 tablespoons)
for a small handful of grated
cheese)

HOW TO MAKE
Pre-preparation

There are two elements to this meal – the quesadilla itself and the salad elements on the side to serve it with. Make sure you wash the salad vegetables, then drain them in a colander over the sink. For the salad part of this meal, cut all the cherry tomatoes in half. Cut the quarter of the cucumber into circles. Rip a few leaves off the lettuce. Arrange on a plate and set aside for later. Grate a small handful of cheese and also set aside for later on.

Method

1. Put a capful of oil in the frying pan and begin to heat up over the hob at a medium temperature. Slowly increase the temperature to avoid the oil spitting.

2. Cover one side of a wrap liberally with salsa, as if buttering a sandwich (this is about 2 tablespoons of salsa). Add the wrap to the pan, salsa side up, by using the tongs. Bubbles should begin to appear in the wrap. Quickly add the handful of cheese all over.

3. Add the second wrap on top. The cheese should have begun melting. Push down the wraps into the saucepan for up to 30 seconds, in order to stick them together. Flip over using the spatula after around a minute to cook the other side.

4. Serve on a plate with the salad you chopped up and set aside earlier.

EXPAND YOUR REPERTOIRE

Toppings are everything in this recipe – and can be swapped around easily to adapt. Red onions would add a sweeter tang; spring onions, even a few chives, would bring a fresh taste to this recipe. Just make sure, if you decide to use red onions, to sweat them out first.

CHICKEN SKEWERS FOR FOUR PEOPLE

Duration: 1 hour and 30 minutes
Energy rating: Moderate
Skill level: Medium
To make when: it's summer and there's an outside gathering with relatives – for example, to celebrate a significant wedding anniversary in the family; you're hosting dinner with your friends and need something easy to construct; you've had a bit of a meltdown-y day (just quarter the amounts in this case).

This recipe had to be in this book; I associate it with hope for the future. At my great-grandmother's funeral in 2021, a version of this recipe was served at the wake. As I turned to leave the room, I saw a sign etched in the wall of the village hall. I haven't worked out my place in the universe yet, but I do think 'upstairs' send signs occasionally. 'Fight the good fight,' it said. I could hear my great-grandmother saying that – it's exactly what she would have said. If food is about community, then this is a recipe everyone should have in their arsenal. We can fight a good fight against food poverty, as a start, with the first step of increasing accessibility.

EQUIPMENT YOU WILL NEED

1 chopping board
1 chopping knife
1 mixing bowl

1 tablespoon
8 skewers
1 baking tray

INGREDIENTS

2 bell peppers of your preferred colour

1 tablespoon of ground coriander

1 tablespoon of ground ginger

Optional: a pinch of chilli flakes (to be used with caution)

6 chicken breasts (this will be enough for 2 large skewers per person)

1 bottle of olive oil

HOW TO MAKE
Pre-preparation
Cut up the peppers into smaller pieces (think about half the size of your index finger) and set aside for later; these will soon be skewered along with the chicken that needs to marinade for a little while. Make sure all the different spice options are open.

Method

1. Set your oven to 200°C/400°F and allow to heat up for later on. Cut your chicken breasts into bite-sized pieces; in the mixing bowl, cover them and the pepper pieces with oil. Sprinkle in 1 tablespoon of each spice (apart from the chilli flakes) so everything gets an even coating of the spices. If you want to use the optional chilli flakes, only add in a pinch. Allow this to marinade for 30 minutes.

2. Using the skewers, put on the pieces of chicken and pepper until all eight skewers have been used.

3. Put on the baking tray and cook for 25 minutes.

EXPAND YOUR REPERTOIRE
Plain grilled chicken is a good alternative if you are a sensory avoider; in terms of 'autistic popular culture', this has often been anecdotally cited as a particular favourite of some. I would advise adding a pinch of salt, just to bring out the flavour. Avoid adding the spices, and you will still have a chicken skewer at the end of completing the recipe. Sensory seekers might want to experiment with different spices; if you're feeling brave, try paprika! You might want to try adding in additional elements such as tomatoes; they tend to grill relatively well (cherry tomatoes are best in this context). You also don't have to cover everything with the spices. You could also try making additional sauces instead of the seasoning in the recipe; 'sweet and sour' chicken is easily adaptable to skewer form. All you need to do is create the sauce and drizzle over the chicken and pepper.

STUFFED POTATO SKINS FOR THREE PEOPLE

Duration: 2 hours and 45 minutes

Energy rating: Moderate

Skill level: Easy

To make when: the weather is cold outside, and you've come back from work when it is already dark; you need something low maintenance to make with limited use of energy.

Potato skins are a very easy meal to make and something everyone should have in their cooking arsenal. They are also very adaptable to suit most sensory needs. They can also suit a range of budgets – it doesn't matter where you buy the ingredients from. This recipe can be a bit finicky – so leave yourself some time, just in case. Most of the time involved is the potato baking, so it can be baking while doing another task – such as a quick walk with your family dog. (This is exactly what we do in my house.)

EQUIPMENT YOU WILL NEED

1 cheese grater

1 colander

1 chopping knife

1 chopping board

1 baking tray

1 mixing bowl

1 tablespoon

INGREDIENTS

3 large baking potatoes

1 packet of cheese (can be dairy-free if needed – you will need enough to grate a handful)

1 bag of mixed salad leaves

1 cucumber

1 large tomato

Optional: a small handful of chives (you can use the fresh version or dried – it doesn't matter which)

2 capfuls of olive oil

Rock salt

HOW TO MAKE
Pre-preparation
Wash the potatoes and set aside for later. Using the grater, finely grate a handful of cheese and also set aside for later. Use the colander over the sink to wash the bag of salad leaves, drain and allow to dry for serving later on. Cut the cucumber into small discs to go with the leaves; also cut the tomato up. If using fresh chives, chop these into small pieces.

Note: if you are a sensory avoider, cut the cucumber and tomato into smaller pieces; this can sometimes help with texture-related challenges.

Method

1. Set your oven to 120°C/250°F and allow to heat up. Spread a capful of olive oil over the baking tray. Put the three potatoes on the tray, covering them in the oil; stab them all over repeatedly with the knife, then sprinkle a pinch of rock salt on top of each. Bake for up to 2 hours and 30 minutes.

2. Once they have cooked, cut open each potato and, using the tablespoon, scoop out the fluffy centre into the mixing bowl. Combine with the grated cheese and (the optional) chives, then stuff the skins. This should take maybe 30 seconds while steaming hot; between this and serving, the cheese should start to melt.

3. Combine the leaves, cucumber and tomato discs to create a salad on the side. (If you are a sensory avoider, keep all the elements separate.)

EXPAND YOUR REPERTOIRE
If you like a little bit more of a kick to your cheese, you could try experimenting with different flavours. Try sprinkling on a pinch of black pepper or even chilli flakes on top as well (just be sparing if you do decide to try this). For the potatoes, you could also try different flavours of oils, too.

SHEPHERD'S PIE FOR THREE PEOPLE

Duration: 1 hour
Energy rating: Moderate
Skill level: Complex
To make when: there is a family film night and you need something that will keep people quiet while watching the TV; you need to batch cook; it's your first week living independently.

Shepherd's pie is a favourite dish in my family; when it's just my mother, my sister and me, we each enjoy a portion while we watch a film. This happens maybe twice a month. It's also a meal we often have when the weather grows colder towards the end of the year. This is a bit more complicated and can take a while – especially because there are three different parts to this meal, which can be tricky to contend with when executive functioning will not play ball.

Note: you can use mince for this recipe, or you can use a replacement if you are a vegan or vegetarian.

EQUIPMENT YOU WILL NEED

1 chopping board

1 chopping knife

1 peeler

1 kettle

2 saucepans

1 colander

1 frying pan

1 silicone or wooden spoon

1 potato masher

1 tablespoon

1 ceramic baking dish

1 slotted spoon or ladle

INGREDIENTS

1 head of broccoli

2 carrots

Optional: 1 bag of frozen sweetcorn

Optional: 1 bag of frozen petit pois or peas

6 large potatoes

500 grams (17.6 ounces) of lamb mince/ground lamb (vegetarian options can also be used)

1 pack of butter (you will add a small slice of butter to the potatoes)

1 bottle of olive oil (you will need a capful for frying the mince)

HOW TO MAKE
Pre-preparation

Using the chopping board and knife, roughly chop up half of the broccoli into smaller pieces; make sure you limit how long the stalks are. Peel both of the carrots using the peeler and chop up into small discs. Set both aside for later. Take the petit pois and sweetcorn out of the freezer and set aside. You will need both of them in about 10 minutes. Peel all the potatoes and dispose of the potato peel.

Note: this recipe has the optional step of including petit pois and sweetcorn in the shepherd's pie; if you are a sensory avoider, this is best avoided, due to potential challenges with the texture of them both being a 'membrane' food.

Method

1. Set your oven to 180°C/350°F and allow to heat up.

2. Fill your kettle to the halfway point and boil the water in it. Add to one of the saucepans on a medium heat (gauge at the halfway point) on the hob. Put the potatoes in it so they are fully immersed and put the lid on to start boiling them.

3. The potatoes will gradually become soft after around 10–15 minutes; you can test this by poking with a knife or fork. If it passes through the outside of the potato easily, drain using the colander over the sink. Put them back in the pan with the heat off; put a small slice of butter in with them. Now, using the masher, mash into a fluffy pulp to create the 'mash'. This should take 5–6 minutes in total. Once done, remove from the heat and put the lid on to keep it warm.

4. Put the frying pan over another ring on the hob. Add in a capful of oil and

heat up over a medium heat. Add in the mince. There will be a slight hiss; stir every few minutes. The mince will begin to slowly look brown and will break up; make sure that all of the mince looks like this, as this shows it has fully cooked. This usually takes around 15–20 minutes.

5. Optional: add in 4 tablespoons of petit pois and sweetcorn and keep stirring. This should take around another 5–7 minutes to fully cook.

6. Once the mince and potatoes are both completed, get out the ceramic dish. Spoon out the mince along the bottom with a spoon. Spoon the potato on top of the mince and be sure to smooth it out. Put it into the oven and allow to cook for up to 20 minutes or until golden brown. Just make sure to test if this is fully cooked, as every oven is different.

7. While this is cooking, the other vegetables need to be prepared. If you are a sensory avoider, consider using separate saucepans for the broccoli and carrots. Boil the water using the kettle. Put the saucepan(s) over a medium heat, add the vegetables, add the water until they are fully immersed, and allow to boil; this should take 10–15 minutes. Drain with a colander over the sink; return them to the pan and put the lid on to keep them warm. Serve alongside your shepherd's pie for three people!

EXPAND YOUR REPERTOIRE

If you would like to bring out a more juicy flavour in the mince, you could use the technique of broiling the mince with your preferred stock option (cube or stockpot) that has dissolved in boiled water. At the point of it being in the pan, you could also add a sprinkle of pepper, even chilli flakes, for extra sensory input. When serving, you could also add cheese on top of the potato. A vegetable swap could be leeks in black pepper; use the frying pan and cook with boiled water until it evaporates. Sprinkle over the top when serving.

THREE BEAN AND CHORIZO CHILLI – BY MAIA OSBORNE

Duration: 2 hours

Energy rating: High

Skill level: Complex

To make when: you need to entertain family members, perhaps if they are visiting you for the first time in your new home; the weather outside is starting to turn colder and winter is once again on its way; you need to throw some kind of official gathering, such as a dinner party to celebrate a wedding anniversary.

Maia Osborne is a laboratory scientist. She is a self-diagnosed autistic adult; at the time of writing, she was in the process of getting an official autism assessment.

Please note, this is a recipe just for sensory seekers – and is not adaptable for sensory avoiders. You can experiment with the spices, however, if you wish to expand your repertoire. If you want to adapt this recipe to be vegetarian, use meat replacements, vegetable stock cubes, etc. More information about ingredient alternatives can be found in the back of this book.

As a hygiene note: when working with meat and vegetables, it's good practice to use separate tools for each for health and safety reasons. This is why in this recipe there are two sets of chopping boards and knives.

EQUIPMENT YOU WILL NEED

1 small bowl

1 tablespoon

1 teaspoon

2 chopping boards

2 chopping knives

1 large cooking pot or a wok

1 mixing spoon or a spatula

1 kettle

1 measuring jug

INGREDIENTS

4 tablespoons of ground cumin

4 tablespoons of paprika

4 tablespoons of mild chilli powder

1 teaspoon of pepper

Salt

1 large onion

4 garlic cloves

1 sweet red pepper

1 tin of butter beans (400 grams/15 ounces)

1 tin of kidney beans (400 grams/15 ounces)

1 tin of cannellini beans (400 grams/15 ounces)

1 chorizo sausage (this should be around 225 grams, or 7.9 ounces)

1 bottle of olive oil (just a capful is needed)

300 millilitres of water

1 beef stock cube

1 tin of chopped tomatoes (400 grams/15 ounces)

3 tablespoons of soy sauce

1 tablespoon of tomato ketchup

4 squares of dark cooking chocolate

HOW TO MAKE
Pre-preparation

Measure out all of the spices and add to the small bowl; mix until they are all combined, and set aside for later. Chop all of the vegetables up; dice the onion and the garlic cloves once peeled. Finally, rinse the beans in cold water and also set aside for later.

Method

1. Dice the chorizo. Over a medium heat on the hob, add a capful of oil to your cooking pan or wok and fry the sausage. Once crispy on the outside, add in all of the vegetables you prepared earlier. Keep stirring until the vegetables are also soft on the outside.

2. Add the spice mix you set aside earlier; ensure the chorizo and vegetables are all evenly covered with it, and, once again, continue stirring.

3. Fill the kettle to halfway. Once it has boiled, pour 300 millilitres of water into the measuring jug. Crumble in the beef stock cube and allow to dissolve. Once this happens, add to the pot and stir.

4. Add the chopped tomatoes, soy sauce, ketchup and chocolate to the pot. Keep stirring the mix.

5. Allow the pot to boil by turning up the heat to full; once it reaches this point, reduce the heat to a low level. Put the pot's lid on and simmer for 20 minutes.

6. Take the lid off and add the beans to the pot.

7. Put the lid back and allow to simmer for a further 10 minutes.

8. Turn the hob off and allow to sit for 10 minutes before serving.

EXPAND YOUR REPERTOIRE

For a contrast in flavour, you could serve this with avocado on the side; Maia especially recommends this for the cooling contrast of flavours. Plain long grain rice (prepared after step 5) is also another serving option, she suggests; she also loves to smother the chilli in grated cheese.

ROASTED GREEK LAMB LEG – BY KIERAN ROSE

Duration: 8 hours and 30 minutes

Energy rating: Medium

Skill level: Complex

To make when: you have relatives coming over for lunch at the weekend – usually later in the day in the UK – and you need something that will cater to several people at once, with only a certain amount of extra effort; it's date night and it's your turn to cook.

Kieran Rose is a consultant, writer, trainer, public speaker and researcher in autistic burnout and autistic masking. You can find out more about him and his work at www.theautisticadvocate.com.

This is a recipe that can be left while you go about other activities – this is why the rating for this is medium when it comes to energy. It is also very adaptable for a wide range of preferences, especially when it comes to spices – more on that in a minute. Please note that the preparation for this recipe is not sensory-avoider-friendly – and disposable gloves are advisable for making this dish.

EQUIPMENT YOU WILL NEED

1 chopping board

1 chopping knife

1 large baking tray

1 roll of foil

INGREDIENTS

1 leg of lamb (size does not matter in this recipe – just go for one that is a bit bigger if you have, say, three or more people to cater for)

1 punnet of cherry tomatoes

1 pack of feta cheese (you will use half a pack)

1 bottle of olive oil

1 jar of thyme*

1 jar of oregano*

1 pack of rock salt*

1 bottle of lemon juice*   Optional: 1 small jar of olives

*Quantities will depend on the size of the leg of lamb – you will be covering it all over later in the recipe.

HOW TO MAKE
Pre-preparation

Keep your leg of lamb in your fridge overnight, as you will be taking it out in the morning. Quarter the cherry tomatoes and dice up half of the feta cheese with the chopping board and knife; also set aside for later.

Method

1. Take the leg of lamb out in the morning and allow to come to the temperature of the room. Rest on a baking dish while doing this.

2. Now, we need to prepare the meat; cover the leg in olive oil, and make sure it is completely evenly covered. (This may mean having to use your hands.) Sprinkle over the diced feta, along with the cherry tomatoes, olives if using, and the thyme and oregano. Sprinkle the salt and drizzle lemon juice evenly across the top.

3. Wrap this up in the foil and allow to sit for two hours in your fridge; this just allows the herbs to set, and will bring the flavour out more, kind of like when you marinade something.

4. Set the oven to its full temperature (200°C fan/425°F). Once it is hot, put the lamb in. After 30 minutes, reduce the temperature to 120°C/250°F. (This is a hygiene measure.) Cook slowly for 6 hours. Serve while still warm.

EXPAND YOUR REPERTOIRE

As always, you can try using other herbs when it comes to creating the flavour of the leg of lamb; this could be ground cumin and ground coriander, or even paprika for an extra 'kick'. (That may be something for sensory seekers.) However, if you are an avoider, it would be advisable to limit the number of different flavours used. To make this into a bigger meal, and therefore suitable for more people, try cooking roasted and/or boiled potatoes or serving with extra vegetables on the side, such as asparagus or (buttered) leeks.

TWO-HOUR ROAST DINNER FOR THREE – BY NATHAN GOKHOOL

Duration:	2 hours
Energy rating:	High
Skill level:	Complex
To make when:	you need to serve your relatives – traditionally, this is made for a Sunday afternoon in the UK; you are hosting a friendly gathering; you are serving people Christmas dinner.

Nathan Gokhool is a writer. In his spare time, he likes to keep active and is a keen climber/hiker.

This is a pared-down version – things to add are at the end of this recipe. This recipe makes three generous portions to serve that number of people – however, leftovers can be repurposed afterwards. Scale up if you wish to serve more.

EQUIPMENT YOU WILL NEED

2 chopping boards	1 large baking tray
2 chopping knives	2 large saucepans
1 potato peeler	1 silicone or wooden spoon
1 cheese grater	1 kettle
1 serving bowl	1 small saucepan
1 measuring jug	1 small baking tray

INGREDIENTS

1 head of broccoli	1 packet of rock salt (you will only need a little)
6 carrots	
15 potatoes in varying sizes	1 bag of plain flour/all-purpose flour (you will need 2 tablespoons of this)
1 leg of lamb	

½ packet of cheese of your choice (cannot be an alternative cheese)

Milk (approximately 250 millilitres)

1 jar of goose fat (or olive oil as an alternative, you will need enough to drizzle on the lamb and potatoes)

HOW TO MAKE
Pre-preparation

Use the chopping board and knife to cut the broccoli in half. Next, roughly chop off the broccoli florets of one of the halves; set aside for later. Peel the carrots and chop into small circles. Peel the potatoes and cut into large chunks of a similar size. Grate the cheese into the serving bowl and set aside for later. Cut off half the broccoli by using the chopping board and knife. Measure 100 millilitres of milk in the measuring jug.

Method

1. Heat your oven to the temperature given in the instructions on the packaging of the leg of lamb. Put the leg of lamb on the large baking tray; cover all over by drizzling the olive oil. Sprinkle a small amount of rock salt across. Put into the oven to cook as per the instructions.

2. Put the peeled potatoes in one of the smaller saucepans. Fill with cold water until all are submerged and sprinkle with rock salt. Allow to sit for 30 minutes.

3. In a separate saucepan, add the flour, cheese and a pinch of salt. Add the milk gradually. Stir with the silicone or wooden spoon until thick to create the sauce for the cheese sauce. Once that's done – it takes a few minutes – allow to simmer.

4. Put the carrots and broccoli pieces into the other pan. Fill with boiling water from the kettle until all are submerged and begin to heat up over the hob; allow them to simmer for the moment.

5. Back to the potatoes. Put on the final baking tray; cover with salt and optionally goose fat. Put in the hot oven and cook until golden brown.

6. Back to the vegetables. Boil until they are all soft and can easily be cut up; you can test this with a knife and fork. This can take 5 minutes.

7. Take the lamb out and carve up once cooked; add the potatoes to your serving plate. When you add the vegetables to your plate, cover with the cheese sauce to finish off.

EXPAND YOUR REPERTOIRE

If you are feeling brave, you could angle the potatoes to be underneath the leg of lamb – enough so that the fat from the meat drips down. If you would like to recreate this for a Christmas dinner, you could add things such as pigs in blankets, boiled/buttered leeks, peas and sweetcorn – even sauces such as mint or cranberry.

FROZEN SEAFOOD CHOWDER
– BY PAULINE DUNNE

Duration: 1 hour

Energy rating: Moderate

Skill level: Medium

To make when: there is an evening in with friends during the winter; it's cold and blustery outside and you need to serve more than just three people with as little effort as possible.

Pauline Dunne is a former animation student based in Ireland. They like cooking for large groups – and this recipe will serve approximately six people as a result. Chowder is suitable for meal prepping – it can be frozen if needed – and is also budget-friendly, too.

EQUIPMENT YOU WILL NEED

1 chopping board

1 chopping knife

1 potato peeler

1 kettle

1 measuring jug

1 butter knife

1 large saucepan

1 garlic crusher

1 tablespoon

1 teaspoon

1 silicone or wooden spoon

INGREDIENTS

1 white onion

1 stick of celery

1 green bell pepper

3–4 Rooster potatoes

3 garlic cloves (you can double this if you are a more ardent sensory seeker)

1 small tin of sweetcorn (198 grams/7 ounces)

1 vegetable stock cube

1 packet of butter (you will only need a little)

1 tablespoon of smoked paprika

Optional: 1 teaspoon of cayenne pepper

1 tablespoon of tomato paste/purée from a tube

1 tin (410 grams) of evaporated milk

1 bag of frozen seafood mix (350 grams/12 ounces) (available from most supermarkets – just make sure it's gluten-free if needed)

HOW TO MAKE
Pre-preparation

Using the chopping board and knife, peel and then dice up the onion. Chop up the celery into small discs and then chop up the green pepper into small bite-sized pieces. Set all vegetables aside for later. Peel the potatoes and quarter them. Peel the garlic cloves. Drain the tin of sweetcorn.

Method

1. Fill up your kettle to about halfway and begin to boil. Once boiled, add 450 millilitres to the measuring jug and put in the stock cube to begin dissolving.

2. Use the butter knife to cut a tiny piece off the end of the butter packet; add this to the saucepan and begin to heat up on the hob with the gauge turned to the halfway point. Add the onion, celery and pepper and begin to sweat them out for about 5–7 minutes. (You should really begin to smell them!)

3. Crush in the garlic cloves with the garlic crusher, followed by a tablespoon of the smoked paprika, then the (optional) teaspoon of cayenne pepper. Continue stirring with the silicone or wooden spoon.

4. Once that is fully mixed in, add a tablespoon of the tomato paste and keep cooking until it starts to become more of an orange colour.

5. Add the drained tin of sweetcorn and the evaporated milk to the pot, and continue stirring in.

6. Once that is all mixed in (as in step 4), add all of the potatoes into the pot; they take a little while to cook, and that can be tested by cutting them open to see if any steam comes out. Keep stirring meanwhile.

7. Add in the frozen seafood mix of your choice and keep cooking until the

seafood starts to have a more flexible texture. All in all, this recipe should take approximately 60 minutes.

EXPAND YOUR REPERTOIRE

Instead of the evaporated milk, you could try using cream – for a fuller taste. (Evaporated milk is a cheaper alternative.) Depending on the various spices you like, you could try experimenting with the flavours of your own preference – thyme, rosemary, even tarragon could be alternatives to try. Rooster potatoes are not always widely available – so you could also try experimenting with potato types when making this chowder, to suit your own preferences. If you would prefer to try something fresher, you could always try adding in prawns (shrimp), mussels or squid rings – they can come in frozen form or are sometimes available from a fishmonger or a deli counter in a supermarket. (Using a frozen seafood mix just happens to be budget-friendly, as well as saving an amount of the energy this recipe could otherwise take up.) Just make sure that you use non-breaded types as this can become a problem when it comes to the physical production of this recipe. When it comes to serving, this is best served with a crusty loaf of bread of some sort – some supermarkets make these fresh every day, or you could also have a go at making your own, too.

PART 4

Desserts, Snacks and Miscellaneous Recipes

KETO KOOKIES – BY LYRIC HOLMANS

Duration: 25 minutes
Energy rating: Low
Skill level: Easy
To make when: you are after a quick snack to eat – and there isn't anything in the immediate vicinity you fancy eating; you've had a stressful day and want to bake as an act of self-care.

Lyric Holmans is the founder of Neurodivergent Consulting and is based in Texas. They are known for the award-winning blog Neurodivergent Rebel, which has the tagline 'Rebelling against a culture that values assimilation over individuality'. Neurodivergent Rebel can also be found on YouTube as well as other platforms. Lyric is also the founder of the hashtag #AskingAutistics.

Editor's note: Lyric follows a specific diet, on the advice of their doctor. Always consult a medical professional before following diets; however, this recipe is suitable for everyone in moderation.

Keto Kookies are an executive functioning 'win' – in that they stay fresh for up to a week and require little to no planning. Using stevia makes this a keto-friendly recipe. Organic stevia can be hard to find – and you can use alternatives for this reason, such as sugar.

EQUIPMENT YOU WILL NEED

1 set of digital scales

1 mixing bowl

1 wooden spoon

1 baking tray

1 teaspoon

1 roll of greaseproof paper

INGREDIENTS

225 grams (8 ounces) of organic stevia (If you are using brown sugar, double this)

480 grams (17 ounces) of peanut butter

2 eggs

Optional: ¼ of a teaspoon of cinnamon

HOW TO MAKE
Pre-preparation
Measure out all the ingredients into their quantities as stated above. Measure out the greaseproof paper to fit the baking tray and cut to size.

Method

1. Set the oven to 185°C/365°F and allow to heat up.

2. Having measured everything out, combine all ingredients together. Mix the ingredients together enough to get a mix that should be ball-shaped.

3. Separate into smaller balls and place on the greaseproof paper that is on the baking tray. Squish to make them more biscuit-shaped. Bake for 10–13 minutes, or until golden brown.

EXPAND YOUR REPERTOIRE
Dust the top of this recipe with brown sugar; you can do the same with the stevia.

BASIC BUTTERCREAM ICING MIX

Duration: 10 minutes

Energy rating: Low

Skill level: Easy

To make when: you have just created a sponge cake and need something to 'sandwich' the two halves together.

It is more of an 'art' than a straightforward recipe – and will require some patience, as well as practice. Please note that this recipe does not rely on specific amounts. The problem with making icing for a cake is that it is more of an 'art' than anything else; the quantities can be hard to predict.

EQUIPMENT YOU WILL NEED

1 mixing bowl

2 tablespoons

Optional: 1 mixer

1 paring knife

INGREDIENTS

1 pack of butter (you will only need a quater of the pack)

1 bag of icing sugar (you will only need 3½ tablespoons)

HOW TO MAKE

Pre-preparation

Make sure the butter is at room temperature or cut up a quarter of a standard pack into smaller pieces. This will make the process a lot easier to contend with, as it will be easier to manipulate.

Method

1. Take about a quarter of the butter packet out and put in a bowl. Add about 3½ tablespoons of icing sugar to the butter. Now, blend. You can do this manually – such as by using the back of a tablespoon to combine the two

ingredients – or with a mixer; it doesn't really matter, but both methods are just as good. The result should look yellow and gooey.

2. Taste it to see how sweet the mix is. Keep adding a tablespoon of sugar, and then mix again, until you get the flavour you would like.

EXPAND YOUR REPERTOIRE

Icing sugar is really malleable and can be adapted pretty much any way that you like. That means it is pretty much suitable for anyone when it comes to different sensory needs – you just need to decide what flavour and consistency you would like. Sensory seekers may like to try out stronger flavours. Chocolate buttercream can be created by adding a tablespoon of cocoa powder at a time to the mix, as well as to the sponge; the more you add, the more chocolatey the flavour with be of both. Most supermarkets also sell small bottles of flavouring that you could try adding to the icing; in the past I have made gin-flavoured cake, or a more simple vanilla one for friends. It's cheap and keeps for ages. Sensory avoiders should steer clear of any strong flavours and keep any matching sponge as 'clean' as they possibly can by limiting the flavours used.

LALAINE'S VICTORIA SPONGE CAKE

Duration: 1 hour and 30 minutes
Energy rating: High
Skill level: Complex
To make when: it's summer and you need to entertain relatives; you need to construct a cake when it's someone's birthday; you're hosting a dinner party or a night in, and your meal needs a dessert to finish it off.

'You're wearing pink today.' I nervously glance up at the lady boss, apprehensive and awkward in this new office. I nod. In the shrillest, loudest voice possible, the lady boss draws attention to the situation, so everyone in the room stares: 'Pink to make the boys wink!' A friendship of many years was born out of my cringing embarrassment while trying to fade into the background. Lalaine is my oldest friend and was one of the first people to fully accept me as an autistic individual. For a few years I ducked out of her Christmas wish – for a freshly baked Victoria sponge – so this recipe deserves its place here in this book.

EQUIPMENT YOU WILL NEED

1 set of digital scales	1 piece of kitchen roll paper
1 mixing bowl	1 standard cake tin
1 chopping board	1 palette knife
1 paring knife	1 butter knife
2 tablespoons	1 small bowl
1 silicone or wooden spoon	1 wire rack

INGREDIENTS

3 eggs

170 grams (60 ounces) of caster sugar

170 grams (60 ounces) of butter + extra for greasing your cake tin with and to make the buttercream icing

170 grams (60 ounces) of self-raising flour

1 bottle of vanilla essence (you will only need a small amount)

1 bag of icing sugar (you will only need 3½ tablespoons)

1 jar of strawberry jam/preserve (about 3½ tablespoons)

1 small handful of strawberries

HOW TO MAKE
Pre-preparation
Using the digital scales and the mixing bowl, measure out the caster sugar and butter. Use the chopping board and paring knife to cut the strawberries into halves.

Method

1. Set your oven to 190°C/375°F and allow to heat up.

2. With the back of a tablespoon, cream together the butter and sugar in the mixing bowl. Set on the digital scales and then turn it on so it says the weight is at zero; next, measure out the flour. Add in the eggs and mix together with the silicone or wooden spoon. Add in a drop of vanilla essence and stir again.

3. Use the extra butter and kitchen roll paper to grease your cake tin; once you have done that, spoon in the cake mixture and bake until golden brown. Put a butter knife in the middle to test if cooked; if it comes out clean, it's safe to eat. This can take up to 45 minutes or longer, because everyone's oven is different.

4. Take the cake tin out of the oven and put on the wire rack. Gently take off the tin and use a palette knife to extract the bottom of the tin after about 10 minutes. Allow to cool completely.

5. While cooling, we are going to be making the icing. Use the **Basic Buttercream Icing Mix** recipe to create your icing.

6. Once the cake has cooled, use a knife to cut it into two. Cover one side of one half in buttercream; on the other half, spoon out the strawberry jam and cover. Sandwich the two together to assemble the cake.

7. Once you have assembled the cake, decorate the top with the strawberries from earlier, and sprinkle over with a pinch of icing sugar.

EXPAND YOUR REPERTOIRE

Try using different flavours instead of vanilla essence; you could even add in a tablespoon of cocoa powder. Decorations can be different, too, as most shops sell different icing and more.

ETON MESS FOR FOUR PEOPLE

Duration: 20 minutes

Energy rating: Moderate

Skill level: Easy

To make when: you need to cater for someone who does not like cake, and needs an alternative dessert option; there's a family barbecue and 'afters' are needed; it's a 'girls' night' or there's a social occasion like a hen do.

There are two ways to serve this – one because I dislike cream; the two different methods (with and without cream) are described below. This is for four people; if you need to make more, you can easily multiply the quantities.

EQUIPMENT YOU WILL NEED

1 chopping knife

1 chopping board

1 colander

1 mixing bowl

1 whisk

4 bowls to serve in

4 spoons or forks to eat with

INGREDIENTS

1 box of strawberries

1 box of blueberries

1 box of raspberries

1 medium pot of double cream (you will need to whip this later)

1 box of meringue nests (vegan versions are available)

HOW TO MAKE
Pre-preparation

Cut up all the different fruits into small pieces separately and rinse through the colander over the sink. Set aside for later. Take the cream out of the fridge.

Method 1 – Traditional Eton Mess

1. In the mixing bowl pour out half the bottle of cream. Use the whisk to whip it; it should start to look thick and peaky. This will take about 10 minutes.

2. Pile up the cream, meringue (crumbled) and the different fruits in the serving bowl. Repeat this pattern for all four portions, until all the ingredients are finished up.

Method 2 – Eton Mess Deconstructed with No Cream

This is for anyone who detests cream like I do; this can also be adapted further, such as with plate dividers, to keep the majority of the flavours separate. This is more of a friendly option for sensory avoiders, too. If you're like me, you can also try leaving out the blueberries – one of the only fruits I detest.

1. In the serving bowl, add the strawberries, then the raspberries. Do this for the four portions.

2. Crumble a meringue on top of each portion, then serve.

EXPAND YOUR REPERTOIRE

I know of a few autistic individuals who have a hard time with fruit, particularly citrus fruit. Once you have used the colander and the fruit has had enough time to dry, try sprinkling a little sugar on top of the fruit. This will bring out the flavour and dampen down a potentially bitter flavour. If you dislike meringue, you can always try swapping this with a small amount of ice cream.

ICE-CREAM PICNIC FLOATS

Duration: 15 minutes
Energy rating: Low
Skill level: Easy
To make when: there's an outside picnic – such as in your back garden; you want an alternative to sitting in a café; you need a date idea.

If you watch the old-fashioned American movies – think Golden Age of Hollywood – then ice-cream floats were probably almost always a fixture. This recipe is very much for people who have a sweet tooth. Just bear in mind that there is an element of pre-preparation for this.

EQUIPMENT YOU WILL NEED

1 ice cube tray

1 paring knife

1 chopping board

1 ice-cream scoop

1 ice-cream float/sundae glass

INGREDIENTS

1 can of cola or an equivalent drink

1 small handful of strawberries

1 banana

1 carton of ice cream in a flavour you like (vanilla seems a good call for sensory avoiders) – gluten-free, vegetarian and vegan options are available (you will need a few scoops)

1 bottle of maple syrup (you will only need a small amount)

HOW TO MAKE
Pre-preparation
The night before, you will need to prepare the ice cubes. Pour the fizzy drink into the ice cube tray and freeze overnight; this will add an extra sensory input element, thanks to the extra 'fizz' that will be added to the float. When you come to construct the float, make sure you start by slicing the strawberries and bananas as thinly as you can.

Method

1. Pop out the ice cubes from where you froze them overnight. Put them in a cold place for now, to avoid melting; they will be used in a minute.

2. In the float/sundae glass, use the ice-cream scoop to add in ice cream to the bottom, making sure that it is fully covered.

3. Add your fruit and then add a small amount of the maple syrup on top.

4. Pour in your fizzy drink of choice and pair with the ice cubes. Add a straw and spoon to serve it with.

EXPAND YOUR REPERTOIRE
Conventional wisdom seems to suggest that if you add the ice cream to the bottom of your glass, and then the drink on top of that, then the ice cream will somehow magically float to the top. I have never been able to replicate this, but if you do, try adding crushed nuts as a topping. There are also several easy-to-make recipes of chocolate sauce online; try adding this to the bottom of your glass.

TWELVE 'TASTE OF ROTTERDAM' CUPCAKES

Duration: 1 hour and 15 minutes

Energy rating: Medium

Skill level: Moderate

To make when: you'd like a snack for after a meal, such as after lunch or dinner; when you have to entertain younger relatives; when you have to prepare dessert, such as when hosting a dinner party, and need something simple to make when feeling burnt out.

If ever there was such a city, Rotterdam is my home from home. I love the city, its history, the architecture, the street art. It is also where I met one of my closest friends, Envy. Rotterdam is a multicultural hub, a mixing pot; this was my tribute to the city that taught me to not be ashamed of being curious.

EQUIPMENT YOU WILL NEED

1 set of digital scales

1 mixing bowl

1 silicone or wooden spoon

1 standard cupcake tray with 12 holes for 12 muffins

1 sheet of kitchen roll paper

1 palette knife

1 wire rack

1 tablespoon

1 butter knife

INGREDIENTS

170 grams (60 ounces) of caster sugar

170 grams (60 ounces) of butter plus extra for greasing your cupcake tray and to make the buttercream icing

3 eggs

170 grams (60 ounces) of self-raising flour

2 tablespoons of speculaas spice (1 tablespoon for the cake mixture and 1 tablespoon for the buttercream icing)*

1 bag of icing sugar (you will only need 3½ tablespoons)

* This is a Dutch spice and can be found on the internet or in the Netherlands.

HOW TO MAKE
Pre-preparation

Using the digital scales and the mixing bowl, measure out the caster sugar and butter.

Method

1. Set your oven to 190°C/375°F and allow to heat up.

2. With the back of a tablespoon, cream together the butter and sugar in the mixing bowl. Set on the digital scales and then turn it on so it says the weight is at zero; next, measure out the flour. Add in the eggs and mix together with the silicone or wooden spoon. Add in a tablespoon of speculaas spices and stir again.

3. Grease the cupcake tray with the kitchen roll and extra butter; once you have finished, divide the mixture between the 12 holes. Bake until golden brown, which is around 30 minutes – but may take slightly longer, as everyone's oven is slightly different.

4. Take the cupcake tray out of the oven and put on the wire rack. Gently ease the cupcakes out of the tin after about 10 minutes. Allow to cool completely.

5. While cooling, we are going to be making the icing. Use the **Basic Buttercream Icing Mix** recipe to create your icing and add in a tablespoon of the speculaas spice. Cream until you get the icing texture and then ice your cupcakes.

EXPAND YOUR REPERTOIRE

Once you have added the icing on top of the muffin, you could dip it in crushed nuts to add a degree of an extra texture. Walnuts are a great example of this; you could even bake them, when crushed up, into the batter. If you add icing on top of the muffin, sprinkle on a little extra speculaas spice and/or cinnamon. You could even add in a Biscoff biscuit, right on top, if you like. This kind of decoration seems to be popular in some coffee shops.

BROWN SUGAR AND CINNAMON APPLE SLICES

Duration: 20 minutes

Energy rating: High

Skill level: Complex

To make when: dinner has finished and you are not entirely sure what you would like for dessert; there is an influx of apples in the fruit bowl (happens in my family all the time); you need something 'extra' to go with vanilla ice cream; you are having an evening in with your oldest friend.

This is one of my mother's favourite desserts – and it combines very few ingredients with just enough flavour to not be boring! (Because let's be honest, sometimes a plain apple for after you have finished dinner is sometimes just not cutting it.)

This recipe is marked as complex as it requires a lot of fine motor skills and other skills.

EQUIPMENT YOU WILL NEED

1 chopping board

1 corer

1 paring knife

1 butter knife

1 saucepan

2 teaspoons

1 silicone or wooden spoon

INGREDIENTS

1 apple

1 pack of butter (you will be using a medium-sized slice)

1 teaspoon of ground cinnamon

1 teaspoon of brown sugar

HOW TO MAKE
Pre-preparation
Using the chopping board, you need to prepare the apple; first, use the corer to take out the centre and discard. Quarter the apple and continue chopping each quarter so that you have wafer thin slices. Take the butter out of the fridge and allow to come to room temperature; this will make it more malleable and a lot easier to work with.

Method

1. Put the saucepan on the hob at a medium heat. Use the butter knife to cut off a medium-sized slice from the end of the packet and add in; add in a teaspoon of the ground cinnamon and brown sugar. They should all melt together to create a brown liquid.

2. Add in the slices of the apple to the saucepan. Use the silicone or wooden spoon to continue stirring, to ensure all apples are evenly covered with the mixture. Keep stirring until the apples are soft and have a brown tinge.

3. Optional step: serve with a scoop (or two) of vanilla ice cream.

EXPAND YOUR REPERTOIRE
It might be a little bit basic, but this recipe can act as a complement to other dishes, should you choose to build the apple slices into anything else; there is a recipe in this book later on involving pastry that this would be perfect for! You could also try out different flavours to coat the apple in. This is perfect for Christmas time and would taste great in a crumble as well.

LEBKUCHEN – BY ALLIE MASON

Duration: 1 hour and 30 minutes
Energy rating: High
Skill level: Complex
To make when: you need to give someone a Christmas or birthday present, such as a parent or older relative; when you're in a cozy mood and want to have a film night topped off with hot chocolate; you're waiting for Father Christmas to arrive.

Allie Mason is a children's author and keen roller-skater. She also blogs about her writing projects and her training for the Berlin Inlineskating Marathon. She was formally diagnosed as autistic when she was 23 years old. Lebkuchen, Allie says, is a form of German gingerbread. It is also something those of us in the UK may associate with celebrations such as Christmas. This recipe makes 32 biscuits. Sensory avoiders should be aware that some of the ingredients in this recipe are quite strong in flavour.

EQUIPMENT YOU WILL NEED

1 sieve

1 mixing bowl

1 wooden spoon

1 china mug or an extra china bowl

2 baking trays

1 pair of digital scales

1 roll of greaseproof paper

1 tablespoon

1 teaspoon

1 rolling pin

1 cookie cutter in a shape of your own preference

1 cooling rack

INGREDIENTS

100 grams (3.5 ounces) of clear honey

100 grams (3.5 ounces) of light brown sugar

60 grams (2 ounces) of butter

220 grams (7.5 ounces) of plain flour/all-purpose flour

100 grams (3.5 ounces) of ground almonds

1 teaspoon of cinnamon

1 teaspoon of ground ginger

1 teaspoon of cocoa powder

2 tablespoons of chocolate chips

½ a teaspoon of bicarbonate of soda (this does not have to be exact)

½ a teaspoon of salt (this does not have to be exact)

1 egg

HOW TO MAKE
Pre-preparation

Measure out all the ingredients that have grams or ounces as their quantity; the rest we will come to later.

Method

1. Using the sieve, add the flour to the mixing bowl. Repeating the same method, add the almonds, cinnamon, ginger, cocoa powder, salt and bicarbonate of soda to the mix. Mix all of these dry ingredients together.

2. Add the egg and mix.

3. Add the butter, sugar and honey in the mug or the extra china bowl. Melt together in the microwave for 30 seconds only. Stir. Repeat the same microwaving process until the butter has melted and the sugar dissolved. Add to the dry mixture and stir in using the wooden or silicone spoon.

4. As you stir, you will notice a dough beginning to form, as it will become harder to stir the mix. Chill in your fridge for 60 minutes.

5. While waiting, line the two baking trays with greaseproof paper. Heat the oven to 180°C/350°F.

6. Take the mix out of the fridge once 60 minutes is up. Mix the chocolate chips in.

7. Sprinkle flour across the work surface and your rolling pin. Roll out the dough so it is about half a centimetre thick. Cut out the dough with your cookie cutter in your preferred shape. Space the shapes out on the baking tray.

8. Bake for 10 minutes and allow to cool on the rack.

EXPAND YOUR REPERTOIRE

Once you have baked your Lebkuchen, you could dust with icing sugar for decorative purposes. This is just a little 'extra'.

ELDERFLOWER FAIRY CAKES

Duration: 1 hour and 15 minutes

Energy rating: Medium

Skill level: Moderate

To make when: you need a picnic essential for a park meet-up; when a younger member of the family has a birthday party and you need to contribute something; you have no idea as to what to give your grandparents for a Christmas or birthday present; you need a snack later on, such as if you are having a film night with your friends.

Fairy cakes were a staple of my childhood, especially at the end of the school year in primary school; a Christmas party would require every child to bring something for the rest of the school, and this often resulted in the same cupcake brand year after year. While testing out another prototype, this came to mind as a recipe. It was also the first thing I baked from scratch in my first flat.

EQUIPMENT YOU WILL NEED

1 mixing bowl

1 silicone or wooden spoon

1 set of digital scales

1 cupcake tray with 12 holes for 12 muffins

1 piece of kitchen roll paper

1 palette knife

1 tablespoon

1 butter knife

1 wire rack

INGREDIENTS

170 grams (6 ounces) of caster sugar

170 grams (6 ounces) of butter plus extra for greasing your cupcake tray and to make the buttercream icing

3 eggs

170 grams (6 ounces) of self-raising flour

1 bottle of elderflower cordial (you will need 2 teaspoons of this)

1 bag of icing sugar (you will only need 3½ tablespoons)

HOW TO MAKE
Pre-preparation
Using the digital scales and the mixing bowl, measure out the caster sugar and butter.

Method

1. Set your oven to 190°C/375°F and allow to heat up.

2. With the back of a tablespoon, cream together the butter and sugar in the mixing bowl. Set on the digital scales and then turn it on so it says the weight is at zero; next, measure out the flour. Add in the eggs and mix together with the silicone or wooden spoon. Add in a teaspoon of the elderflower cordial and stir in.

3. Grease the cupcake tray with the kitchen roll and extra butter; once you have finished, divide the mixture between the 12 holes. Bake until golden brown, which is around 30 minutes – but may take slightly longer, as everyone's oven is slightly different.

4. Take the cupcake tray out of the oven and put on the wire rack. Gently ease the cupcakes out of the tin after about 10 minutes. Allow to completely cool.

5. While cooling, we are going to be making the icing. Use the **Basic Buttercream Icing Mix** recipe to create your icing and add in a teaspoon of the elderflower. Cream until you get the icing texture, and ice your cupcakes.

EXPAND YOUR REPERTOIRE
Smother the top of the fairy cake with the icing. Consider dipping this into sprinkles or crushed nuts as a decoration. This will add an extra texture – so, if you are a sensory avoider, consider carefully if you can cope with this. Try experimenting with the flavourings. Some supermarkets sell other flavourings that you can add to the cake; you could even try with other liquids, including things such as lemonade. Some shops also offer edible flowers; a matching elderflower would add satisfying coordination.

MAKE YOUR OWN FIDGET CHOCOLATE BAR

Duration: 1 hour and 15 minutes
Energy rating: Low
Skill level: Easy
To make when: you need a quick and easy snack to make; you have to entertain younger family members such as cousins; you teach individuals who have additional needs.

When it comes to sensory aids, I'm aware that a lot of autistic people use 'pop its' in some form or another. Often in the shape of an animal, they are placed on a flat surface, and you press certain pieces to make a 'popping' sound. This recipe incorporates your 'pop it' of choice to act as a mould for your own chocolate bar.

This is suitable for both sensory seekers and sensory avoiders.

EQUIPMENT YOU WILL NEED

1 mixing bowl

1 kettle

1 saucepan

Pop it (the fidgets you can pop) – make sure it is clean and dry

1 silicone or wooden spoon

INGREDIENTS

1 bar of cooking chocolate (200 grams/7 ounces) – vegan cooking chocolate is available

1 bottle of edible glitter (you will need enough to sprinkle)

A small handful of your favourite sweets, small enough to sit in the holes of the pop it

HOW TO MAKE
Pre-preparation

In the mixing bowl, smash the chocolate into smaller pieces; this will make it a lot easier to melt in the long run. Make sure the edible glitter is open. Set the kettle up ready to boil the water. The bowl should be big enough that the water will not touch it or the bowl will not fall into the water, when it comes to melting.

Method

1. Pop the 'pop it' all over; this will mean that you have several different compartments for where your favourite sweets will sit. Put your favourite sweets in the holes, and then sprinkle glitter across the pop it.

2. Use the process of bain-marie to melt the chocolate bar – by using the kettle, saucepan and mixing bowl. Keep gently mixing with the non-stick spoon until there are no lumps and bumps.

3. Cover the 'pop it' with the chocolate. (The sweets you have just covered will be the 'front' of the bar.) Smooth to level off and freeze for up to an hour to harden. To pop it back out, all you have to do is pop the 'pop it' as you do when fidgeting!

EXPAND YOUR REPERTOIRE

There are some individuals who really like chilli chocolate. You can use a sprinkling of chilli flakes mixed in with the chocolate in the melting bowl, but extreme caution should be used while putting this together. Food colouring could also potentially be experimented with while making chocolate; just make sure you use white cooking chocolate. You could also try making a marble effect, by combining three different chocolate types, and mixing them all together.

IRENE'S CHOCOLATE AND LAVENDER SPONGE CAKE

Duration: 1 hour and 30 minutes
Energy rating: High
Skill level: Complex
To make when: you have visitors for the day, and coffee and cake needs to be offered after a long drive; times are hard and you need a hug – this is a hug in cake form; you need to create a birthday cake.

My great-grandmother Irene died while I was writing this book. She was one hell of a Legendary Little Lady. In the hours after she left this world, staff who looked after her at the care home raised a glass, reminiscing about the hilarious daily utterances often bellowed at full volume. And woe betide Hospital Food – capitals intended. She may have hated 'bad language', but that didn't stop her fun. Trying to convince her to eat a chocolate pudding while hospitalized received a loudly childish response, with the petulant stuck out lip: 'Tastes like ****.' She 'got me', even if it wasn't in the most politically correct of terms. In our correspondence spanning almost a decade, she always urged me to 'fight the good fight'. She was the original storyteller in our family. I miss her, so much that I can still summon her voice.

EQUIPMENT YOU WILL NEED

1 set of digital scales   1 standard cake tin

1 mixing bowl   1 butter knife

2 tablespoons   1 palette knife

1 silicone or wooden spoon   1 small bowl

1 sheet of kitchen roll paper   1 wire rack

INGREDIENTS

170 grams (6 ounces) of caster sugar

170 grams (6 ounces) of butter plus extra for greasing your cake tin with and to make the buttercream icing

170 grams (6 ounces) of self-raising flour

3 eggs

1 bottle of vanilla essence (you will only need a drop)

1 bag of edible lavender for baking with (you will need a tablespoon)

1 bag of icing sugar (3½ tablespoons)

1 tablespoon of cocoa powder

HOW TO MAKE
Pre-preparation
Using the digital scales and the mixing bowl, measure out the caster sugar and butter.

Method

1. Set your oven to 190°C/375°F and allow to heat up.

2. With the back of a tablespoon, cream together the butter and sugar in the mixing bowl. Set on the digital scales and then turn it on so it says the weight is at zero; next, measure out the flour. Add in the eggs and mix together with the silicone or wooden spoon. Add in a drop of vanilla essence and stir again. Then add in a tablespoon of the lavender and stir in once more.

3. Use the extra butter and kitchen roll paper to grease your cake tin; once you have done that, spoon in the cake mixture and bake until golden brown. Put a butter knife in the middle to test if cooked; if it comes out clean, it's safe to eat. This can take up to 45 minutes or longer, because everyone's oven is different.

4. Take the cake tin out of the oven and put on the wire rack. Gently take off the tin and use a palette knife to extract the bottom of the tin after about 10 minutes. Allow to completely cool.

5. While cooling, we are going to be making the icing. Use the **Basic Butter-cream Icing Mix** recipe to create your icing. This won't take very long; just add a tablespoon of the cocoa powder.

6. Once the cake has cooled, decorate the top and sides with the icing; spread over with the butter knife.

EXPAND YOUR REPERTOIRE

You could try flavouring the icing – such as with gin flavouring, strawberry flavouring or any other flavour that is available from most supermarkets. KitKats make an excellent decoration when stuck vertically around the edge of a cake. (Just stick with buttercream icing, to ensure they stay in place.)

GRANNY B'S PEANUT BUTTER COOKIES – BY TED AYRE

Duration: 30 minutes

Energy rating: Low

Skill level: Easy

To make when: you need a quick and easy recipe to give to an older relative at Christmas; it's raining outside and you have nothing else to do; you want to entertain visitors when you start to live independently. This recipe has a gentle flavour, so is suitable for sensory avoiders.

Ted Ayre is an admin manager for the National Health Service (NHS) and was recently diagnosed with autism spectrum condition (ASC) through an occupational health referral.

EQUIPMENT YOU WILL NEED

1 set of digital scales

Bowls for the individual ingredients

1 baking tray

1 roll of greaseproof paper

1 silicone or wooden spoon

1 electric mixer (or a bowl and whisk to do this manually)

1 tablespoon

1 fork

INGREDIENTS

115 grams (4 ounces) of salted butter or margarine

115 grams (4 ounces) of crunchy peanut butter

115 grams (4 ounces) of brown sugar

115 grams (4 ounces) of white caster sugar

2 eggs

285 grams (10 ounces) of self-raising flour

HOW TO MAKE
Pre-preparation
Using the digital scales and bowls, measure out all of your ingredients separately and set aside for later.

Method

1. Set your oven to 170°C fan/375°F, and cover your baking tray in greaseproof paper. (This will mean that your cookies will not stick to the tray once baked.)

2. Using the silicone spoon, mix both types of butter and sugar, as well as the eggs, together.

3. Next add in the flour and mix until all ingredients are combined.

4. Using the spoon, scoop out a small bit of mixture and place on the baking tray. Flatten with the fork on top so that there is an imprint of lines. Do this for all of the mixture, but make sure to leave enough space in between, as these cookies will spread and expand while baking.

5. Bake for 15 minutes, or until they begin to look golden brown.

EXPAND YOUR REPERTOIRE
Dried nuts or fruit add an extra layer of texture and could provide sensory feedback; add these at step 3. If you prefer cookies to be smooth, make sure you use smooth peanut butter. Slightly overcooking these cookies by up to two minutes will also add an extra 'crunch'.

MADEIRA CAKE POP STICKS

Duration: 1 hour and 25 minutes
Energy rating: Moderate
Skill level: Easy
To make when: you are hosting some sort of party and need to create 'party favours'; you're hosting a hen do or a baby shower; there's a night in on the cards; when it's raining outside and there's nowhere to go.

Sometimes cake can be a bit sickly in too great a quantity; a cake pop solves this problem fairly well, and can even be colour-coordinated for events, such as if you want to create an arrangement to be mounted on a table, similar to a pot plant. This needs an element of hand preparation when constructing with the 'pop', so it might not be the best for sensory avoiders. As a potential solution, gloves that are appropriate for dealing with food could be worn.

EQUIPMENT YOU WILL NEED

1 pair of scissors

1 roll of greaseproof paper

2 small baking trays

2 cooling wire racks

1 kettle

2 saucepans

3 small mixing bowls of around a similar size

A handful of cake pop sticks (not lolly sticks)

1 tablespoon

INGREDIENTS

1 Madeira cake – around 300 grams (10.5 ounces)

2 packs of the same cooking chocolate – these are usually each around 200 grams (7 ounces)

Optional: a selection of icing pens for decoration

1 pack of butter (start with a knob of butter and add more if needed)

HOW TO MAKE
Pre-preparation

Take out the icing pens and put them in a warm place for later; this will make the process of decoration a lot easier. Do the same for the butter; this will make it easier to cut later on. Using the scissors, cut two pieces of greaseproof paper out to fit and cover the baking trays. Put the wire cooling rack on top; this will stop the cake pop dripping and making it messy while in the fridge.

Method

1. Boil water in the kettle to start making the cake pops. We will be using the method of bain-marie to start melting the chocolate and butter. In the saucepans, add the boiled water, and then place the bowls into the sauce-pans, just so the bottom starts to heat up. Add the butter and chocolate separately to each so they begin to melt. This will take around 10 minutes.

2. While this is happening, slowly begin to break up the Madeira cake into small pieces; do not make into crumbs.

3. Once the butter has melted, combine with the Madeira cake pieces. They will slowly bond together; roll around to create small balls, and then poke the stick in to create the 'pop'.

4. Dunk the 'pop' (the Madeira cake butter ball) in the melted chocolate to cover it all over. Prop up on the wire rack; continue until all ingredients are used up, and then put in the fridge for the chocolate to set.

5. Optional step: Once the chocolate has hardened, decorate with the icing pens.

EXPAND YOUR REPERTOIRE

If this is for a themed celebration – such as a bridal party or a baby shower – think about the colours that go with that. (On this occasion it would be probably pink, blue, white.) Most shops sell a wide range of different-coloured cooking chocolate. You could also experiment with dyeing the Madeira cake with food colouring, just for an added 'oomph'.

CHOCOLATE-COVERED STRAWBERRIES FOR TWO

Duration: 1 hour and 20 minutes (includes setting time)
Energy rating: Low
Skill level: Easy
To make when: it's a special occasion – like a bridal party, Christmas Day, baby shower, on receiving good exam results; there's a sleepover happening; just 'because'.

Chocolate-covered strawberries have been a huge fixture in my family for so many years now; I have lost count of how many times we have eaten this dessert, or even when and how it began.

One of my favourite Christmases will always be when, for breakfast, my mother presented me and my sister both with a glass pot that was stacked to the top with chocolate-covered strawberries; it was a breakfast of kings! This is one of my favourite recipes for this reason; it was just the three of us, united by something very simple. This recipe can be fiddly, and also opens up a range of textures and other sensory input. If you are a sensory avoider, wear disposable gloves for this.

EQUIPMENT YOU WILL NEED

1 chopping board

1 chopping knife

1 mixing bowl (needs to rest inside the saucepan)

1 roll of greaseproof paper

2 baking trays

1 kettle

1 saucepan

1 silicone or wooden spoon

1 fork

INGREDIENTS

1 box of strawberries (227 grams or 8 ounces is the average size)

2 bars of cooking chocolate (bars are usually 150 or 200 grams) – vegan cooking chocolate is available

HOW TO MAKE
Pre-preparation
Using the chopping board and sharp knife, chop up all of the strawberries and set aside; if you are a sensory avoider, chop them into quarters, as the smaller the piece is, the easier it will be to cope with. Break up the chocolate and also set aside; this is just to make it melt more easily and can be done roughly. Cover the baking trays with the greaseproof paper; this will protect the trays from any dripping chocolate sticking, which is difficult to remove.

Method

1. Boil the kettle; we are going to be using the process of bain-marie to melt the chocolate, to dip the strawberries in. Once this is boiled, pour into the saucepan, and place the mixing bowl on top.

2. Add all of the chocolate to the mixing bowl; the boiled water underneath will begin to melt it into a gooey liquid. Use the non-stick spoon to stir every 2 minutes, in order to prevent burning.

3. Use the fork to spear a piece of strawberry. Dunk into the chocolate, to cover the strawberry all over. Then ease off on to the baking tray. Repeat until all strawberry pieces are covered.

4. Put in the fridge to set the chocolate to harden. This can take up to an hour; once that is done, enjoy!

EXPAND YOUR REPERTOIRE
If you're really good with your decoration skills, you could try melting two different types of chocolate; you could experiment by creating patterns, or just different combinations of chocolate. You could also use food colouring to dye white cooking chocolate other colours, which would be great if a special occasion has a specific colour scheme. Most supermarkets also stock a range of icing pens, or even edible glitter; you can use all of these options to decorate your strawberries!

CHOCOLATE LOG FOR FOUR PEOPLE

Duration: 1 hour
Energy rating: Moderate
Skill level: Medium
To make when: you need a dessert for Christmas Day – such as if seeing
                    relatives, or if there is a party or gathering; just 'because'; as
                    an alternative to a birthday cake. (It's true – there are people
                    who don't like cake.)

A chocolate log was one of my favourite desserts as a child, and we'd only really have it around Christmas time; after the Christmas dinner had been eaten, this was my favourite part of the meal. Although this is a 'cheat' version – in that we won't be creating the actual log from scratch – this is still perfectly valid, as well as being budget-friendly, too.

EQUIPMENT YOU WILL NEED

2 mixing bowls   1 saucepan

1 pair of scissors   1 silicone or wooden spoon

1 roll of greaseproof paper   1 butter knife

1 baking tray   1 tablespoon

1 kettle

INGREDIENTS

1 pack of butter (you will use   1 plain Swiss roll
a quater of the pack)
                                  Optional: Christmas-related
1 bar of cooking chocolate   cake decorations, such as a
(200 grams/7 ounces)   robin, to create a Christmas
                                  scene on top of the chocolate
1 bag of icing sugar (you will   log
only need 3½ tablespoons)

1 tub of cocoa powder
(1 tablespoon is needed)

HOW TO MAKE
Pre-preparation

Take out the butter and leave to soften up at room temperature; being more malleable will mean it's easier to create the buttercream icing. Roughly break up the chocolate bar into small pieces and set aside for later. This will make it a lot easier to work with. Using the scissors, cut out a square of greaseproof paper to fit the baking tray; this will prevent the chocolate from sticking to it, and is generally a good executive functioning hack to always remember.

Method

1. Boil water in the kettle. We'll be using the process of bain-marie to melt the cooking chocolate, in order to flavour the buttercream icing later on. Pour the water into the saucepan, place the mixing bowl on the top and then add the chocolate into the bowl. The boiled water will begin to slowly melt the cooking chocolate. Stir every 3–4 minutes with the non-stick spoon to prevent burning.

2. Using the spoon, cream together the butter and the icing sugar. (Should be to a rough ratio of 1:2, to create the sweet taste – see the **Basic Buttercream Icing Mix** recipe.) Add in a tablespoon of cocoa powder and keep creaming together in order to create the buttercream icing.

3. Once you have completed step 2, pour the melted chocolate into the butter mixture. Stir. Take out the Swiss roll and put it on the baking tray you prepared earlier. Use the butter knife to cover with the buttercream icing you prepared earlier; the ridges on the knife will create a log-like texture. Cover both ends. Put in the fridge so the icing sets.

4. Optional step: once you have covered the log in the buttercream icing, add decorations to the top of the log. You could create a Christmas scene with the various decorations that are available in supermarkets. Sprinkle a small amount of icing sugar on top to look like snow.

EXPAND YOUR REPERTOIRE

Once you have covered the Swiss roll in the icing, you could dribble across another colour of just chocolate; white cooking chocolate could be used, for example, to create a snowy scene. You could also cover the top of the log with something like small fudge pieces, edible glitter, honeycomb pieces – there is a range of potential decorations you could use. Go completely wild with your decorative equipment – there is a huge range of items available. Icing pens are also a bonus, such as for lettering, patterns and more.

FRUIT CRUMBLE – BY VERA, AKA HAPPY AUTISTIC LADY

Duration:	1 hour
Energy rating:	Low
Skill level:	Easy
To make when:	you need a dessert for a special occasion, such as a birthday; you have been asked to contribute food at a family gathering, such as when there is an anniversary; the weather has become more autumnal and you need a dessert for the season.

Vera describes herself as a 'nature nerd', as well as being 'proudly autistic'. She was diagnosed while studying for her BSc in Biology, later going on to complete a MSc in Geographical Information Science. She has since started a job in the environmental sector.

Please note that while this is recipe is for sensory seekers in its current form, there is a note at the end as to how to adapt this for sensory avoiders.

EQUIPMENT YOU WILL NEED

1 chopping board	1 set of digital scales
1 chopping knife	1 mixing bowl
1 butter knife	1 ovenproof dish
Optional: 1 potato peeler (if you use apples, this may be advisable for sensory avoiders)	1 wooden or silicone spoon

INGREDIENTS

100 grams (3.5 ounces) of plain flour/all-purpose flour	50 grams (1.5 ounces) of granulated sugar

50 grams (1.5 ounces) of butter	400 grams (14 ounces) of assorted fruit (apples work well throughout the year; however, rhubarb, raspberries and blackberries also work well)

HOW TO MAKE
Pre-preparation
Take the butter out of the fridge to begin to warm up to the temperature of the room. Cut up all of the fruit into small cubes and set aside for later. (If the fruit is quite hard, simmer in a saucepan of boiling water and a dab of butter to soften it.)

Method

1. Mix together all of the ingredients (except the fruit) in the mixing bowl, using the silicone or wooden spoon to do so. It should eventually have the texture of breadcrumbs – not too fine but still fully combined all together. If it looks too stiff and is not mixing well, add a splash of water and continue mixing.

2. Add your fruit to the ovenproof dish; this will be the base of the crumble.

3. Sprinkle over the mix of the dry ingredients that you made in step 1.

4. Set your oven to 180°C/350°F and allow to heat up. Bake in the oven for 30–40 minutes. (You can check if it is cooked in between by inserting a butter knife; if it comes out clear, then it's cooked.) Allow to cool for 10 minutes when you take it out of the oven. When it comes to serving, you have a variety of options – you can eat it hot or cold, with custard or ice cream.

EXPAND YOUR REPERTOIRE
Adding spices to the fruit can add an additional layer of sensory input – try to think in terms of combinations of flavours that would go well with the fruit you have used in the crumble. Cinnamon or lemon goes well with various apple varieties, ginger goes well with raspberry; there are several options you could try experimenting with. If you are a sensory avoider, you can try modifying this by making the fruit into a purée beforehand, as well as having a smaller layer of the actual crumble.

CHOCOLATE CEREAL BARS

Duration: 1 hour and 30 minutes

Energy rating: Low

Skill level: Easy

To make when: it's a rainy day, and you are grounded inside, bored with nothing to do; you are seeing younger relatives, such as younger children; for an occasion like Christmas (chop up the bars small and put in a pretty cellophane bag for your relatives); you need to get rid of a few ingredients prior to going food shopping.

When I was very little, this was a recipe that was strategically deployed at various intervals, probably as a great distraction device. But this is really adaptable – you can even make it so it's in the shape of an animal, for example – and is suitable for a wide range of ages, too. Besides, no one is ever going to say no to a chocolatey treat if you offer it to them!

EQUIPMENT YOU WILL NEED

1 mixing bowl

1 kettle

1 saucepan

1 baking tray

1 roll of greaseproof paper

1 silicone or wooden spoon

1 fork

INGREDIENTS

2 bars of cooking chocolate (200 grams/7 ounces)

75 grams (2.5 ounces) of cereal of your choice

Optional: for extra sensory input, you could also use a pinch of popping candy (only suitable for sensory seekers)

HOW TO MAKE
Pre-preparation
Break up the cooking chocolate roughly into smaller chunks and set aside for later; this will make it easier to work with later on, as well as speeding up the process of bain-marie when it comes to the melting. Cut out the greaseproof paper to cover the baking tray and also set aside for later.

Method

1. The cereal of your choice will be bound together with chocolate melted by the process of bain-marie, which has been used throughout this book. Using the kettle, boil up some water and pour into the saucepan. Add the mixing bowl on top.

2. Pour in the chocolate to the mixing bowl. The boiling water sitting below it in the saucepan will begin to slowly melt it. Using the non-stick spoon, stir at regular intervals to prevent burning.

3. Once melted, add in the cereal and stir! Coat all of the cereal with the chocolate. (If you are using the optional popping candy, add this in now, too, and stir in evenly.)

4. Pour the mix into the baking tray with the greaseproof paper you prepared earlier. Use a spoon to squish down without crushing the cereal. Leave in your fridge to set, then chop up into the portion sizes you'd like from the tray to enjoy. (This would make multiple serving portions for my little family.)

EXPAND YOUR REPERTOIRE
You can experiment with the binding agent that holds the cereal together. Melting marshmallows is one possible way and could turn this into a snack just right for Halloween. (You could even add on scary faces, complete with goggly eyes! Just crack out the icing pen.) You can also add in other ingredients like small pieces of fudge to the actual bar itself, too. Honeycomb pieces are also great for extra sensory input. Smarties are a great decorative tool – you could even use them to create a miniature snowman; just melt some extra white chocolate, cover the top, and draw the relevant features with an icing pen. The Smarties would act as the button on the 'tummy' of the snowman or could even be eyes. Think about what you could serve this with. You could present this to older relatives as a Christmas present; cut up the bar into smaller, bite-sized chunks and serve in a pretty cellophane bag. If you're hosting a party, you could serve it with fruit, and dribble chocolate over both in a slightly whacky geometric fashion; the possibilities are endless!

CONVENTIONAL AUTUMN CRUMBLE FOR FOUR TO SIX PEOPLE

Duration: 45 minutes to 1 hour
Energy rating: Low
Skill level: Easy
To make when: you need to entertain family relatives – such as if they have
                     driven a long way to see you to stay over for the weekend;
                     your housemates have all decided to stay in for the evening
                     and you need a pudding of some sort.

We have already had a crumble recipe in this book, but this is a slightly more elaborate version, and it is also a bit more seasonally specific. It is also a smell I strongly associate with my childhood.

This recipe has a hands-on element, so sensory avoiders may wish to use disposable gloves.

EQUIPMENT YOU WILL NEED

1 butter knife

1 mixing bowl

1 set of digital scales

1 ceramic baking dish

1 piece of kitchen roll paper

1 tablespoon

1 silicone or wooden spoon

INGREDIENTS

250 grams (9 ounces) of butter plus a little extra to grease your ceramic baking dish

4 tablespoons of plain flour/ all-purpose flour

1 bag of frozen blackberries and raspberries

2 pinches of brown sugar

HOW TO MAKE
Pre-preparation
Take the butter out of your fridge and allow to come to room temperature; this will make it easier to work with in the long run. Chop up into rough small chunks and put it all in the mixing bowl; measure out the flour and also add to the mixing bowl. Grease your ceramic baking dish with a little butter on the kitchen paper. Put the fruit into it.

Method
1. Set your oven to 180°C/350°F and allow to heat up.

2. Rub together the flour and the butter together to get a crumb-like mixture; this can take up to 10 minutes and will be the top of your crumble. Spread it evenly on top of the fruit, covering the fruit completely.

3. Sprinkle 2 pinches of brown sugar across the top of the crumble. Bake for 30 minutes or until golden brown.

EXPAND YOUR REPERTOIRE
Try sprinkling other things on top of the crumble in addition to or instead of the sugar; desiccated coconut is one thing you could try! Porridge oats could also make a healthier mix during step 2: replace half of the flour with the oats.

MARSHMALLOW SANDWICHES FOR SIX PEOPLE

Duration:	10 minutes
Energy rating:	Moderate
Skill level:	Easy
To make when:	you need a small snack that is low-energy to make and budget-friendly to serve several people at once; the season is turning to autumn and Halloween is on the way; you need a sociable task for people to get involved with.

American readers may know this recipe as a s'more; as a child, this was a task while away on a social weekend with people at a club I attended. If you need an activity to distract people to conserve your energy, such as if you are hosting a small get-together, this is the ideal recipe for that. This recipe is for six people, but it can be adapted accordingly. I prefer the title of sandwich, simply because you can sandwich pretty much anything between two biscuits – there are also endless ways to expand this recipe, particularly if you have an artistic side.

Note: if you are a vegan, make sure that you use vegan marshmallows. They are available at most supermarkets – and it means you won't miss out.

This recipe makes 18 sandwiches, so there should be three sandwiches for each person eating.

EQUIPMENT YOU WILL NEED

1 pack of matches – or a rechargeable lighter

6 tealight candles

6 skewers

6 plates for serving

6 pieces of kitchen roll

1 chopping board

1 chopping knife

INGREDIENTS

1 large packet of marshmallows (vegan and vegetarian types of marshmallows are available)

2 packets of biscuits of your choice

HOW TO MAKE
Pre-preparation

Count out 3 marshmallows, 1 tea light candle and 6 biscuits for each individual who will be eating this dessert. There are no other steps you need to prepare for this, as this is one of the simplest recipes you will ever come across.

Method – how to make 1 sandwich

1. Using the matches or lighter, light a tea light. This will be the flame that you melt your marshmallow on in just a minute.

2. Stab the marshmallow on to the skewer and hold above the flame. It will gradually begin to toast and you will see the colour of its skin change slowly.

3. Sandwich the marshmallow between 2 biscuits and gradually ease it off the skewer. Using the chopping board and knife, chop it in half.

4. Repeat the process so that everyone has 3 biscuit sandwiches each.

EXPAND YOUR REPERTOIRE

If you have a sweet tooth, you could create more of a dessert dish; you could serve this with ice-cream sauce in a funky pattern.

The sandwiches can be dipped into melted chocolate and allowed to set, and you could decorate the top in whatever way you wish. If you are looking after younger children – for example, if you are babysitting – you could get them involved with icing pens and stick-on edible eyes in order to create the faces of animals. You could also dip into the chocolate to create more of a sweet 'lolly' that will not melt.

GLUTEN-FREE, MILK-FREE, PEANUT BUTTER OATMEAL COOKIES – BY MIRANDA DRESSLER

Duration:	45 minutes to 1 hour
Energy rating:	Moderate
Skill level:	Medium
To make when:	you need to undertake some self-care – baking can be a form of that; you feel like you need a snack; you need to serve a dessert option to a wide variety of individuals of varying ages.

Miranda Dressler is an artist working in animation and product design in Los Angeles. Miranda is also known for the Wrong Planet comic on Instagram. She was diagnosed as autistic in 2017. Her hobby is baking cookies; she is coeliac, and making the traditional cookie recipe gluten-free is a challenge willingly taken on.

Editor's note: this recipe can be frozen – so if you need to store any cookies, put them in your freezer for another time. Miranda also recommends using a spring-loaded cookie scoop (in the UK this is sometimes referred to as an ice-cream scoop). This means the individual making this recipe can avoid direct contact with the dough, if this is a potential sensory issue.

EQUIPMENT YOU WILL NEED

1 set of digital scales

2 mixing bowls

1 fork

1 ice-cream scoop (known as a spring-loaded cookie scoop in the US and other places)

1 small bowl

1 roll of plastic wrap (in the UK this is called clingfilm)

1 baking tray

1 roll of greaseproof paper

1 wire rack

INGREDIENTS

240 grams (8.5 ounces) of crunchy peanut butter

100 grams (3.5 ounces) of brown sugar

1 tablespoon of molasses*

1 egg

½ a teaspoon of vanilla extract

1 teaspoon of baking soda

½ a teaspoon of cinnamon

60 grams (2 ounces) of old-fashioned rolled oats

140 grams (5 ounces) of dairy-free chocolate chips

*This is not always vegan, due to the production process.

HOW TO MAKE
Pre-preparation

Using your digital weighing scales, weigh out all of the 'wet' and 'dry' ingredients separately. This will be handy for later on; while doing this, combine all of the dry ingredients into one mixing bowl. Prepare the baking tray by covering with greaseproof paper.

Method

1. Using a fork, beat the egg in the small bowl until the yolk is broken up fully. Add the egg to the bowl of other wet ingredients. Once you have done that, add the dry ingredients to the same bowl.

2. Fold in the chocolate chips to the mix. Cover the bowl with plastic wrap and put in the fridge to chill for 35 minutes. (This will make the cookies chewy and fluffy when it comes to eating.)

3. Heat your oven to 180°C/350°F. Use the cookie scoop to scoop out the dough and place on the baking tray; when you do this, press down gently with the back of the scoop to create a criss-cross pattern. There should only be 8 cookies on the baking tray.

4. Bake for up to 10 minutes; check in regularly to prevent burning.

5. Remove from the oven and allow to cool for 10 minutes on a wire rack; but first whack the cookie sheet on your kitchen top counter to prevent air bubbles.

EXPAND YOUR REPERTOIRE

Chocolate chips are optional; not everyone likes them. However, you could combine and mix them up – such as white or milk chocolate or both together in one deliciously chocolatey combination. Instead of peanut butter, you could try using a spread such as Biscoff.

HOT CHOCOLATE CHRISTMAS HOLIDAY FLAVOUR BOMB SHAKERS

Duration: 2 hours and 30 minutes
Energy rating: High
Skill level: Medium
To make when: you need to give someone like your grandparents a Christmas present and you aren't sure what to give them – because this is the sort of person who 'has everything'; you're seeing a friend you haven't seen in a long time during the colder months; you need to create a housewarming gift.

Christmas – or the holidays – is a time of lights, delicious food, glitter and, well, family. It can be a time that may well be fraught for autistic people – as there is a lot to contend with, such as changes in routine, new foods, social expectations that aren't explicit and so much more.

Hot chocolate stirrers are often on sale around this time of year – and they can even be adapted into other forms, including decorative truffles. These have something of a 'flavour bomb' in the middle. This serves six people in total.

EQUIPMENT YOU WILL NEED

1 mixing bowl

1 baking tray

1 roll of greaseproof paper

1 kettle

1 saucepan

1 tablespoon

1 silicone or wooden spoon

spherical-shaped chocolate mould, 12 half spheres are needed to create 6 of the 'flavour bombs' in total

---

INGREDIENTS

300 grams (10.5 ounces) of
cooking chocolate

1 tub of cocoa powder

1 bottle of peppermint
flavouring (you will need a
few drops)

Optional: a selection of icing
pens in the colours of your
choice

HOW TO MAKE
Pre-preparation

Break the chocolate into smaller chunks, as this will make it easier to work
with later on. Put it in the mixing bowl and set it aside for later. Prepare the
baking tray by covering with greaseproof paper.

Method

1. Boil the water in the kettle, put in the saucepan and heat up on your hob
   with the heat set to halfway. It should be bubbling slowly, not aggressively;
   rest the mixing bowl with the chocolate inside the pan. It will begin to melt;
   keep stirring with the silicone spoon.

2. Once all the chocolate is melted, add to the moulds; this will form the base
   of the chocolate shaker. As soon as all moulds are filled, put in the fridge
   to set. This should take 45 minutes to 1 hour; however, this can vary from
   fridge to fridge.

3. Once the moulds are set with the chocolate, gently pop them out. You need
   two to create one stirrer; fill one up halfway with the cocoa powder. Repeat
   the same process for each pair that will create each stirrer. Add a drop of
   the peppermint flavouring in the middle of the shell with the cocoa powder
   in it; this will be the 'flavour bomb'.

4. Seal them up using either the icing or melted chocolate; dribble on the
   edge, and place the not filled half on top. Set again in your fridge on the
   baking tray you covered with the baking tray paper earlier. This can take
   up to 45 minutes.

5. This should eventually be set in place. Decorate with the icing pens once that is the case, and then put back once again to set more, for up to half an hour. Serve these with a mug; pour in the boiling water to begin the melting to create your hot chocolate. Gently shake it around the base of your mug with a spoon to make sure it melts, in order to create your hot chocolate.

EXPAND YOUR REPERTOIRE

Experimenting with different flavours of cooking chocolate can dramatically change the flavour of your beverage in the end; you could also consider adding tiny pieces of fudge or even chocolate chips into the chocolate shells prior to sealing them up. You could also consider converting the chocolate stirrer (the overall product) into a chocolate truffle, or even adding cake into the middle of it before sealing up, for a more moreish type of dessert to eat.

RUDOLPH THE RED-NOSED REINDEER ICE-CREAM SUNDAE

Duration: 15 minutes
Energy rating: Low
Skill level: Medium
To make when: you are entertaining at Christmas time – for example, you have relatives visiting for the first time; there is a friendly gathering – such as a party among friends; you need to entertain younger relatives.

Working with ice cream you already have is quite simple – and you just need a few things to make it seasonally appropriate. Sundaes are one of my favourite treats – and this can suit a wide range of ages and social contexts, too. This serves one person – just scale up to make more if needed.

EQUIPMENT YOU WILL NEED

1 ice-cream scoop
1 cocktail glass (to serve in)
1 teaspoon

INGREDIENTS

2 icing pens – in black and white

1 Curly Wurly chocolate bar

1 packet of Smarties (you will need 1 red Smartie, or an alternative is any red round sweet)

1 tub of chocolate ice cream (vegan brands are available) (you will need 2 scoops)

1 pair of edible googly eyes

1 pot of brown sprinkles (known as chocolate vermicelli)

HOW TO MAKE
Pre-preparation
Bring out the icing pens so that they warm up to room temperature; this will make them a lot easier to work with when it comes to creating the face of the reindeer. Break up the Curly Wurly bar so that two pieces can be used as antlers. Open your packet of Smarties and find a red one for later. Count out two eyes for later, too. Sometimes ice cream takes a while to be malleable enough to get out of the tub – so extra time has been built in for this reason. Ice cream obviously melts really fast – so working quickly is most important when preparing this recipe.

Method
1. Using the ice-cream scoop, scoop out one large serving of ice cream into the glass. This will be the body of your reindeer. Add a smaller scoop on top to be the head of the reindeer.

2. Stick the Curly Wurly pieces on either side of the 'head' of the reindeer to create the antlers. Add the two eyes and the red Smartie (nose) to create the face.

3. Draw a smile with the black icing pen and outline the eyes with the white icing pen. Sprinkle all over with brown sprinkles to create the appearance of fur. Enjoy!

EXPAND YOUR REPERTOIRE
You could use moulds for a more ambitious take on this very simple recipe; using the process of bain-marie, you could melt chocolate and create a mould this way. Hiding ice cream underneath it could mean the person eating could pour on something like hot fudge sauce, in order to reveal the ice cream under-neath. You can put faces on the chocolate mould by using icing pens and edible eyes. (Just make sure you use enough icing from the icing pen to make it sticky enough.) Using that process, you could also make several other animals – a polar bear, for example. Try changing up the brands of ice cream you use as well – you could have a salted caramel flavour reindeer. There is also edible glitter that you could sprinkle all over, to give the sundae a more 'Christmas' feel. (Because if Christmas is about one thing, it has got to be glitter, right?!)

FRUIT PASTRY PLAIT

Duration: 45 minutes
Energy rating: Moderate
Skill level: Medium
To make when: you have been asked to bring a dessert to an event – such as if you are at a wedding or a party for a significant birthday; extended family is assembling for Christmas dinner; you go back home weekly for a family dinner (we have weekly Sunday roasts in my family).

'Plaits' usually get a bad reputation for being too complex and, frankly, exhausting to make; besides, what is the point in taking so long in making something if it will just be gone in seconds and not really appreciated for its appearance? This is a kind of 'cheat version', to make a fruit-flavoured version – and is also adaptable to sensory needs, too.

EQUIPMENT YOU WILL NEED

1 small bowl   1 roll of greaseproof paper

1 empty water bottle   1 silicone brush

1 fork   1 teaspoon

1 baking tray   1 rolling pin

INGREDIENTS

1 egg   Plain flour/all-purpose flour

Salt   1 sheet of ready rolled puff

1 bag of frozen, pre-prepared   pastry (in the UK you get 1
fruit of your choice   sheet per packet)

HOW TO MAKE
Pre-preparation

In the smaller bowl, crack open the egg; use the empty water bottle to suck out the yolk and discard (you can find videos online showing how this is done). Add in 2 pinches of salt to the egg white and mix together with a fork; this will be your egg glaze for later. Take the fruit out of the fridge and break up into whole pieces of each individual fruit if it is all stuck together. Cover your baking tray in a sheet of greaseproof paper for baking later on. Finally, open up the packaging of the pre-rolled pastry.

Method

1. Set your oven to 180°C/350°F and allow to heat up.

2. Sprinkle a pinch of flour across your work surface and on to your rolling pin. This is to stop your pastry sticking to it in the next step; this also plays a part in it cracking less easily. (Sometimes I prefer to use the spoon, just to keep things a bit tidier; this may be useful if you experience issues with interoception.)

3. Now, get your pastry out to roll out; this should be one nice sheet that is rolled out around a centimetre thick. Imagine that this is in thirds, horizontally across the pastry. In the second third, add your frozen fruit, leaving around an inch at the edges.

4. Fold the pastry over like a sausage roll and wrap it up. Using the brush and egg mix from earlier, cover the top in a sticky layer. Now, put it on the baking tray.

5. Bake for 20 minutes, or until the pastry goes golden brown.

EXPAND YOUR REPERTOIRE

If you wish to add to your own skill set, it may be worth the challenge of creating your own pastry; however, this is a more adaptable version for people who may experience challenges when it comes to executive functioning. You could always use fresh fruit – however, take into consideration that some fruit, such as strawberries, can be very watery. (Peaches may be a good option to begin with.) You could always try making the **Brown Sugar and Cinnamon Apple Slices** from earlier in this part, and adding into the middle as well. For a more stylized finish, try crimping the edges of the plait when sealing it up.

DECORATIVE MARZIPAN MUSHROOMS (CAKE TOPPERS OR INDIVIDUALLY EATEN)

Duration: 1 hour and 15 minutes
Energy rating: Moderate
Skill level: Complex
To make when: it's Christmas time; you need a quick gift to make for older relatives or for someone when you aren't quite sure what to give them; when it's a 'special interest day' (more on that in just a moment); as a cake topper.

While writing this book, I often saw other autistic individuals posting online at times about their special interest – namely, mushrooms of every shape, size and possible origin. I can't claim to understand this – but mushrooms and photos of mushrooms have popped up frequently on my social media feeds. They still do. So, here's how to make a decorative marzipan mushroom, suitable as a cake topper – or it can be eaten solo. Please note that this recipe is very tactile – and to make this accessible, you could use a pair of disposable gloves when working directly with the marzipan. This recipe is marked as complex; although there is no baking or cooking, it requires fine motor skills to assemble the mushroom. Additional time has been built into this recipe for this reason, as this is quite often something autistic individuals can struggle with.

EQUIPMENT YOU WILL NEED

1 butter knife
2 mixing bowls
1 wire rack tray

Optional: 1 pair of disposable gloves
1 fork
1 silicone or wooden spoon

INGREDIENTS

1 packet of marzipan (500 grams or 17.5 ounces)

A selection of icing pens in various different colours of your own choosing

2 bottles of food colouring of your own choosing (you will need a couple of drops)	1 bottle of vanilla essence (you will need a couple of drops)

Most marzipan available in supermarkets is vegan- and vegetarian-friendly, but check that the brand you are using does not contain eggs.

For traditional mushroom colours, I'd use red for the mushroom top and keep the base (stem) plain.

HOW TO MAKE
Pre-preparation
Allow the marzipan to warm up to room temperature; this will make it a lot easier to work with.

Method

1. Use the butter knife to roughly divide the packet of marzipan into three different sections; being precise about this doesn't really matter. Put two of these slabs into separate mixing bowls, and set aside the third slab for later on.

2. Add a drop of one type of food colouring and one drop of the flavouring to one of the bowls; use the base of your hand to pummel the marzipan to mix the colouring into it. By the end, it should be dyed the colour of the food colouring. Do the same again with the other slab in the other bowl with the other bottle of food colouring.

3. Using the slab of marzipan we set aside earlier, begin to fashion (with your fingers) it into the base of the mushroom – the 'stem' that the mushroom head will sit on. This can be fiddly – make sure it's thick enough to support the top of the mushroom later on.

4. Fashion the top of the mushroom from one of the dyed slabs of marzipan by using your fingers. This can also be fiddly – and there is no real way to do this 'right'. Add the head to the stem you made in step 3 to assemble your mushroom. Repeat steps 3 and 4 until all of the marzipan has been used up.

5. Place all the mushrooms on the wire rack, and place in your fridge to set for up to 30 minutes.

6. Decoration time! Use your icing pens to decorate the tops of the mushrooms; you could add spots like a traditional red toadstool from a fairytale, or even use stripes. You could even attempt some piping.

EXPAND YOUR REPERTOIRE

There are various ways that you can expand this recipe if you want to practise other skills you may have or wish to refine. Using the process of bain-marie, you could melt cooking chocolate and dip the top of the mushroom in it to set for later. You could also dribble it across the top of the assembled mushroom. Supermarkets sell a host of different bottled flavours that you could try experimenting with. Edible glitter can be used for decorative purposes; if you had to create something for a child's birthday party – this could give the mushroom more of a 'magical toadstool' look.

CHAMELI'S COCONUT AND CHOCOLATE SPONGE CAKE

Duration: 1 hour and 30 minutes

Energy rating: High

Skill level: Complex

To make when: you need to bake a cake for a friend's birthday – and they have a 'sweet tooth'; when you need something for other celebrations such as Christmas, a significant anniversary or Diwali.

This recipe was inspired by Chameli Meir, sister to Dee – who is mentioned in the first part of this book. Chameli has a sense of mischief about her that meant we were instantly friends, as if we had known each other for many years; this was especially true when it came to delicious (probably unhealthy) snacks. Her eyes were exactly like those of a child let loose in a sweet shop! Whenever we speak – such as if one of us is in a foul mood – her solution is 'go out and eat cake!'. Note: in the UK most sugar brands are vegan, but this is not the case in the US. Make sure to always check the label. Some icing sugar brands are also not vegan-friendly due to their use of egg white; most are gluten free. Make sure to check the label on these ingredients before starting. Sensory avoiders may prefer to add the coconut on after they cut themselves a slice, or to go without.

EQUIPMENT YOU WILL NEED

1 set of digital scales	1 cake tin
1 mixing bowl	1 butter knife
2 tablespoons	1 palette knife
1 silicone or wooden spoon	1 wire rack
1 sheet of kitchen roll paper	1 small bowl

INGREDIENTS

170 grams (6 ounces) of caster sugar

170 grams (6 ounces) of butter plus extra for greasing your cake tin with and to make the buttercream icing

170 grams (6 ounces) of self-raising flour

3 eggs

1 bottle of coconut flavouring (you will only need a drop)

Cocoa powder (you will need 1 tablespoon)

1 bag of desiccated coconut (you will need 1 tablespoon)

Icing sugar

HOW TO MAKE
Pre-preparation
Using the digital scales and the mixing bowl, measure out the caster sugar and butter.

Method

1. Set your oven to 190°C/375°F and allow to heat up.

2. With the back of a tablespoon, cream together the butter and sugar in the mixing bowl. Set on the digital scales and then turn it on so it says the weight is at zero; next, measure out the flour. Add in the eggs and mix together with the silicone or wooden spoon. Add in a drop of the coconut flavouring, a tablespoon of cocoa powder and a tablespoon of desiccated coconut and stir once again.

3. Use the extra butter and sheet of kitchen roll paper to grease your cake tin; once you have done that, spoon in the cake mixture and bake it until golden brown. Put a butter knife in the middle to test if cooked; if it comes out clean, it's safe to eat. This can take up to 45 minutes or longer, because everyone's oven is different.

4. Take the cake tin out of the oven and put on the wire rack. Gently take off the tin and use a palette knife to extract the bottom of the tin after about 10 minutes. Allow to completely cool down before doing anything else.

5. While the cake is cooling, we are going to be making the icing. Use the **Basic Buttercream Icing Mix** recipe from earlier in this book to create your icing. Just add in an extra tablespoon of cocoa powder to make it into chocolate icing.

6. Once the sponge is fully cool, cover the top and sides with the buttercream icing by using the palette knife; sprinkle a pinch of the desiccated coconut on top to finish it off.

EXPAND YOUR REPERTOIRE

You could use two cake tins in order to make a bigger cake and sandwich them together; just make more icing to do that. For extra sensory input, consider adding in other things to the sponge; you could add in small pieces of honeycomb, popping candy or fudge (see the next recipe to make your own). Just make sure it is not too overpowering or you will lose the flavour of the coconut.

BASIC FUDGE MIX

Duration: 90 minutes to 2 hours
Energy rating: Moderate
Skill level: Medium
To make when: you want to practise a bit of self-care (cooking/baking definitely counts as self-care); you have guests visiting; there is a birthday or other celebration coming up – putting fudge in a nicely presented cellophane bag with a ribbon would make a lovely gift for older relatives.

Fudge seems to be a recurring food for a lot of autistic people – and I had some wonderful conversations with some interviewees who rhapsodized over the delicious substance, enough so it would make anyone's mouth water. It's quite sensory-friendly, too. This is a very basic recipe – and can be adapted to pretty much any preference going. Just bear in mind that it can be sticky and can become very sickly, quickly.

EQUIPMENT YOU WILL NEED

1 mixing bowl

1 roll of greaseproof paper

1 baking tray

1 saucepan

1 silicone or wooden spoon

1 tablespoon

INGREDIENTS

300 grams (10.5 ounces) of white cooking chocolate

150 grams (5 ounces) of condensed milk (from a 397 gram tin)

1 bottle of vanilla essence (you only need a drop)

A pinch of sea salt

HOW TO MAKE
Pre-preparation

Break up the chocolate bars into smaller pieces in the bowl; this will make it easier to work with when we begin melting it later on. Use the greaseproof paper to line the baking tray for later on; this will prevent the fudge sticking to it.

Method

1. Heat up your hob at the halfway point. Put the chocolate into the saucepan and stir it as it begins to heat up; it will start to turn into more of a liquid gradually.

2. Add the condensed milk and slowly stir in; you will notice that the mixture starts to become thicker and more sticky. Eventually, it should start to take more of a solid form; add a drop of the vanilla essence and stir in.

3. Use the silicone or wooden spoon to spread out the mix in the baking tray, on top of the greaseproof paper. Sprinkle a pinch of sea salt on the top of the fudge and allow to set in your fridge.

EXPAND YOUR REPERTOIRE

This is a really basic mix to start experimenting with – you can create a wide variety of different fudge flavours and types by using this basic mix. Most supermarkets sell small bottles of flavouring of the sort that you add to cake mixes, but you could easily add these to the fudge mix. (To repurpose!) Using food colouring could change the colour of the fudge – and if you are feeling very brave, you could try making rainbow fudge! Other things can be stirred into the fudge, too, such as small pieces of crumbled biscuit or chocolate chips. You could also decorate the top, with an icing pen, dusting glitter across the set top, adding sprinkles – there are many possibilities.

Ideas for Other Meals You Can Make

With the information in this book, you should have the basic information to experiment and adapt to your own sensory needs while cooking. These are just some ideas of meals you could adapt and experiment with, in order to further build up your skills.

Salad
Just cut up your favourite vegetables – peppers, lettuce, whatever. Cut into smaller pieces and keep all items separate if you are an avoider; consider adding extra flavouring if a sensory seeker. This could be lemon, lime, more traditional dressings such as when it comes to specific oils, vinegar, etc.

Jacket potatoes
These are probably one of the easiest meals to make – and you can dress them up or down however you like. They require minimal effort, not too many skills, and are quite easy to contend with when executive functioning becomes an issue. Toppings vary – a few have been suggested in the recipes in this book.

Curry
You can pretty much make most sorts of curries with the help of a blender; all you would then need to do is to heat it up and serve with rice and/or a flatbread.

Rice bowls
Rice does not take a lot of energy to prepare and is one of the quickest food types to make – but adding different spices, 'extras'

like bits of sausages or salad leaves, even pieces of paneer, can create a more substantial quick meal. I quite like salmon, flavoured with lemon and a chilli sauce, shredded into rice that has been flavoured with ground coriander and other spices.

Smoothies

Frozen fruit can save a lot of time and energy – something to keep in mind when you are autistic – just make sure you add enough banana and yogurt, as some fruits are water-based. (The more you add, the thicker it will be.) Orange juice or water helps to liquify this to a smoothie state. Or make a fruit milkshake by adding milk in the blender!

Wraps

You can buy them all ready and prepared – just add your favourite ingredients and wrap up. Just don't bulk it up too much as it will cause difficulties folding the wrap. Or – as in the recipe for the **Naan Hut Chicken Wrap** – you can always use a cocktail stick to do this for you. Just be careful you don't hurt yourself. Some supermarkets also sell pre-prepared wrap kits, too.

Couscous

Just add salad leaves with a little bit of dressing. It should take maybe five minutes, possibly longer if you need to wash the salad leaves. Couscous is very adaptable and can be used in multiple formats.

Sandwiches

If you like planning, you could try planning ahead of time to make bread. If not, you can get most elements of sandwiches in a supermarket. You can also be very elaborate with making sandwiches – such as by combining chicken, pieces of bell peppers, and more.

Lettuce boats

Essentially, the lettuce leaf is the 'boat' – and you can top with something like mince.

IDEAS FOR OTHER MEALS YOU CAN MAKE

Sweet potato fries

Cut a sweet potato into strips, lightly coat with oil and spices of your choice and slowly roast at 180°C/350°F. Try different oils and spices for different sensory input.

New potatoes

Boil new potatoes with mint leaves in the water, and serve with chilli mince (can be made with vegetarian/vegan alternatives) and salad. This is quite simple and can be made for either sensory seekers or sensory avoiders. If you hate salad, try serving with boiled vegetables instead.

Katsu curry

Katsu sauce can be found in most supermarkets, as well as the spice to cook with. Just be sparing in how much you use when cooking a piece of chicken and rice, as it can be a bit rich.

Salmon and salad

Bake the salmon in foil, having smothered it in lemon, parsley, mint and a teeny tiny amount of black pepper. The salad can have any dressing.

Lazy Susan

It's essentially a rotating circle with lots of different dishes – salad, pasta, anything you want. If executive functioning is not playing ball today, this is a great option to use.

Cheesy grilled toast

Cook in the oven and sprinkle a tiny amount of black pepper on top. You could also use a blow torch for quicker results, but that could pose motor skill difficulties. This is also really nice when you have come inside out of horrible weather, for example.

Bruschetta

Bruschetta is thick toasted bread with chopped tomatoes and other things on top of it. There are easy recipes available online.

Breakfast muffin

You can prepare the mix to construct this in advance. Robin Van Creveld, who was interviewed for this book, has a delicious recipe for breakfast muffins – and everyone should have a copy of his book *Man with a Pan*.

Vegetable tacos

You can buy the shells in a pre-prepared state. The 'guts' would just need to be heated over a hob, which should not take too long. Grab a saucepan, a dash of oil, some vegetarian mince, a spice of your choice and spring onions, and combine all together.

Soup

Always follow the instructions on the back of the packaging while making soup; you can also make soup with stock and almost any blended vegetables, too. The texture can range from smooth to chunky, and some are also meant to be served cold, too.

Panini

Just add the ingredients to a pre-bought roll and heat up.

A bacon, lettuce and tomato sandwich

Sometimes I am 'between' things in the evening – that period of time between finishing work and going out. Still hungry, you might just need something to eat quickly instead of a full meal, that can be prepared very quickly.

Pizza bases

There is a recipe in this book that will provide you with more details about this (see Fat Head Pizza Dough for Two). They are great for batch cooking.

Bread

Consider experimenting by adding in extras like walnuts or tiny pieces of onion for a more savoury flavour. Add toppings as well – sprinkling a tiny amount of black pepper, for example, can add an extra flavour. Just be sure to eat fairly soon. Recipes for bread can be found online.

Sauces

If you make sauce for a dish, such as if it is tomato based, it can usually be re-frozen for using on another day.

Ingredients and Their Alternatives for Allergies, Sensory Needs and More

When it comes to eating, what is not always taken into consideration is that there are other needs — those related to allergies or digestive issues, for example. In writing this, there were multiple requests from autistic individuals who have coeliac disease, as well as to cater for those who were vegetarian or vegan. A lot of the recipes in this book can be adapted if need be — the illustrations from the key indicate this, usually when all you would need to do is change an ingredient or two. It can take a bit of experimenting to find your rhythm with this, but having the information in one place should be useful. This is by no way a complete list; make sure you read the labels of brands you pick up in supermarkets when buying your food, too.

Eggs
Honey can be a great replacement when it comes to baking. (It depends on what you are making, however, as honey can burn quite quickly.) This could even be agave honey, if you are a vegan. Water can be used as a way to bind some recipes instead of eggs. Chickpea water, also known as aquafaba, can be used when it comes to making meringues.

Oil
If needed, replace with chia seeds or flax seeds. Mix with a few tablespoons of water to expand them. This only works for some particular dishes and baking recipes.

Flour

Until I started looking into it, I had no idea just how many different types of flour there are. They all have different functions depending on what recipe they are used for. There are particular brands that would be coeliac-friendly, as well as others for vegans and/or vegetarians. Just make sure to check the label when shopping. There are specific types such as almond flour; just be aware that some recipes cannot be adapted.

Marshmallows

There are vegan and vegetarian alternatives of marshmallows available in most supermarkets; just be aware that they may not be under the same title as 'marshmallows'.

Meat

When it comes to mince (ground meat), most supermarkets have alternatives that are vegetarian and vegan. If you are concerned about making the switch, remember to use liberal amounts of stock as flavouring, to mask if you think alternatives taste unpleasant. Traditional meat brands also offer products like meat-free sausages that are suitable for a range of dietary and sensory needs. Some recipes cannot always be adapted, however.

Milk

Oat or almond milk is a good replacement you can use, if you are vegan or need a dairy-free diet; most supermarkets now stock different options. Soy milk is also another possible alternative; just note that some vegans and some vegetarians do not eat soy-based products. Sometimes if a recipe says 'add milk' – for example, when creating a dough or a cake – you can usually use water instead.

Cheese

There are alternative brands available in supermarkets – essentially, cheese without the cheese! It's worth shopping around for alternatives.

Soy

Soy-based products are vegan and vegetarian, but there are concerns about the production of it and the impact of creating the soy. While the product itself is vegan, it's a matter of how much you wish to follow through with this.

Molasses

While this is vegan and vegetarian as a product, it is similar to soy in that some vegans will not eat it due to concerns about the production of it.

While this is by no means a complete list, it is always worth shopping around for alternative products; make sure to check labels, too. Some brands also now use the terms of vegan/vegetarian as a unique selling point, and this can easily be found on their packaging. Just take care to research before you buy.

Terminology, Decoded

To be on the autistic spectrum can be as if you have been transplanted to a country outside your homeland, but are expected to be fluent in all of the customs, culture, language. Making mistakes is seen as being the end of the world – and this unreasonable expectation is only matched by the knowledge that you are highly likely to be misunderstood at least from the moment you wake up. Yes, I went there; people ask me what it's like to be autistic, and this has been a metaphor I have heard for years from many autistic people. The world of cooking, baking and food preparation can seem like a strange and coded world. Language is fluid, ever changing – and can be difficult to interpret at times. Cooking and baking are imprecise – more an imperfect art than anything else. Compiled here are some expressions and phrases for ease of reference, especially if you have trouble understanding what is being asked of you.

A capful of...
This usually applies to adding liquid, quite often when it is being added to dry ingredients. A capful is a literal direction: take the cap off the bottle of liquid, add some of the liquid to the cap, then add to your ingredients. Of course, a cap can vary by size depending on the bottle you are using at the time.

A knob of...
This is usually used for essential items such as butter. It's a small amount of butter just chopped off the corner or the end of a packet – and is usually smaller than your thumb or finger.

A dab of...

I like to think of this as when you dab at a child's face to clean them up, when they are very little and have just finished eating. It's kind of the same gesture when it comes to cooking – to dab something on.

A dollop of...

This usually means a spoonful of liquid, or a spoonful of a soft cooking dough that you put on a baking tray.

A drizzle of...

This usually applies to if you are using something like olive oil when it comes to roasting – it means to distribute some of the oil from the bottle across whatever it is you are cooking.

A medium heat

Generally speaking, this is used when heating something in a saucepan over a heat on a hob or stove. The heat indicated by a dial or button can be mostly divided into three parts – small, medium, large. (Yes, it makes no sense.) The small heat is the first third, the medium the second, and so forth. If you have a gas hob with a flame, the size of the flame will change as well. A medium heat on a hob is usually halfway up the dial.

A pinch of...

The use of pinches often applies to the use of salt or spices. So, between your thumb and forefinger, pinch up whatever it is and add to what you are making. This is a small measure but also indeterminate in size.

A sprinkle of...

Sprinkle usually refers to sweeter edible products, such as chocolate chips, hundreds and thousands, silver balls. Gather up a small amount of whatever it is with all your fingers and sprinkle on to dust what you are making.

Brown

This applies to meat; when cooking in a frying pan with a little oil, the texture and colour will change.

Butter/grease

When baking something, this will usually mean you need to use a baking tray or dish of some sort; in order to stop the food sticking to the dish once baked, you're going to need to grease it or butter it up. Rub butter all over the insides, up the sides, to cover the dish in a thin layer of butter. Next, add whatever food it is you're cooking – then bake!

By eye

Measuring ingredients, in preparing for a recipe, can be done 'by eye' – taking a rough visual guess that you've probably reached the required amount of what is needed, rather than measuring precisely, to the exact measurement, of whatever it is that you need.

Crimp

This is a technique often used when working pastry; using a fork and sometimes an egg wash, this refers to sealing the filling up in the pastry, and marking the edges with a fork to create a shell-like texture. For example, the edges of a Cornish pasty have been crimped closed.

Dribble

This usually means when you have to pour something on top of something else; you 'dribble' a tiny amount across the top, usually for just a few seconds.

Drop consistency

When working with a cake mix or a dough, it may need to be a 'drop consistency'; get a spoon and, over the bowl, see if it easily drops off. It shouldn't be liquid, and it should not be so sticky that it sticks to the spoon and stays there. If that's the case, add a drop of water or milk to create a softer mix.

Dry

This term applies to types of ingredients and is the opposite of 'wet'; as an example, brown sugar is a dry ingredient.

Flavour bomb

A sudden burst of flavour when you bite down; this could be from something like sun dried tomatoes, capers, etc.

Quarter

To chop something into four different pieces. Take an apple, for example. You would cut it in half, and then you would cut those halves in half again. This term can apply to anything – from carrots to cucumbers, etc. I'm not sure if this term is used a lot outside of the UK, however; I haven't heard it elsewhere.

Roughly

This is usually used in relation to the preparation of ingredients for whatever dish it is that you are baking, and most of the time the sentence will be that the ingredient you are preparing should be either chopped or broken up roughly. That means without precision – for example, break up a chocolate bar, but it doesn't have to be so each square is neatly preserved. The presentation will not be impacted as a result; your dish will still look nice.

Sand consistency

When making dough, sometimes you need to rub several dry elements together; in order for this to work in baking, it needs to have the consistency of fine sand.

Wet

Wet refers to liquids such as water, but can also refer to ingredients and their properties. For example, olive oil would be a wet ingredient and so would an egg. This is a term that very often crops up when baking, especially when it comes to recipes like cookies.

Resources for Further Reading

Please note that, even though included here, the author and Jessica Kingsley Publishers do not necessarily endorse the views put forward, such as if the website is a personal blog or website. As many expert resources were included here as possible for that exact reason.

For day-to-day support
Assert

https://assertbh.org.uk

Assert is a charity that is based in Brighton; the organization supports young people and adults who are on the autistic spectrum, with the values of neurodiversity at its core.

Lorna Wing Centre

www.autism.org.uk/directory/t/
the-nas-lorna-wing-centre-for-autism

The Lorna Wing Centre is run in connection with the National Autistic Society in the UK and provides diagnostic services and professional training.

For further reading

Autistic Not Weird

https://autisticnotweird.com

Chris Bonnello is the author behind the *Underdogs* series and often speaks internationally, too. Autistic Not Weird has many different articles about his personal experiences, as well as easily adaptable tips.

Neurodivergent Rebel

https://neurodivergentrebel.com

Lyric Holmans, whose recipe is featured in this book, runs this personal lifestyle blog and associated business Neurodivergent Consulting. This website focuses a lot on neurodiversity, as well as advocating for yourself. Lyric also created the hashtag #Asking-Autistics and creates content for a wide variety of platforms, including Instagram and YouTube.

Perfectly Autistic

www.perfectlyautistic.co.uk

Run by the neurodivergent husband-and-wife duo Kelly and Hester Grainger, this is a website with all sorts of resources about being on the autistic spectrum. There is also a Perfectly Autistic Facebook group, which acts as a support network for parents, children and autistic individuals that anyone can join.

Quantum Leap Mentoring

www.qlmentoring.com

Quantum Leap Mentoring is a website run by another Jessica Kingsley Publishers author, Siena Castellon. Siena is the author of *The Spectrum Girl's Survival Guide*, and this website focuses on peer mentoring for autistic children and others.

The Aspie World

www.youtube.com/channel/UCOKKRcJey93Ms-dL630UNIQ

The Aspie World is a popular YouTube channel that is run by Dan Jones; he also has a website, as well as merchandise and clothing created in connection with Born Anxious. Dan covers a variety of topics in a quick, punchy style that is accessible for a wide variety of audiences.

The Autistic Advocate

https://theautisticadvocate.com

Kieran Rose is a researcher as well as a consultant; there are a lot of resources available for – and written by – autistic people (well, person in this case). This can be found in places such as the blog section.

YoSamdySam

www.youtube.com/c/YoSamdySam

Samantha Stein is a YouTuber by trade and was one of the interviewees for this book. She posts regular content on her YouTube channel, YoSamdySam, about neurodiversity, autism and other related topics.

21andsensory

www.instagram.com/21andsensory

Emily of @21andsensory illustrated this very book you hold in your hands; Emily posts regular illustrations on her Instagram page, and the podcast of the same name is also very comforting to listen to. (Okay, I'm biased – but the interviews have a comforting ASMR quality.)

1800 Seconds on Autism

www.bbc.co.uk/programmes/p06sdq0x/episodes/downloads

1800 Seconds on Autism is a podcast that is hosted by two autistic individuals, Robyn and Jamie. Subjects range from bedtime routines to employment, stimming and sensitivities to hospital stays and how to cope with the Covid 19 pandemic. Like most podcasts, 1800 Seconds on Autism is available from all good podcast directory apps.

For dealing with eating disorders

There is ongoing research that suggests that eating disorders have a higher prevalence in autistic individuals; while the reason for this is not entirely known, these are some resources for individuals who may require help or assistance. Obviously, this is a subject that needs to be talked about a lot more, and there should be a greater awareness among health professionals. Please note, however, that advice should always be sought from your GP or doctor. If you need help, or know someone who may be affected, these are a few services you can contact. These are just some resources that everyone ought to be aware of.

ARFID Awareness UK

www.arfidawarenessuk.org

According to researchers, people who are autistic are more likely to develop avoidant restrictive food intake disorder (ARFID); one of the individuals who was interviewed for this book specifically mentioned ARFID Awareness UK as a resource that had been helpful to them.

Beat

www.beateatingdisorders.org.uk

Founded in 1989, Beat is the UK's eating disorder charity. It offers resources for those with an eating disorder or those supporting someone with an eating disorder, and information for anyone wanting to know more.

Mind

www.mind.org.uk/information-support/types-of-mental-health-problems/eating-problems/treatment-support

An organ lth, the website also offers reliable information, as well as other potential avenues to explore when looking for help.

NAS (National Autistic Society)

www.autism.org.uk

The National Autistic Society is a UK-specific organization, and the website provides useful and simplified breakdowns of complex information; the website has information specific to eating disorders, as well as information about where to get help and seek advice.

NHS (National Health Service)

www.nhs.uk/mental-health/feelings-symptoms-behaviours/behaviours/eating-disorders/overview

The NHS is the body responsible for healthcare in the UK that is free at the point of use; the website, which is written by medically trained professionals, has an overview of eating disorders and potential treatment pathways for recovery. The website may not have autism-specific resources or information in exploring such a subject, but it does have information about how to seek help in the UK.

People Who Contributed to *The Autism-Friendly Cookbook*

This book would not have happened without the autistic individuals who gave up their time to have their recipes collated and written up – often during lockdowns and restrictions brought about by the Covid 19 pandemic. Each and every individual included in this book has their name included below – in no particular order. A roll call, please:

Emily of the 21andsensory Instagram page and the illustrator of this book

India, Hester and Kelly Grainger of Perfectly Autistic

Loz Young, communities manager at Sensooli, formerly known as Chewigem

Pauline Dunne

Sarah Hackert, physical therapist based in the United States

Victoria Ellen, blogger at Actually Aspling and PhD student

Karl Knights, writer and poet

Lyric Holmans, content creator at the Neurodivergent Rebel brand

Allie Mason, upcoming fellow Jessica Kingsley Publishers author

Samantha Stein of the YoSamdySam YouTube channel

Dan Jones, social media influencer and creator at The Aspie World (YouTube channel)

Barb Cook, co-author of *Spectrum Women* and fellow Jessica Kingsley Publishers author

Nathan Gokhool, writer, hiker and climber

Kieran Rose, public speaker, consultant and researcher

Ted Ayre, admin manager for the NHS (National Health Service) in the UK

Miranda Dressler, illustrator and the creator of Wrong Planet comics

Rebekah Gillian, blogger at rebekahgillian.co.uk

Siena Castellon, founder of Neurodiversity Celebration Week and author of *The Spectrum Girl's Survival Guide*

Gavin Davey, engineer

Laura James, journalist, columnist and author of *Odd Girl Out*

Chris Bonnello, writer, speaker and founder of the website Autistic Not Weird

Leonia Czernysz

Anonymous

Aoife Bear Casson, internal communication manager for Alzheimer's Research UK and Etsy shop owner of KumaRooma

Maia Osborne, laboratory scientist

Vera, also known as @happyautisticlady on Instagram

April Lloyd

And thank you also to Robin Van Creveld and Julia Martinez. They may not be autistic but they have worked with neurodiverse adults – and it is one of their key values. This book would not have been possible without their expertise.

Every single individual person is bound by one single, inalienable truth: we all need to eat. It is around food that we begin important relationships, share pivotal moments that define our lives, create communities – hundreds of tangible moments, bundled together, frozen in time. This is something that we all have in common, something more powerful than what can divide us. The information just needs to be more accessible – and we can ensure that we do that by becoming the start of a conversation.

Index

The Young Autistic Adult's Independence Handbook
Haley Moss

£14.99 | $19.95 | PB | 240PP |
ISBN 978 1 78775 757 8 |
eISBN 978 1 78775 758 5

Are you living away from home for the first time, graduating from school, or perhaps getting a new job? These transitions can be especially overwhelming to deal with as a young autistic adult. This handbook is bursting with neurodivergent-friendly advice from autistic people themselves (and a few neurotypicals too) for young adults embarking on their own journeys of self-discovery and independence.

From guidance on managing your own money, looking after your home, and organizing your social life to tips on self-advocacy and important life skills such as driving, voting, and volunteering, Haley Moss has you covered. Using personal stories, interviews with experts, and advice from other young people, this book gives you tips and tools to boost your confidence, ready to make your mark on the world!

Haley Moss is an autistic attorney and the first openly autistic lawyer admitted to The Florida Bar. She is an educator and presenter on autism, neurodiversity, and the law

Shake It Up!
How to Be Young, Autistic, and Make an Impact
Quincy Hansen

£13.99 | $18.95 | PB | 256PP |
ISBN 978 1 78775 979 4 |
eISBN 978 1 78775 980 0

This inspiring book by autistic blogger Quincy Hansen encourages autistic teens to find their voice and make a difference in the world around them. Featuring interviews with young autistic change-makers such as Siena Castellon, and addressing issues like self-image, harmful stereotypes, and communication barriers, *Shake It Up!* aims to build readers' confidence and inspire them to take action towards changing the world into a better place.

Quincy Hansen is a young autistic activist, blogger, and public speaker residing in Colorado, USA. Quincy's advocacy revolves around correcting stereotypes and misconceptions about autism in order to bring about greater acceptance, understanding, and inclusion of autistic people.

The Autism and Neurodiversity Self Advocacy Handbook

Developing the Skills to Determine Your Own Future

Barb Cook and Yenn Purkis

£14.99 | $19.95 | PB | 176PP | ISBN 978 1 78775 575 8 | eISBN 978 1 78775 576 5

Being autistic, you might come across more challenges than others around you, such as dealing with ableism, discrimination in employment or difficulties in your relationships.

Written by two autistic activists, this book will give you the tools and strategies to advocate for yourself in any situation. It covers specific scenarios including work, school, and family and relationships, as well as looking at advocacy for the wider community, whether that's through social media, presentations or writing. Additionally, the book provides advice on building independence, developing your skills, standing up for others and resolving conflict.

The authors explore the overall impact of self-advocacy in all areas of your life, building a sense of confidence, resilience and control. Drawing on the authors' extensive experience, this book will help you to success-fully prioritize your needs and rights, challenge what is unfair or unjust and make your voice heard.

Yenn Purkis is autistic and non-binary and has published a range of books with JKP since 2006. They actively speak at autism conferences and have increasingly spoken and written on autism and LGBTQ+ identities and received the ACT Volunteer of the Year award for work in autism advocacy. Yenn lives in Canberra, Australia.

Barb Cook is a Neurodivergent Developmental Educator and holds a Master of Autism degree from the University of Wollongong. Barb is a prolific writer, speaker and advocate on neurodivergence, and is founder of *Spectrum Women Magazine*, NeuroEmploy and the NeuroDiversity Hub, based in Gympie, Australia.